**Forensic
Hypnosis**

Forensic Hypnosis

Psychological and Legal Aspects

Roy Udolf
Hofstra University

LexingtonBooks
D.C. Heath and Company
Lexington, Massachusetts
Toronto

Library of Congress Cataloging in Publication Data

Udolf, Roy.
  Forensic hypnosis.

  Bibliography: p.
  Includes indexes.
    1. Hypnotism—Jurisprudence—United States.
  2. Forensic hypnotism. I. Title.
  KF8965.U26 1983   347.73'066   81-48558
  ISBN 0-669-05418-6   347.30766

Copyright © 1983 by D. C. Heath and Company

Published simultaneously in Canada

Printed in the United States of America

International Standard Book Number: 0-669-05418-6

Library of Congress Catalog Card Number: 81-48558

In memory of Milton J. Hoffman, Esquire.

Contents

Foreword

During the first century of the history of hypnosis, from the time of Mesmer to the Victorian era, an important focus of legal concern was the alleged ability of hypnotists to coerce an innocent person into antisocial, criminal, or self-destructive behavior. Indeed, such claims have continued to be heard and have even been brought into court proceedings in relatively modern times. These claims at times have been supported by the conclusions of laboratory experiments using college students as subjects, as well as by evidence offered in notorious courtroom trials, mainly in Europe. Reiter and others have summarized such reports, and they are available elsewhere. While the claims of hypnotic coercion have not entirely survived the scrutiny of scientific objectivity, interest in the broader forensic implications and applications of hypnosis has continued.

At the present time, forensic, or investigative hypnosis, as it has variously been termed, has increasingly become a technique employed for refreshing the memories of victims, witnesses, and others. A significant impetus for these developments was the sensational Chowchilla, California, kidnapping case of little more than a decade ago, which was solved by the hypnotic examination of a bus driver who was then able to remember most of an automobile license number. In this timely book, Roy Udolf—who is trained in both psychology and law—describes the methods, case law, legal status, and problems associated with forensic hypnosis, with a wealth of documented detail that will clarify the issues for the reader.

The claims of some health professionals and law enforcement personnel—that hypnosis uncritically and fully facilitates a perfect tape-recorder-like retrieval of past experience—have been shown to be invalid. Memory recall, even with hypnotic assistance, can be imperfect under the best of circumstances, due to the influence of emotion, confabulation, and other variables, all of which occur normally in human beings. But it has been repeatedly observed that hypnosis, when properly and competently utilized as an investigative technique in real-life settings, can indeed facilitate the retrieval of memory details that had not been previously elicited from victims and witnesses in both criminal and noncriminal situations.

An important point that Udolf makes in this book is that hypnotically refreshed memories are not necessarily true (although they may well be) and should be regarded as leads for subsequent investigation, clarification, and validation. In addition, while there may be potential for misuse of forensic hypnosis, this can be minimized and controlled only by the strictest adherence to professional ethics and techniques and by the insistence on professional competence of the highest order. Forensic hypnosis is simply a tool, whose effectiveness is no better than the qualifications of the person using it.

The admissibility of hypnotically facilitated recollections as evidence in courtroom proceedings has become an important legal question on the Supreme-Court level in several states. By no means, it should be noted, have these state-court decisions been uniform. In the landmark 1981 *Hurd* case in New Jersey, the court established a well-considered set of procedural rules to be followed by the forensic hypnosis professional, who, to begin with, must be either a psychologist or psychiatrist with special training. In the 1982 *Shirley* case in California, the court virtually excluded hypnotically based testimony. (In the latter, it was unfortunate that the court apparently confused the possibility of memory distortion under hypnosis with probability.) The significance and usefulness of hypnotic hypermnesia in forensic applications will undoubtedly bring the matter to the attention of the United States Supreme Court before long.

As one who has been engaged in the practice of forensic psychology and forensic hypnosis for more than two decades, I welcome the publication of this book. It comes at a critical moment in the history of hypnosis and in the special considerations that are provided by the forensic applications of this technique.

Melvin A. Gravitz, Ph. D.
Editor,
American Journal of Clinical Hypnosis
Former President,
American Society of Clinical Hypnosis

Preface and Acknowledgments

The purposes of this book are to consolidate in one source a variety of materials, concepts, and techniques with which the forensic hypnotist needs to be conversant, and to inform him or her of the legal issues, principles, and problems that are involved with forensic applications of hypnosis. To achieve this goal the literature and the applicable case law, both recent and not so recent, have been surveyed.

It is also intended to acquaint lawyers, prosecutors, judges, legislators, law-enforcement personnel, and other interested professionals with the characteristics, capabilities, and limitations of hypnosis; the scope of its potential applications; and its dangers as a forensic and investigative tool.

The book will deal with the psychology of hypnosis and hypnotic phenomena as it relates to forensic applications, and the legal principles and case law related to these applications.

It is not intended as a book to train psychotherapists unfamiliar with hypnosis in this specialty (as is the author's *Handbook of Hypnosis for Professionals*). It is aimed at the experienced hypnotherapist interested in forensic applications and legal problems of hypnosis.

It is also designed to provide an introduction and overview of the subject for the legally trained reader so that legal controversies can be evaluated in the context of the facts of hypnosis.

In short, this book will examine the area of forensic hypnosis from the viewpoints of both the psychotherapist-expert and the attorney in the hope that this will aid each profession to understand the other's special problems and thus make interaction more harmonious and productive.

Acknowledgments

The following people must share much of the credit for the publication of this book, for it could not have been completed without their help.

Professor Alfred Cohn of Hofstra University's New College and Professors Richard O'Brien and Hadassah Paul of the Psychology Department of Hofstra University reviewed the manuscript and made many helpful suggestions concerning the psychological portions of this book.

Adrian DiLuzio, J.D.; Barbara Tinsley, J.D.; and Jeffrey Scott Berkerman also reviewed the manuscript and graciously gave the author the benefit of their legal expertise.

Though the comments of all of these consultants resulted in many improvements in this book, the author did not always accept their suggestions and hence he reserves for himself full credit for any remaining errors, omissions, and for all opinions expressed.

Without the generous help provided by Dean Sherry J. Friedman, formerly of the Hofstra University School of Law, and the efforts of the Hofstra Law Library staff members Joseph Burk, Fred Johnson, and Marguerite Pidoto in providing the author with copies of hundreds of case reports, this book could not have been written.

Gerard E. Giannattasio, Esquire, Hofstra University Reference Law Librarian, constantly provided the author with invaluable and highly skilled professional assistance in contending with the intricacies of legal research.

Dean David C. Christman of Hofstra's New College, as always, provided the author with encouragement and support in this undertaking.

Dagmar Santangelo, Joan Dale, and Mary Joan DeMarco converted an illegibly marked-up rough draft into a finished manuscript with their customary dispatch and skill.

1 Introduction

Basic Conceptions of Hypnosis

Hypnotic phenomena have been observed and utilized since the beginning of recorded history and probably well before this, yet many misconceptions about the nature of hypnosis persist. Before investigating the potential forensic value, limitations, and dangers of hypnosis, it is necessary to present a few basic concepts concerning the nature of hypnosis and the trance state.

Many people believe that a hypnotic trance is an invariant state with definite signs, and that an expert can detect whether or not a subject is truly hypnotized. They also believe that it is a dichotomous situation—that a subject is either hypnotized or not. Finally, they believe that it is this special "altered state of consciousness" that produces all of the phenomena commonly associated with hypnosis. All of these ideas are inaccurate.

First, there is an almost limitless variety of trance states, ranging from the conventional deeply relaxed state, through what Gibbons (1976) called *hyperempiric* or *active* trance, to the type of Crisis reaction obtained by Mesmer in which patients experienced convulsions and unconsciousness. It is also possible to induce a trance state that cannot be distinguished from the normal waking state. The type of trance attained is a function of the type of trance-inducing suggestions made to subjects and of their expectations of what is to happen. Once subjects have experienced hypnosis, their reactions in subsequent trances tend to be very similar to the initial ones unless something contrary is suggested (Udolf 1981). In fact, people enter trance states spontaneously in everyday life (in the absence of any hypnotist), and these spontaneous trance states are rarely recognized for what they are. Spiegel (1980) makes the point that witnesses, subject to the stress of questioning by police, may slip into such a state as a way of defending themselves from a traumatic situation. He claims that opponents of hypnosis in police work may fail to recognize the danger of its inadvertent presence. Hence, it is not really possible to outlaw the employment of forensic hypnosis by the police even if this were universally deemed desirable. He asserts that it is a better safeguard to train lawyers and law-enforcement personnel to be aware of the problems that hypnosis may cause rather than to assume that these can be eliminated by legislation.

Because most modern hypnotists suggest a relaxed trance state there are certain common concomitants of the resulting trance, such as a lack of

1

spontaneous movement or speech, an expressionless facial mask, postural slumping, alterations in the respiratory rate, and so forth. However, none of these signs is invariant and there are great individual differences from subject to subject in these criteria. In point of fact, no expert can say with certainty whether or not a particular subject is hypnotized. He can merely give an educated estimate of the likelihood that the subject is in a trance. Orne (1959) has noted that the presence or absence of a trance is a matter of clinical diagnosis. In research utilizing unhypnotized subjects instructed to simulate hypnosis and to try to deceive the experimenter, it has been demonstrated that experts are often unable to detect simulators, at least over a short period of time (Udolf 1981).

The question of whether or not a subject is hypnotized is really not a very meaningful one, for a variety of reasons. For one thing, a hypnotic trance can vary in depth from a very light (*hypnoidal*) state to a very deep (*somnambulistic*) one. One of the most important characteristics of the hypnotic state, for forensic and other purposes, is the hypersuggestibility associated with it. Trance depth is generally measured in terms of the kinds of suggestions that the subject will accept. Suggestions that are more difficult, that is, that have a lower probability of being accepted, are indicative of a deeper trance state when they are acted upon. Udolf (1981) points out that the difficulty of a suggestion is a statistical concept. It relates to how many out of a large group of hypnotic subjects are capable of effectuating the suggestion. Statistics enable good predictions to be made about groups but are not valid for making inferences about individuals. Hence it is not uncommon to find a subject who is capable of producing a statistically difficult response, such as a visual hallucination, who fails to produce a much easier response, like arm catalepsy.

Trance depth is not very important clinically. It is a common observation that a very light trance can be clinically productive with a well-motivated patient, while a deeper state may not be if the patient lacks the desire to attain the goal of the hypnosis. Most clinicians recognize that the best predictor of success in relatively direct applications of clinical hypnosis, such as antismoking suggestions, is not the trance depth obtained but patient motivation (Gravitz 1980; Udolf 1981).

This probably holds true in such forensic applications as memory enhancement, but forensic hypnotists would be well advised to obtain as deep a trance as possible and to test its depth carefully, because opposing counsel is likely to make this an issue. This is particularly so if the opposing counsel has the misconception that a deep state of hypnosis precludes a witness from lying or assures the accuracy of his recollection. (Gravitz 1980; Salzberg 1977; Spector and Foster 1977).

Hypnotic susceptibility or trance capacity is to trance depth as potential is to actual. In other words, it is a measure of the ability of a subject to attain a certain depth of trance under a given set of conditions. Typically, it is measured by the use of a standardized induction procedure followed by a test of hypnotic depth. Since all subjects get the same induction procedure, differences in depth produced must be because of differences in the subjects' intrinsic hypnotic abilities rather than extrinsic factors (Udolf 1981).

Although the essential nature of hypnosis remains unknown and is subject to widely different theoretical views, hypnotized subjects generally display most of the following characteristics to a greater or lesser extent (Hilgard 1965; Orne 1982):

1. A literalness in understanding and in following directions;
2. A narrowing of the perceptual field and the focusing on a single idea (*monoideism*);
3. Hypersuggestibility and compliance, or a desire to please the hypnotist;
4. The suspension of critical judgment and reality testing and a tolerance for incongruous situations (*trance logic*);
5. Susceptibility to alterations in perception, affect, and memory;
6. The assumption of role-appropriate behavior.

It is popularly believed that a hypnotic subject has no memory of the events that occurred during hypnosis, but a spontaneous posthypnotic amnesia for the events of an experimental hypnotic session is rare. However, such an amnesia can be produced easily by suggestion. When it does occur spontaneously it probably results from autosuggestion by a subject who believes that is is supposed to occur. In clinical hypnosis, however, spontaneous amnesia for the hypnotic session is more common and is probably because of the traumatic nature of the material dealt with under hypnosis.

Note that hypnotized subjects are in no sense of the word *unconscious*, nor are they asleep. They are aware of everything going on around them, although they tend to ignore everything on which they are not focused. Subjects never lose control of the situation nor surrender their volition to the hypnotist. They can come out of hypnosis at any time they desire.

From a clinical and a forensic viewpoint, it is most important to realize that hypnosis is not a condition in which the ordinary principles of human behavior are suspended. Quite to the contrary, these principles may become intensified. Any hypnotic procedure used must take into account the personality characteristics of the subject if it is to be successful. There is nothing that can be accomplished by using hypnosis that could not be done by using some alternative procedure.

Hypnosis is not a method of therapy. It is simply a naturally occurring phenomenon that can be used as an ancillary technique in a variety of psychotherapies. Like any technique, if used competently in an appropriate application, it can be useful. If misused or used when inappropriate, it can be counterproductive.

The common view that a trance produces the heightened suggestibility and other characteristics of hypnosis is partially true but somewhat misleading. A trance is simply a response to a set of trance-inducing suggestions, as is any other phenomenon obtainable under hypnosis. However, as the subject begins to act on suggestions made to him, his confidence in the effectiveness of the procedure increases making him more suggestible and more likely to respond as requested to the later, more difficult suggestions. Conventionally, there comes a point in the hypnotic induction procedure at which the hypnotist stops making suggestions to go into hypnosis and starts making trance-deepening suggestions. These suggestions differ not in kind but merely in name. Generally, the hypnotist begins with suggestions that are easy for the subject to effectuate and works up to suggestions as difficult as the subject can handle successfully (Udolf 1981).

There are theorists like Barber and his associates, who, while not denying the reality of hypnotic phenomena, do not believe that the concept of a trance state is necessary to account for them. Indeed, these researchers have been able to produce most of these phenomena in well-motivated waking subjects given what they call *task-motivating instructions*. These, they believe, are usually integrated into and confounded with most hypnotic induction procedures. Certainly most of the simpler but dramatic hypnotic effects such as arm levitation or hand attraction can be obtained in waking subjects quite readily and are therefore often incorporated into induction procedures.

Hypnosis and the Legal System

The modern history of hypnosis (from the time of Mesmer) has been punctuated by periods of renewed interest and popularity interspersed with periods of disinterest and neglect (Ladd 1902; Udolf 1981). Recently there has been renewed interest in hypnosis among clinicians coupled with an increase in both the quantity and quality of research in the field.

Today hypnosis is finding practical applications in psychotherapy, medicine, and dentistry as well as in a variety of nonclinical fields such as sports, advertising, research, education, and others (Udolf 1981).

It would be strange indeed if such a ubiquitous phenomenon did not begin to interface with the legal system, as indeed it has. As the use of hypnosis becomes more widespread, this interaction with the law can be expected to become even more frequent.

There are two main interfaces between hypnosis and the law: the use of hypnosis as a tool in legal controversies; and the defining of legal rights and liabilities arising from the use of hypnosis.

To date, the first area has been the major type of interface between the two disciplines. Hypnosis has been used or advocated for all of the following purposes and others:

1. Hypnotic memory enhancement
   a. As an investigative or discovery tool to obtain leads to independent evidence (Ault 1980; Douce 1979; Graham 1980; Kassinger 1979; Kleinhauz, Horowitz, and Tobin 1977; Levitt 1981; Millwee 1979; Reiser 1978, 1980; Robinson 1979; Salzberg 1977; Schafer and Rubio 1978; Stratton 1977; Wilson 1979).
   b. To enhance the memory of witnesses to and victims of crimes (Conour 1980; Gold 1980; Haward and Ashworth 1980; Spector and Foster 1977, 1979; Teitelbaum 1963a; Teten 1979; W. S. 1969).
   c. To enhance the memory of witnesses and parties in civil actions (Dilloff 1977; Gold 1980; Levy 1955; Raginsky 1969; Teitelbaum 1963b).
   d. To enable the defendant in a criminal case to break an amnesia and aid in the preparation of his defense (*Cornell* v. *Superior Court* 1959; Anon. 1969; Davis 1960; Dilloff 1977).
2. As a truth-seeking device, analogous to a lie detector or truth serum (Arons 1977; Danto 1979; Mutter 1979; Weinstein, Abrams, and Gibbons 1970).
3. As a technique by which an expert evaluates a defendant's sanity, state of mind, or specific intent, that is, *mens rea* (Haward and Ashworth 1980; Sarno 1979; Spector and Foster 1979).
4. To aid in the preparation of witnesses or parties for trial (Bryan 1962; Haward and Ashworth 1980).
5. To detect malingering or antisocial uses of hypnosis (Levy 1955; Teitelbaum 1963b).
6. To aid in obtaining statements, admissions, and confessions (Arons 1977; Teten 1979).
7. As a defense in a criminal case (Lehan 1970; Levy 1955; Sarno 1979; Teten 1979).

Some of the foregoing uses of hypnosis, such as the development of leads to independent evidence, represent sensible and potentially valuable contributions to the search for truth. Others, such as the use of hypnosis as a lie detector, are based on false beliefs concerning hypnosis and what it is capable of accomplishing. Some of these proposed applications, such as the use of hypnosis to obtain statements from a defendant in a criminal case, reflect a serious lack of understanding of the basic principles of our legal system.

In any proposed forensic application of hypnosis, three questions must be asked:

1. Has hypnosis been demonstrated to be capable of producing the result sought?
2. Is there an alternative procedure that can accomplish this result with fewer problems? (See Wagstaff 1980, 1981a, 1981b).
3. Is what is sought to be accomplished legally acceptable?

Often a given application of hypnosis (for example memory enhancement) may be of value for one purpose (such as discovery) and be unacceptable for another (such as eliciting testimony). Even without consideration of legal factors, the value of hypnosis may vary greatly from one specific situation to another. For example, hypnosis may be of great value in the retrieval of memories that are unavailable because of psychological trauma, but prove to be of little help in recovering a lost memory for meaningless material like a license number or unrecorded events.

One of the major problems in the forensic applications of hypnosis is that most judges, lawyers, and potential jurors are laymen whose knowledge of hypnosis is frequently based on popular and sensational literature or stage hypnosis. The latter is often more showmanship and misdirection than actual hypnosis. Hence, they may harbor many misconceptions about what hypnosis is and what it can or cannot accomplish. Some probably credit hypnosis with a power to compel subjects to do almost anything from telling the truth to committing crimes. Others, equally naïve, assume it is a total fraud. Even mental-health professionals without special training in hypnosis harbor many false beliefs about hypnotic phenomena. In addition, most mental-health professionals are as uninformed about legal principles as lawyers are concerning hypnosis.

Hence, the literature of forensic hypnosis is really three separate literatures. There is the legal literature consisting of law-review articles and case reports. This literature recognizes the legal problems involved in hypnosis, but often cites a curious mixture of valid and invalid psychological principles in support of legal reasoning. Legal conclusions are often unsound because of the falsity of the psychological premises upon which they are founded. Then there is the psychological literature, more likely to be accurate with respect to hypnosis, but often failing to recognize the legal nuances involved in proposed forensic applications. The third literature, which often propagates extremely naïve and inaccurate views about hypnosis and the psychological facts concerning memory and perception, is essentially a lay literature written by police officers who use or advocate the use of hypnosis in police work and are generally inadequately trained in both hypnosis and psychology.

In view of these often contradictory literatures, and because forensic hypnosis is an interdisciplinary field requiring training in both psychology and law, courts and lawyers are often unable to recognize real controversies in hypnotic research versus controversies caused by misconceptions.

Among the issues and pseudoissues frequently raised in the literature are the following:

1. The possibility of hypnosis against a subject's will (versus without his consent or knowledge, or *covert* hypnosis);
2. The extent of the hypnotist's power over the subject, (the hypnotist's ability to victimize the subject or compel or deceive him or her into committing antisocial actions);
3. The extent to which memory can be improved by hypnotic means and the variables involved;
4. The value of hypnosis as a lie detector and its supposed ability to compel a subject to tell the truth; and
5. The ability of an expert to detect the faking of hypnosis and to estimate the depth of a trance accurately.

Although there is some legitimate controversy associated with all of these issues, there is enough experimental evidence available to resolve most of these questions with a considerable degree of confidence. Often an appreciable amount of confusion is caused by purely semantic problems. For example, the evidence appears overwhelming that it is not possible to hypnotize a person who actively resists hypnosis, since his or her co-operation must be enlisted in the process. However, it *is* possible to hypnotize persons without their awareness by using a variety of techniques. These include describing the procedure as a relaxation exercise and avoiding the use of the terms *sleep* or *hypnosis*, or using a *chaperone* technique, that is having the subject undergo hypnosis by watching a confederate ostensibly being hypnotized (Udolf 1981). A great deal of pointless semantic contro-versy can be created if covert hypnotism is described as hypnosis against the subjects's will, which it really is not. (For an example of this see Watkins' (1947) hypnosis of a soldier "against his will" by having him stare at a ten-dollar bill).

Many of the court decisions concerning hypnosis and its legal effect on testimony discussed in chapter 3 can only be understood in the light of the widespread naïvete of the legal profession with respect to hypnosis and hypnotic phenomena. Even when courts reach what appears to be the correct decision in the case at hand, they may reach it for the wrong reasons.

Finally, an important and recurring legal issue in forensic hypnosis is the question of how adequately existing law is able to deal with problems involving hypnosis and its applications. There are those legal authorities who believe that existing legal principles, intelligently applied, are adequate to deal with problems posed by hypnosis without the need for special legislation, while others believe only the latter can deal adequately with these problems (Diamond 1980; Herman 1964; Ladd 1902; Levy 1955; Swain 1961; Warner 1979). Theoretically there is room for a wide range of opinion between these two extreme positions. But most legal writers seem to fall at one of the two extremes, advocating either minimal or extensive legislation.

If the legal profession became educated about hypnosis, the existing body of law, worked out over many generations of legal experience, especially the rules of evidence, should be adequate to deal with most hypnotic problems. If the legal profession is not cognizant of the current state of the art in hypnotic research, no special legislation is likely to help the situation. Indeed, legislation based on misconceptions and false premises is likely to do more harm than good. One of the goals of this book is to supply enough factual information concerning forensic hypnosis to provide a sound basis for forming a personal opinion.

2 Hypnosis as an Investigative or Discovery Procedure

Perhaps the least controversial forensic use of hypnosis is as a discovery device, that is, as a means of obtaining independent evidence (Spiegel 1980). Typically this involves the use of hypnotically refreshed recollection on the part of witnesses, victims of crimes, or parties in civil actions. If the subject of such hypnotic investigation never has to be called as a witness in the subsequent court proceedings because the information he or she has is either unimportant or redundant or because the hypnosis leads to the discovery of independent evidence, there would be few if any problems associated with preliminary hypnotic investigations.

However, if pretrial hypnosis is to be used on a prospective trial witness for the purpose of enhancing his recollection of the facts in issue, then a whole Pandora's Box of problems arises concerning the effect of the hypnosis on the accuracy and admissibility of the future testimony and, indeed, on the vulnerability of the witness to future cross-examination.

This chapter will deal with the area of investigative hypnosis, on the assumption that the hypnotized subject is not likely to be used as a witness in the subsequent trial. Chapter 3 will deal with the legal and psychological consequences of the employment of hypnosis on a trial witness. However, it is often impossible to be sure that a subject hypnotized during the investigative stage of a legal proceeding will not be needed subsequently as a witness. If it seems at all probable that the subject may be needed as a witness, counsel should be very reluctant to permit a hypnotic examination of such a subject by his investigators. At best, the fact of the pretrial hypnosis may be used to impeach the credibility of the witness, and in some jurisdictions it may lead to the exclusion of testimony, in whole or in part. However, if the jurisdiction in question permits the introduction of hypnotically refreshed testimony, as many do, and the value of the information obtained is likely to exceed any adverse effect of a cross-examination highlighting the possibility of hypnotic distortion of facts, then it might be justifiable to hypnotize a potential witness. Hypnotizing a potential witness would also be justified when human life is threatened, such as when the witness might help to identify or locate a kidnapper.

Investigative hypnosis, like most applications of hypnosis, is more likely to be effective with volunteer and highly motivated subjects (Gravitz 1980; Kleinhauz, Horowitz, and Tobin 1977). It is a fundamental mistake to think that investigative hypnosis assures truth. Even hypnotic subjects in a deep trance are capable of lying if they are so motivated. They may also make honest errors. Stratton (1977) reports a dramatic account of a chaplain's hypnotic recall of his experiences as a prisoner of war in Vietnam. He had, in fact, never been there. What hypnotic investigation actually produces is a mixture of fact and fantasy in indeterminate proportions, that provides a basis for seeking independent verification (Gravitz 1980; Udolf 1981). This is the sole legitimate purpose of investigative hypnosis and, as long as the material elicited under hypnosis is not used as testimony, the fact that much of it may be in error is not important. Such inaccuracies merely increase the cost of the investigation, to disprove them. But some of the elicited material may be accurate, in whole or in part, and may lead to the discovery of valuable new information and evidence.

The Extent of Hypnotic Investigation by Law-Enforcement Agencies

Investigative hypnosis is primarily used by local police departments and federal investigatory agencies on witnesses and victims of crimes. Among the law-enforcement agencies utilizing hypnosis in investigations and providing special training for their personnel are:

> Police departments in Los Angeles, New York City, Portland, Seattle, Denver, Houston, San Antonio, and Washington, D.C. (Diamond 1980; Monrose 1978; Reiser 1976, 1978; Reiser and Nielson 1980; Wilson 1979);
>
> the Los Angeles County Sheriff's Office (Stratton 1977);
>
> the FBI (Ault 1979, 1980; Diamond 1980; Douce 1979; Kroger and Douce 1979, 1980; Monrose 1978; Teten 1979);
>
> the Alcohol, Tobacco and Firearms Bureau of the Treasury Department (Diamond 1980; Monrose 1978);
>
> the U.S. Air Force Office of Special Investigations (AFOSI) (Diamond 1980; Hibler 1979; Monrose 1978);
>
> the Civil Aeronautics Board (Raginsky 1969); and
>
> the Israeli national police (Kleinhauz, Horowitz, and Tobin 1977; Robinson 1979).

For constitutional reasons to be discussed in chapter 4, law-enforcement agencies in this country generally prohibit the use of investigative hypnosis on any subject who is or is likely to become a suspect in the case. Again, it is not always possible to predict in the early stages of an investigation who is likely to be a suspect. Decisions about which witnesses should be subjected to investigative hypnosis should be deferred until this issue has been determined. Once hypnosis has been undertaken, should information be elicited suggesting that the subject may be guilty of the crime being investigated (or another one), merely stopping the hypnotic session immediately is not likely to repair the damage done to the *People's* case.

The defense may, however, wish to hypnotize a defendant in order to break an amnesia and permit him to aid in his own defense, to elicit information about his mental state at the time of the alleged crime, or to determine his sanity or capacity to stand trial. Such use of hypnosis by the defense is analogous to a discovery procedure, but it necessarily carries with it complications should the defendant later choose to testify at his own trial. In those jurisdictions disqualifying previously hypnotized witnesses, there would be serious constitutional issues raised in the application of such a rule against a defendant, for it would appear to deny him his right to defend himself. No case has been found to date dealing directly with this constitutional issue.

It should also be obvious that a victim of a crime is likely to have to testify at the subsequent trial and, except in special cases, he should not be subjected to investigative hypnosis. Nevertheless, it is the practice of most law-enforcement agencies to use hypnosis as readily on victims as on other witnesses.

The Effectiveness of Investigative Hypnosis

Statistics reported by law-enforcement proponents of investigative hypnosis are generally impressive if taken at face value. Kleinhauz, Horowitz, and Tobin (1977) report a significant increase in recall in twenty-four out of forty cases as a result of investigative hypnosis. In sixteen of these twenty-four cases the quality of this additional information was assessed as to whether it led to the uncovering of other evidence or to the apprehension of the criminal. They found that in fourteen of these cases there was a "significant" increase in accurate information, while in two cases the results contradicted other evidence available.

Kroger and Douce (1979, 1980) report that in twenty-three cases involving fifty-three witnesses and victims new information was developed in 60 percent of the cases. Three of the subjects were unable to be hypnotized. Between 1976 and 1979 the Los Angeles Police Department (LAPD) conducted some 350 hypnotic-case investigations. Wilson (1979) reports that a survey disclosed that 101 of these cases had been solved. Of the detectives involved, 78 percent said that hypnosis had provided new information about their cases, 16 detectives said that the information obtained was extremely useful, and 8 said that the case could not have been solved without hypnosis.

In another sample of seventy cases from the LAPD it was claimed that important information, not obtained by routine interrogation, was obtained from witnesses and victims under hypnosis in fifty-four cases (Reiser 1980; Robinson 1979). Eleven of the seventy cases were solved solely through hypnosis. In a later report Reiser and Nielson (1980) note that in 374 hypnotic sessions conducted by the LAPD (through March 1979) 92.5 percent of the subjects achieved some degree of hypnosis. A memory improvement, from slight to marked occurred in 85.2 percent of the cases and additional information was produced in 82.2 percent of the cases. In 67.5 percent of the cases the information was considered valuable. Where corroboration was possible, 90.7 percent of the material was found to be accurate and 6.8 percent inaccurate. Thirty-one percent of the cases were solved and hypnosis was considered valuable in 65 percent of these. Reiser and Nielson also claim that a follow-up has not revealed any instances of ill effects on any subject from the use of hypnosis, and 39.8 percent reported some benefit from the hypnotic session.

Robinson (1979) reports that twenty-five cases of terrorism were solved by means of hypnosis by the Israeli national police. In a pilot program in the Los Angeles County Sheriff's Office, 90 percent of the investigators in fifty cases of major felonies (murder, rape, kidnapping, and robbery) reported that hypnosis was helpful in their investigations (Stratton 1977).

Most of these reports are too general to be used in the critical evaluation of the effectiveness of hypnosis in the cases cited. To do this we would need to know not merely the percentage of new information obtained, but what percentage of the new information was actually relevant to the investigation, the standard employed for determining relevance, what percentage was accurate and inaccurate, and how veracity was determined. Furthermore, the percentage of new, accurate, and relevant information is not necessarily synonymous with the value of hypnosis in a case. Often a single bit of information may prove pivotal while a large amount of other information may be of little value. In addition, there is no way of determining from these data whether the information obtained could have been elicited by other investigative and interrogative techniques had an equal amount of time, skill, and effort been employed. It is known that in clinical work there are many ways of eliciting historical information from a patient. Hypnosis has not been demonstrated to be invariably superior for this purpose.

The only conclusion that can safely be drawn from the data reported is that police officers associated with hypnotic investigations have generally positive feelings toward them. This may be because hypnosis is actually a better method in certain cases, but officers may also find it interesting and dramatic, or that it increases their feelings of control and potency in their work.

The Uses of Hypnotic Investigations

Hypnosis has been used in the attempt to uncover crucial facts and details that have been forgotten by witnesses and victims. Investigators have purported to recover information concerning:

details of crime scenes (Douce 1979);

makes, models, colors, dents, stickers, descriptions, and license numbers of cars (Douce 1979; Kleinhauz, Horowitz, and Tobin 1977; Kroger and Douce 1979, 1980; Robinson 1979; Stratton 1977);

detailed physical descriptions of witnesses and suspects (leading to accurate composite pictures constructed by police artists) (Douce 1979; Kleinhauz, Horowitz, and Tobin 1977; Kroger and Douce 1979, 1980; Robinson 1979);

descriptions of weapons (Kleinhauz, Horowitz, and Tobin 1977); and

details of conversations (Kroger and Douce 1979, 1980; Robinson 1979).

Industrial security investigators have used hypnotic questioning to recover a combination in order to avoid having to damage an expensive safe. Hypnosis has been used to locate misplaced documents (Graham 1980). Mutter and Gravitz each report hypnotic investigations that were effective at a date seven years after the events in question (Gravitz 1980). Holden (1980) cites a forty-four-year-old woman who remembered her mother's murder and dismemberment by her father thirty-five years earlier.

Kroger and Douce (1980) describe a series of cases in which hypnosis was used for investigative purposes with varying degrees of success. In a kidnapping and rape case involving two young girls and in a federal prison gang-murder case many important details were elicited under hypnosis. Yet in another case involving a kidnap and murder the six witnesses interviewed under hypnosis had no significant information about the case, which was ultimately solved by nonhypnotic investigation. Stratton (1977) describes how a hypnotized fifteen-year-old victim of an attempted kidnapping recalled the kidnapper's license number and was able to describe him under hypnosis. Douce (1979) cites the contribution made by hypnosis to the investigation of organized crime in a case involving professional hit men. Salzberg (1977) relates how hypnosis aided a soldier, who had accidentally shot and killed another soldier, to remember where he had hidden the body. But hypnosis failed to help a group of rape victims to remember enough details to identify the rapist, an army captain, who was finally apprehended because of the similarity of the *modus operandi* to that of a series of rapes at his last post.

Spiegel (1980) reports two cases in which hypnosis was successful in lifting a retrograde amnesia. In one case, an eighteen-year-old passenger whose father was killed in a collision with a truck was able to remember the events that closely preceded the accident. In the other case, a woman was able to remember that it was her ex-husband who attacked her with a knife.

These cases are particularly interesting because it is characteristic of retrograde amnesia following a physical trauma that memories of events immediately preceding the injury are never recovered (Russell 1959). This is generally thought to be because the injury interferes with the consolidation process necessary to convert a short-term memory into a long-term one. If these memories were in fact veridical, it would suggest that the mechanisms involved in organic and psychological retrograde amnesias differ and that in these cases the amnesia was caused by the psychological rather than the physical trauma.

In the case of *McGraph* v. *Rohde* (1972), hypnosis, more typically refreshed a plaintiff's memory of events just prior to an auto accident but failed to help him remember the collision itself.

In *People* v. *Heintze* (1980) the defendant moved to suppress a statement made after his arraignment was unnecessarily delayed for sixty-two hours. The jail administrator was unable to account for the delay and testified that the administrator had been hypnotized twice in an unsuccessful effort to recall the circumstances surrounding what the court labeled a "prolonged inadvertence."

Reiser (1978) describes the case of a police officer who was shot, and under hypnosis described his assailant so accurately that the resulting police artist's sketch was a "dead ringer" for the assailant later apprehended. This reasoning is somewhat circular. It is not surprising that the suspect apprehended closely resembled the sketch—that is probably why he was arrested in the first place. Although the article cited did not publish this sketch and a photograph of the suspect for comparison, in a subsequent book Reiser (1980) published three such sets of pictures. The resemblance between the suspects and the sketches was not particularly impressive. In one case a huge sebaceous cyst located between the left eye and the nose, which appeared in the photograph, was omitted from the sketch. It was so prominent a feature that any witness would have been expected to notice it.

There are probably hundreds of faces that would match these sketches as well as or better than the pictures actually shown.

Reiser and Nielson (1980) report a kidnapping and sexual abuse case that was solved by memory under hypnosis of an auto license number and names mentioned by the three assailants. The victim also aided in the drawing of a composite sketch.

A more interesting case reported by the same authors involved a woman who was too drunk at the time of her boyfriend's murder to remember any details of the event, but was able to recover them under hypnosis. What makes this case interesting is that research in memory suggests that alcohol may prevent a memory from forming and a nonexistent memory trace should be unrecoverable by any means. This type of hypnotic recall ought to be subject to very careful scrutiny to assure that it is memory and not fantasy or confabulation. The fact that a conviction is obtained in a case is no evidence at all that the material elicited was accurate. It merely indicates that a lay jury was impressed with the witness's testimony. If anything, it demonstrates how dangerous forensic hypnosis may be if it renders intrinsically unreliable evidence believable.

Hypnosis has been employed in the investigation of many well-publicized crimes, including the Coppolino case (1963), the Boston Strangler case (1965), the Sheppard case (1966), and the assassination of Attorney General Robert Kennedy (1969) (Teten 1979). It was also used (unsuccessfully) to investigate the 1975 bombing of La Guardia Airport in New York City (Wilson 1979).

An Israeli bus driver was able under hypnosis to identify a terrorist who planted a bomb on his bus (Holden 1980; Reiser 1978; Wilson 1979). By means of hypnosis, the California police were able to get the license number (except for one digit) of a vehicle involved in the Chowchilla schoolbus kidnapping of twenty-six schoolchildren (Douce 1979; Kroger and Douce 1979, 1980; Monrose 1978; Spector and Foster 1977; Wilson 1979). Orne (1979) points out that even though in this case the license-number recall was fairly accurate, in other cases license numbers have proved to be completely wrong. The results in the Chowchilla case seem to be typical of hypnotic memory recovery inasmuch as they were a mixture of correct and incorrect information.

It is for this reason that all hypnotically obtained information must be independently verified before it can be regarded as reliable. Some authors maintain that hypnotically refreshed memories should be corroborated by independent evidence (Kleinhauz, Horowitz, and Tobin 1977). This author does not agree with that view. What is necessary is not corroboration of this material but independent proof of the facts so that hypnotically facilitated testimony need not be offered in evidence at all.

This author recalls an occasion when a guest at his home was worried about her sick mother and wanted to call her but had completely forgotten her unlisted phone number. Since he knows her to be a good hypnotic subject he offered to try to help her retrieve the forgotten number through hypnosis. The offer was accepted, and while in a trance the subject very readily recalled a number. She was utterly convinced that it was correct. Despite her sense of discovery and excitement she was disappointed to learn, when she dialed the number, that it was wrong. Though the error in this case resulted in no more than a temporary inconvenience, had this phone number been at issue in a trial or a criminal investigation, much graver consequences could have resulted. This is particularly so since the subject would have been fully prepared to swear that the number was correct. This example is cited because, unlike the situation in most forensic hypnotic sessions, the accuracy of the information obtained was subject to external validation with ease and certainty.

The Types of Memory Impairment against which
Hypnosis Has Been Utilized

Hypnotic recall has been attempted in cases ranging from a total retrograde amnesia for the events in question (from trauma or drugs), to cases in which it was desired to enhance a nonamnesic witness's recollection of specific details (Spiegel 1980). Some of the common causes of forgetting on the part of witnesses have been:

1. The fact that certain events appeared to be unimportant at the time of their occurrence and hence the witness did not try to remember them, until later developments made these memories critical;
2. The passage of time; and
3. The repression or suppression of the memory of traumatic events (such as rape or robbery) as a defense against anxiety (Kleinhauz, Horowitz, and Tobin 1977; Robinson 1979; Teten 1979).

In some cases hypnotic investigation has been resorted to because the witness had a waking recollection of the events in question at variance with other evidence in the case (Kleinhauz, Horowitz, and Tobin 1977). Such an application of hypnosis is least justifiable, for it lends itself to abuse. It could be used to get a witness to say what the police or investigators need him to say. In spite of the optimistic reports of law-enforcement personnel who use investigative hypnosis, there is little reason to believe that hypnosis is likely to retrieve much accurate new information in cases 1 and 2 mentioned above. In the first case the material is unlikely to have ever been transcribed into long-term memory, and in the second, hypnosis is likely to do little to enhance the ordinary retrieval process available to waking subjects (Udolf 1981).

It is in the case of memories made unavailable by a repressionlike process (to defend the witness against the anxiety that such memories evoke) that hypnosis, with its ability to contain anxiety, would be expected to be of most value. Hypnosis is capable of producing profound states of relaxation that are incompatible with anxiety, since these two conditions involve antagonistic reactions of the autonomic nervous system. Thus it may minimize the psychic pain that the subject would otherwise endure while retrieving the forgotten material to a level he or she can tolerate. Most writers agree that hypnosis is most valuable for the recovery of traumatic memories, particularly those of rape or robbery victims (Haward and Ashworth 1980; Kassinger 1979; Robinson 1979). Since it would be expected that a crime was more traumatic for a victim than a witness, investigative hypnosis may be psychologically more effective on the former, even though hypnotizing a victim is more likely to present subsequent legal problems.

Salzberg (1977) describes the critical factors in predicting the success of hypnosis in augmenting recall:

1. The subject's motivation to recall;
2. The subject's hypnotic susceptibility;
3. The amount of emotional blocking present; and
4. The actual knowledge that the subject has of the events in question.

Kleinhauz, Horowitz, and Tobin (1977) think that the two most important predictors of enhanced hypnotic recall are the amount of anxiety produced by the event to be remembered and the meaningfulness of the material. The more anxiety produced and the more meaningful the material, the more likely hypnosis is to succeed. The least important factor is the subject's hypnotic susceptibility. The other factors are all crucial.

The Principles of Memory and Forgetting

The ordinary psychological laws governing the processes of memory and forgetting are not suspended when a subject is in a trance (Orne 1979). In order for the reader to appreciate which claims made for hypnotic hypermnesia are reasonable and which require careful scrutiny because they conflict with the known facts concerning memory, a brief survey of some of the experimental findings in the area of memory and hypnotic hypermnesia is necessary.

Learning and memory are related like the head and tail of a coin; one cannot exist without the other. Studies that test retention immediately after acquisition are generally labeled learning studies, while studies that permit a time lapse to occur between acquisition and testing are generally termed memory studies. Most authorities believe that there are three stages involved in memory:

1. *Acquisition*, during which the material to be remembered is learned;
2. *Retention*, or the interval between acquisition and testing, during which the material is stored in the nervous system; and
3. *Retrieval*, during which the material stored is brought back into consciousness (Gleitman 1981; Hilgard and Loftus 1979).

Much of the research seems to indicate that there are three separate systems involved in the functioning of memory: the sensory registers; short-term memory (STM); and long-term memory (LTM) (Adams 1976; Gleitman 1981; Houston 1981; Wickelgren 1977).

The sensory registers can best be illustrated by the effect commonly known as a positive afterimage, or persistence of vision. This permits a visual image to be seen for a fraction of a second after a stimulus is gone. It is this effect that makes possible the illusion of smooth motion when the viewer is shown a sequential series of still pictures in a moving picture. All sensory modalities probably have an afterimage, but most research has centered on the visual and auditory senses. There are substantial differences in the duration of sensory afterimages in the various sense modalities. A visual afterimage or *iconic* image has an order of magnitude of around 300 milliseconds, while an auditory afterimage or echo may last for several seconds (Darwin, Turvey, and Crowder 1972; Sperling 1960).

The sensory registers hold information long enough for the cognitive and memory systems to perform operations on them. These operations are necessary for both perception and the creation of permanent memories. Perception encompasses more than the mere reception of sensory information. It involves putting the information into a context and recognizing its significance. People do not normally see a visual pattern as a meaningless array of points of different brightness and color, but organize these points into enduring objects or *figures* against a background or *ground*. The early Gestaltists tried to discover the principles governing the grouping of certain stimuli into figures as opposed to grounds, and developed various laws of perception including the law of proximity, the law of similarity, the law of continuity, and closure.

The Law of Proximity

Things proximate to each other in time or space tend to be grouped together. Examples of this are the grouping of letters into words on a printed page by spacing, or the grouping of sounds into meaningful patterns by the temporal spacing of the *dit* and *dah* sounds in radio code.

This is the reason that figure 2–1 is perceived as three columns of X's and figure 2–2 is seen as three rows of X's.

The Law of Similarity

Things similar to each other tend to be grouped together. This is the reason that figure 2–3 appears to be three columns rather than three rows.

Figure 2–4 is an example of a conflict between the law of proximity (which would cause the figure to be seen as three rows), and the law of similarity (which would cause it to be perceived as three columns). It is an example of an ambiguous figure, like the familiar drawing that can be seen as either two faces or a vase depending on how the viewer organizes the figure and ground elements.

```
X     X     X
X     X     X
X     X     X
```

Figure 2–1.

```
XXX
XXX
XXX
```

Figure 2–2.

```
X   O   X
X   O   X
X   O   X
```

Figure 2–3.

```
XOX
XOX
XOX
```

Figure 2–4.

The Law of Continuity

The viewer tends to follow the natural curves of lines. For example, figure 2–5 is generally perceived as shown in figure 2–6, not as shown in figure 2–7.

Closure

The viewer fills in missing parts of a stimulus complex. For example, figure 2–8 will be perceived as an *A*, not three isolated lines, and figure 2–9 will be perceived as a circle, not a large arc. It is this principle that makes it possible to read badly mutilated writing caused by a bad stencil.

   Because people organize things into enduring figures against backgrounds in accordance with these and other Gestalt principles of perception, they develop certain perceptual constancies such as shape, color, brightness, size, and position, to mention a few. For example, they learn that the shape of a coin does not change if it is rotated. Even if it is positioned to cause an elliptical image to fall on the retina it is still perceived as round. Similarly, a purple surface is one that reflects only blue and red light. If it were viewed under red illumination, the only color it could reflect would be red and hence in reality it has become red. However, a viewer having once perceived a

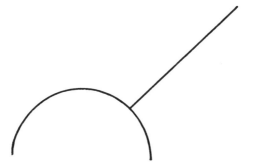

Figure 2–5.

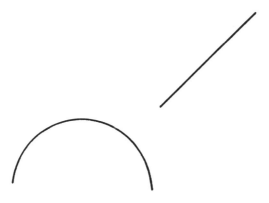

Figure 2–6.

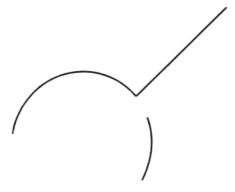

Figure 2–7.

Figure 2–8.

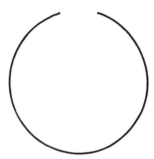

Figure 2–9.

dress as purple will continue to report it as purple even when viewed under a red light because he has learned that colors of a garment do not change with the color of the ambient light.

There are several points to be made concerning these elementary facts of perception.

First, none of this organization is accomplished at the level of the sensory register. Perception is a higher level mental process that requires the interaction of an *icon* or *echo* with material in long-term memory to give it significance and organization. For example, Roger Price's "Droodles" generally consist of a series of simple line drawings that are quite meaningless in themselves until he gives them a title, which immediately places them in a context and makes them funny.

Second, in view of the role of coding and organization in the creation of the kinds of stable long-term memories that witnesses testify from in court, it seems highly unlikely that any material can be remembered unless it is first perceived.

Third, it is probable that most of the material entering a sensory register is never noticed or perceived, because it is not deemed significant enough to be attended to. Most writers on the subject talk about the need to attend to a stimulus in order to perceive it, but it may be that the real factor is the ability of an individual to ignore competing stimuli. The well-known cocktail-party effect is the ability to ignore all conversations except the one in which an individual is engaged, despite the fact that other nearby conversations may be audibly louder. In other words, the essence of attention may simply be ignoring all competing stimuli. Although the ability to remember is regarded positively by most people, it would appear that the ability to forget trivia is just as important. Imagine how chaotic life would be if important information had to be retrieved from a memory bank filled with every bit of trivia experienced since birth! Early in A. Conan Doyle's *A Study in Scarlet*, Dr. Watson was appalled to discover that Sherlock Holmes did not know that the earth rotated around the sun. On being informed of this fact, Holmes' response was that he would do his best to forget it, because he did not want to fill his mind with useless facts that were not of value to him in his work.

In any event, the view commonly expressed by police-officer hypnotists that the mind is like a giant video recorder that records every stimulus it has ever been exposed to is patently inaccurate, if for no other reason than that the majority of stimuli experienced have not been attended to or perceived in the first place. Furthermore, even if every stimulus experienced were perceived and recorded, perceptions themselves are not veridical. The principles of perception all involve distorting processes. For example, closure is a form of confabulation. The person reporting figure 2–8 as an *A* is not reporting objective reality accurately.

Every sensory modality is subjected to distortions that are sometimes referred to as illusions. For example, people are so used to assigning the origin of speech to a pair of moving lips that when the image in a motion picture moves its lips they "hear" the sound coming from the image, even though the speaker is far removed. People "hear" ventriloquists' dummies talking. In the area of proprioception a pilot may actually be flying upside down and believe that he is oriented 180 degrees in the other direction. This is the reason that pilots have to be trained to believe their instruments when they conflict with their senses.

For purposes of the present discussion, perception need not be explored in greater detail. It is sufficient to say that eyewitness testimony is generally regarded by the courts as the best kind of evidence. The study of perception indicates that it may not be (Marshall 1969). Nevertheless, the facts of perception tend to show that the video-recorder or exact-copy theory of memory is untrue even if there were no other objections to it. As will be shown presently, there *are* many other objections.

Material in the sensory registers is transferred into a short-term memory system that is capable of storing items for a period of less than a minute, but items can be held there longer by *rehearsal* (as in continuously repeating a phone number while dialing) (Peterson and Peterson 1959).

Material in short-term memory (STM) has been processed to the point of being perceived, and now must be processed further if it is to be set into long-term memory (LTM). This additional processing is evidenced by research showing that in verbal memories, STM tends to hold items by sound patterns, while in LTM they are filed by semantic meanings (Baddeley 1966). In contrast to short-term memory, long-term memory may retain items for as long as a lifetime (Gleitman 1981).

The storage capacities of these two memory systems vary greatly. Long-term memory holds all memories dating back beyond about a minute, and short-term memory, of the events of the past minute, appears limited to about 7 ± 2 items (Miller 1956).

The fact that short-term memory is limited to about seven items would be a substantial bottleneck to the conversion of material into long-term memory, if it were not for the process generally referred to as the *chunking* of information. This phenomenon in turn depends on the fact that the material has been organized (perceived) in going from the sensory register into short-term memory. If instead of having to deal with twenty-five isolated letters (which it cannot), short-term memory is presented with the same letters organized into seven words, it can handle the task. Indeed, it can handle many more than seven words if the words themselves are organized into larger semantic patterns (Gleitman 1981; Wickelgren 1977).

It appears that the bulk of conscious experience is made up of inputs from the sensory registers and the contents of short-term memory plus material recovered from long-term storage.

The material in long-term memory corresponds to what Freud called the pre-conscious system, because this material is not normally conscious until it is needed. Material in the short-term system apparently enters the long-term system by being encoded into categories. For verbal materials these categories are generally organized semantically. For example, if lists of items such as nonsense syllables or words are presented randomly, they tend to be recalled in organized clusters (Bousfield 1953). Merely rehearsing items in short-term memory does not increase the likelihood that they will enter long-term memory, but organizing or categorizing them does.

Note that this implies an additional opportunity for distortion in the memory process. When an item is assigned to a class, the characteristics of the class are imputed to the individual item. This is essentially the nature of stereotypes. Thus a person classified as a college professor may be more likely to be remembered to have been casually dressed than one classified as a stockbroker.

In order to encode material for transfer to long-term memory it must be compared with material presently in this system. There must, therefore, be two-way traffic between the long- and short-term memory systems. Figure 2–10 is a schematic diagram of the relationships among the three memory systems that have been described.

The material in the sensory registers is constantly being displaced by more recent additions coming from the sense organs. The material in short-term memory is held briefly for processing into long-term memory. Most of it is simply displaced by new material coming from the sensory registers and forgotten without ever entering long-term memory. That portion that is encoded into a long-term memory trace is held in that system, out of consciousness, until it is called upon in the future. The acquisition phase of memory is a selective process, which speaks against an exact-copy theory of memory.

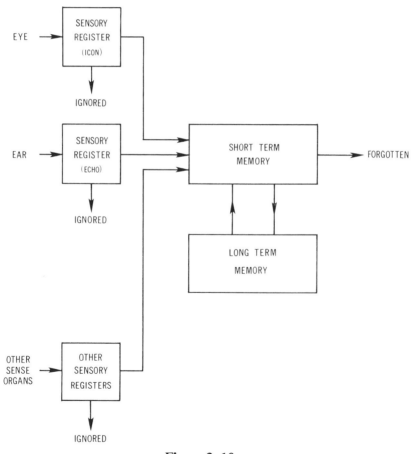

Figure 2–10.

Although it is beyond the scope of this book to consider all of the evidence for this hypothetical division of memory into three systems, it is a model that accounts for much research data, both psychological and physiological. For example, consider the serial-position effect that occurs in learning by rote a list of words or nonsense syllables too long to be within the memory span (that is, within the capacity of short-term memory). There is usually better memory for items appearing at the beginning (*primacy effect*) and end (*recency effect*) of the list than for items in the middle. The recency effect is generally assumed to be indicative of items still in short-term memory and the primacy effect is thought to be a result of items in long-term memory (which have had more time to be processed).

Lesions in the hippocampal area of the temporal lobe generally produce an anterograde amnesia, or a Korsakoff's Syndrome, in which the patient has no difficulties in retrieving previously learned material but is unable to record memories of any recent experiences. This suggests an interference in the process of encoding and recording of long-term memories (Spector and Foster, 1977).

A retrograde amnesia, however, does not interfere with the process of recording new long-term memories, but prevents the retrieval of prior memories. Since some of these memories may return after a time, it suggests that the problem, at least in part, is with the retrieval rather than the recording mechanism. However, since memories immediately prior to an injury are typically never recovered, this implies that memories may require an interval of time to set or become permanent.

Some of the processes involved in the acquisition of permanent memories have been considered. It is now necessary to discuss the retrieval of memory traces into conscious awareness and some sources of difficulty in this process.

Memory is generally tested by either the *recall* or the *recognition* method. The former involves requiring the subject to retrieve the material from storage unaided, and the latter requires him to recognize the target item embedded in a field of other items. An essay examination is an example of the recall method and a multiple choice test is an example of the recognition method. So is an identification made at a police lineup.

In a recognition task the subject must conduct a search of the memory bank to compare the target item with its contents. Sternberg (1969) showed that in searching short-term memory the target item is compared sequentially rather than simultaneously with each item stored. This was evidenced by the increase in reaction time as a function of list size. However, because of the enormous difference in size between the contents of long- and short-term memory, a direct sequential search of long-term memory would be as impractical as trying to find a technical term in a book without using the index. The previously mentioned phenomenon of recall-clustering suggests that this search is conducted by categorizing the target and searching for it under the appropriate categories and subcategories.

The use of the correct category for searching (that is, the same category that was used to encode the item in LTM) will facilitate the search process while selecting the wrong category may impede it (Tulving 1972). For example, if the word *tart* is categorized in the memory bank under the subclassification of food called *desserts*, such a categorization in searching for it will speed up the retrieval and recognition process. If it has been classified under a subclassification of *women*, the same categorization will impede the search.

In general, recognition is a more sensitive measure than recall. It will disclose the presence of some memory when the recall method does not.

There is a third method, devised by Ebbinghaus, that may disclose some memory when even recognition testing does not. This is the *relearning* or *savings* method. If after a period of time following the learning of a list of words or nonsense syllables a subject can no longer recall or recognize any items on the list, he may be able to learn the list to his former criterion of performance in fewer trials than it took him originally. The difference between the number of trials required for the original learning and for the relearning of the list, expressed as a percentage of the original number of learning trials, is called the Savings Score. It is a measure of some level of retention that the recall or recognition tests may fail to disclose.

Forgetting or the failure of memory can result from a failure of any of the three major processes involved: acquisition, retention, or retrieval. It has been shown that failure to learn is a common cause of failure to remember. Indeed, this is generally assumed to be the major reason that students do not get perfect scores on examinations. The law recognizes that a witness cannot testify to something that he has had no opportunity to observe. It should also be obvious, however, that if a witness has failed to record a memory of an event, even if he had the opportunity to observe it, there is no way that such a nonexistent memory can be recovered, hypnotically or otherwise. Such a subject can, however, be deluded by hypnotic suggestion into thinking that a fantasy on his part represents a real memory. He may testify to such "memory" honestly and with conviction. That this is so has been illustrated by experiments in which good hypnotic subjects were made to believe that they had witnessed events that they had not, or even future events through age-progression suggestions (Orne 1979).

In general, memories tend to get weaker with the passage of time. There are at least two major theories that are commonly used to account for this failure of memory. They are not mutually exclusive and since neither accounts for all the data they may both be involved to some extent in most loss of memory retention.

The first theory is called the *passive decay of memory traces*. It simply states that nothing in the world is permanent; just as shorelines are slowly eroded by oceans, and mountains by weather, the chemical encoding of memories breaks down with time. This theory would appear to be wrong, for it would predict that all older memories would be weaker than more recent ones. Everyone knows that some memories from early childhood may seem more vivid than events of last week. The situation is, of course, complicated by the fact that during the interval between the recording of a memory and its retrieval, some memories may have been recalled often and some never. Recalling a memory involves bringing it back into the short-term memory register and this process may lead to its being refreshed, in the sense of being revivified. In addition, it almost certainly means that the memory will not only be restored but modified or distorted in the process. Bartlett (1932) showed that when a story was repeated over a period of time, subjects constantly modified it to make it conform to their own needs and expectations. Changes in a story or memory can take the form of omissions, importations or additions, transportations, confabulations, alterations of structure, and so forth (Hilgard and Loftus 1979). Subjects actually remember only parts of the story and reconstruct the rest in accordance with their ideas about what the story should be. Hence, elements that seem out of place are omitted, those that seem to be missing are added, time sequences are made to accord with the subject's beliefs, and gaps in memory are filled with reasonable confabulations. Note that it is not liars or perjurers, but honest subjects trying their best to reproduce a story accurately, who make these changes unintentionally.

Thus, memory is not a video tape-recording of experience but a subjective record of what the events recorded seemed like to the witness (Hilgard and Loftus 1979). It should also be obvious that once a memory has been reconstructed, the original memory is no longer available to be retrieved. There is good reason to believe that memories start out being inaccurate at best, and become increasingly erroneous with the passage of time. This is especially likely if they are recalled frequently as may be the case with memories of witnesses to crimes.

The second major viewpoint on the failure of memory is the *interference* theory. This holds that what hinders the recollection of memory traces is not their passive decay with time, but the introduction of new material into memory that interferes with the old material.

Actually, because of the huge storage capacity of long-term memory, most memory theorists do not believe that new material interferes with the retention of old memories. Rather they believe such material interferes with the retrieval process by disrupting the organization of the material stored. This is of practical significance, for it implies that material forgotten because of an interference effect is still recorded in the nervous system and may therefore be recoverable.

In a typical interference study, both an experimental and a control group are given a task to learn. Then the experimental group is given a second task to learn while the control group rests. Finally both groups are tested on the original task. If the experimental group performs more poorly than the control group in the final testing, then the interpolated learning has impaired the retention of the first task (retroactive inhibition). If the experimental group performs better than the control group, the interpolated learning has aided retention (retroactive facilitation) (Udolf 1981).

An example of retroactive inhibition can be found in the author's experience in learning foreign languages. During World War II, he learned to speak Japanese to a limited extent. Later, in graduate school, he had to learn Spanish in order to pass a doctoral examination in that language. Although he managed to pass the Spanish exam, from that time forward he was unable to speak Japanese without interposing Spanish words and grammar. In effect, his memory bank seems to have been organized so that all semantic information was classified as either English or foreign, with no adequate subdividision of foreign into Japanese or Spanish.

As previously mentioned, if a memory trace is recorded and the appropriate retrieval cue or categorization is used, the retrieval process is facilitated. Some so-called memory experts on the stage use elaborate encoding schemes that enable them to retrieve a great deal of information rapidly and give the illusion that they have *photographic* memories. Occasionally, however, some children do display a phenomenon called *eidetic imagery*, which is what is usually meant by a photographic memory. It is similar to an iconic image in long-term memory, and such a subject may act as though he or she is actually able to read data from a page no longer in actual view (Leask, Haber, and Haber 1969). This is rare in adults, and Gleitman (1981) says that it occurs in only about 5 percent of school children.

The Exact-Copy versus the Constructive Theory of Memory

Many of the techniques used by law-enforcement agents to enhance the memories of witnesses to crimes, such as the video-recorder technique (to be described) are based on the assumption that the brain records every stimulus that ever impinges on the sense organs and by implication, that it has the potential to faithfully retrieve this information under the proper conditions (Griffiths 1979; Millwee 1979; Reiser 1978). As noted earlier, there is little support for such a theory in the experimental literature and few, if any, workers in the field of memory support such a view. Most believe memory to be a constructive and distortion-prone process (Holden 1980; Miron 1980;

Putnam 1979a, 1979b). Reiser refers to the brain as a cybernetics system. This seems particularly inappropriate, as cybernetics is the science of electronic simulation of brain function, and here the brain itself is being described. The term is probably used because of the tendency that many psychologists have to describe the functioning of the brain in accordance with the latest stage of development of the electronic art. There was a time when analogies between the brain and a telephone switchboard were in vogue. Today it is fashionable to compare the brain with a computer and to talk about memory registers. Perhaps this is done because borrowing the language of the more exact physical sciences gives the comforting illusion that psychology is equally exact.

Reiser (1980) cites the work of Penfield in support of an exact-copy theory of memory. Penfield, in the course of the surgical treatment of epilepsy, electrically stimulated the cerebral cortex of awake patients, who were able to report the subjective feelings produced by the stimulation. A great deal of what is known concerning the functions of the various areas of the cerebral cortex was learned from this work. Penfield found that when certain areas in the temporal lobes were stimulated, patients reported reliving previous memories with perceptual clarity, while at the same time being aware of their present surroundings (Penfield 1958). Presumably it is this work that Reiser and other proponents of a video-recorder theory of memory find supportive of their views. Though such a conclusion would not be unreasonable if it did not contradict so much other psychological evidence, it is not required by the findings. The error seems to be in equating vividness with veridicality. There are other perceptionlike experiences that can be quite vivid, such as nocturnal dreams or hallucinations, which no one would claim were accurate portrayals of past experiences. Penfield's work has caused some people to draw the erroneous conclusion that there are memory centers in the temporal lobe. This is in spite of Penfield's own findings that the visual aspects of a memory are recorded in the occipital lobes, and the auditory aspects in the temporal lobes of both hemispheres. Furthermore, in patients with indwelling electrodes, evoked memories were found to vary with daily events (Levinthal 1979).

The main reason for the persistence of an exact-copy theory of memory among law-enforcement personnel is probably that they are untrained in psychology, and the theory provides them with a rationale to support their findings in court. The theory may seem reasonable to judges and lawyers who are usually not experts in either hypnosis or psychology. Furthermore, these same legal professionals are likely to be less amenable to a constructive theory of memory that implies that most of the eyewitness testimony that our legal system favors is of poor quality, and juries may not be as capable of arriving at the truth from such evidence as is generally supposed.

The basic principles of memory and some misconceptions about them have been described, and the experimental findings regarding the ability of hypnosis to improve memory may now be reviewed.

Hypnotic Hypermnesia

There is an extensive experimental literature dealing with the effects of hypnosis on learning and recall. This literature has been reviewed critically by several authors over the years (Barber 1965; Cooper and London 1973; Dhanens and Lundy 1975; Swiercinsky and Coe 1971; Udolf 1981).

It is difficult to summarize what this literature taken as a whole indicates about the nature of hypnotic hypermnesia since, in many studies, the effect of hypnosis was confounded with the effect of susceptibility, necessary control groups were absent, and the instructions given to the subjects were inadequately reported or were not compatible from study to study. Also some results that appeared impressive have proven not to be replicable.

Nevertheless, subject to these sources of error, the weight of the experimental literature appears to support the following conclusions:

1. Neutral hypnosis, without the use of suggestions of improved learning or recall ability, generally produces no improvement in either (Barber 1965; Cooper and London 1973; Huse 1930; London, Convant, and Davison 1966; Rosenhan and London 1963; Schulman and London 1963; Sears 1954).

2. The amount of hypermnesia produced by suggestions of enhanced recall ability is a function of the kind of material to be recalled and how meaningful it is. There is little if any increased recall of nonsense materials by hypnotic suggestion (Barber and Calverley 1966; Dhanens and Lundy 1975; Huse 1930; Mitchell 1932; Swiercinsky and Coe 1970, 1971; White, Fox, and Harris 1940; Young 1925). With meaningful material, hypnotic hypermnesia is sometimes obtained and sometimes not, but it is more likely to be produced as a function of the meaningfulness of the material. Isolated words produce less hypermnesia than phrases, which produce less than prose or poetry (Das 1961; Dhanens and Lundy 1975; Kleinhauz, Horowitz, and Tobin, 1977; Rosenthal 1944; Stalnaker and Riddle 1932; White, Fox, and Harris 1940; Young 1925).

Orne (1981) points out that, if the video-recorder theory were true, there would be no difference in hypnotic recall of nonsense syllables and meaningful material. Recall for some visual material was found not to be increased by hypnosis, but memory for items scattered on a tabletop was increased (Sears 1954; White, Fox, and Harris 1940). The greatest hypermnesia is obtained under hypnosis with material that is both meaningful and anxiety-producing (Cooper and Lundy 1975; Rosenthal 1944; Stalnaker and Riddle 1932; Stratton 1977; Udolf 1981).

3. There is evidence for and against the view that task-motivating instructions (that is, suggestions that it will be easy for the subject to produce the effect sought and motivating him to achieve it) are equally effective whether the subject is in the waking or hypnotic state (Barber 1965; Dhanens and Lundy 1975; Fowler 1961; Parker and Barber 1964).

Recall of earlier experiences and events of childhood have been found to be enhanced by hypnosis. Often the retrieval technique used in these studies has been age regression rather than a suggestion of hypermnesia.

Age regression is a technique in which it is suggested to a subject that he or she is getting younger and going back in time, either to an earlier period or to some specific event. Typically, good subjects act in a manner indicating that, at some level at least, they are re-experiencing these earlier events. If given standard psychological tests or told to make a drawing, they perform at a level typical of a younger person, but generally more maturely than persons of the age level suggested (Barber 1961b, 1962b; Platonow 1933; Sarbin and Farberow 1952; Spiegel, Shor, and Fishman 1945; Young 1940). For example, subjects regressed to the early school grades usually print instead of write, but often spell and understand words well beyond the age level specified (Orne 1951). Orne takes this to mean that in most age regression there is a form of role playing on the part of the subject, rather than an actual revivification of the past. Role playing means that subjects try to imagine themselves back in the past and to behave as they believe they did then. It is a real effect and the term does not imply that the subject is trying to deceive the experimenter into believing that something is happening that is not. A revivification, in contrast, means that subjects perceptually reexperience the past and all memories after the event in question have been temporarily ablated. This is rarely, if ever, the case. For example, subjects have been regressed to an age at which they spoke a foreign language that has since been forgotten, and recall of that language has been improved (As 1962). In no case reported, however, has the hypnotist been unable to bring such a subject back to the present by instructions in English. If there were a true revivification, with no observing ego left, this would not be the case. When actual records of psychological tests taken on the same day to which a subject has been regressed are available, his performance in the past is found to have been very different from his performance under hypnosis (Sarbin 1950). The writings of police officers, who use the technique of age regression to take a witness back to the scene of a crime, often seem to equate age regression with revivification. One legal writer has gone so far as to argue that a witness should be permitted to testify while under hypnosis because he was, in effect, testifying from perception and not from memory!

From what has been said earlier about memory, it follows that since memory is a selective process, and all stimuli are not recorded, even an event experienced as a vivid revivification would have to include many confabulations of details. In point of fact, a subject can be age progressed as well as regressed, and projected into the future instead of the past. Such a subject will describe with conviction the events occurring at the future date in question (Holden 1980; Orne 1979; Udolf 1981). Few would argue that these future facts are anything other than pure fantasy. The problem with age regression is that in this situation it is possible that some of the facts related may be accurate. It is just as possible, however, that others will be complete fantasy.

Subjects simulating hypnosis seem to perform about as well on age-regression suggestions as real hypnotic subjects, and Barber believes that waking, task-motivated subjects can also do as well (Barber 1961b; Crasilneck and Michael 1957; O'Brien et al. 1977; O'Connell, Shor, and Orne 1970; Perry and Chisholm 1973; Reiff and Scheerer 1959).

One thing that seems quite clear is that the experimental data do not support the many extreme claims made in the clinical and forensic literature for remarkable and highly accurate recovery of previously unavailable memories. One explanation for this apparent conflict is the fact that in experimental work the material to be recalled is rarely of a highly personal or traumatic nature, while in clinical or forensic work it usually is. It may be that in the absence of any inhibitory factors, the normal process of memory retrieval is maximally efficient and hence unlikely to be enhanced by hypnosis or any other technique. However, if the retrieval of a memory is interfered with by psychic pain, or anxiety, hypnosis, with its capacity to inhibit anxiety by the production of a state of deep relaxation, may facilitate recall. If this is the case, the use of hypnosis to break an amnesia may be productive; but its use to enhance a normally functioning memory, particularly of an event that the witness did not find traumatic, may involve all of the risks of hypnotic distortion of memory and provide few benefits.

Orne (1979) notes that when hypnosis is successfully used to treat a traumatic amnesia, the repressed memory typically emerges as an entire experience rather than in pieces. Under such circumstances, it is more likely to be historically accurate than when it is pressured out of a subject with no evidence of pathological memory loss, detail by detail, in response to questions.

Just as there are major differences between experimental and clinical work, there are also major differences between clinical and forensic work. In most clinical applications of hypnotic hypermnesia, the accuracy of the memories retrieved is really quite unimportant. In psychotherapy a patient's subjective reality (and how the world appears to him) must be dealt with, not objective reality (or how it really is). Different people will react to identical events in the real world in totally unique ways. Few if any will remember an occurrence with the accuracy of a video recorder. Pseudo-memories, even those occurring without hypnosis, are really forms of symbolic expression on the part of a subject (just as nocturnal dreams are), and are therefore valuable in therapy. They, like dreams, show how the patient views his life situation and that is what is at issue in therapy.

In forensic work, by contrast, the concern is with objective, not subjective, reality. Here, literally, life and death may depend on the accuracy of the information recovered. In the forensic application of hypnosis, unlike in the clinical situation, the material obtained is not only useless but dangerous unless its accuracy is known. The only way this accuracy can be established satisfactorily is by the development of independent, nonhypnotic evidence.

The evidence from much research in memory retrieval, both hypnotic and nonhypnotic, indicates that when a witness is asked for a free recall of events, with a minimum amount of questioning, he produces less material than when subjected to probing questioning. However, the information obtained tends to be more accurate. If leading questions are used (questions that suggest an answer), the information developed becomes markedly less accurate (Hilgard and Loftus 1979; Orne 1979).

Leading questions are not permitted in the direct examination of a witness in court, for if they were, the lawyer would in effect be testifying and not the witness. Leading questions are, however, permitted in cross-examination (or in the examination of a hostile witness). Because memories can be altered, by a prior retelling of a story, Hilgard and Loftus (1979) believe that pretrial questioning of witnesses weakens the safeguard provided by the rule against leading questions.

Since leading questions inform the witness of the response desired by the questioner, they are thought by many to be even more dangerous when used on a hypnotized witness, who is not only in a hypersuggestible state but is typically anxious to please the hypnotist. Indeed, Diamond (1980) takes the position that hypnotic interrogation of a witness is the equivalent of tampering with him and should render his testimony incompetent. He argues that memory is a reconstructive process and the eliciting of testimony under hypnosis permanently alters future memory. Thus, it changes the testimony that will be given at the trial. This effect may occur with an honest hypnotist, who inadvertently and indirectly leads the witness, and with an honest witness who believes in the objective reality of his "memories." The circumstances of the hypnosis and the fact that an expert conducts the interview may convince the witness that his recollections must be accurate (Orne 1979). Every lawyer knows how difficult it is to conduct a successful cross-examination against a mistaken but honest witness. In effect, hypnosis may render a witness resistant to cross-examination.

The experimental evidence indicates that leading questions can distort the recollections of waking subjects as well as hypnotized ones (Loftus 1975; Loftus and Zanni 1975). Changing a question from the form "Did you see *a* broken light?" to the form "Did you see *the* broken light?" can significantly affect the answers obtained. Changing a question from "How fast were the cars going when they *smashed* into each other?" to "How fast were the cars going when they *collided* into each other?", has affected estimates of speed made by observers of a video recording of an automobile accident (Hilgard and Loftus 1979; Miron 1980).

Putnam (1979a, 1979b) reports no effect produced by the variables of hypnosis versus no hypnosis nor of a time delay of twenty-four hours in the reports of observers of a video recording showing an accident involving a bicycle and an automobile. However, leading questions did increase the number of inaccurate answers in both hypnotized and waking subjects. Subjects asked such questions developed confabulations, and nonexistent details appeared in their stories. So did outright distortions. One subject reported a vivid memory of a blond girl when in fact the girl's hair was black. Information received after viewing the tape was also incorporated into memories of the tape, further supporting the notion that memory is a reconstructive process and is constantly undergoing distortion.

Some writers have expressed the view that since all witnesses are subject to these sources of error, the fact of a prior hypnotic interview should be a matter of no concern, and the remedy for correcting these errors should be a searching cross-examination. This argument ignores the effect of hypnosis on subsequent cross-examination and in effect says that since all testimony is subject to uncorrectable errors, all efforts to keep it as accurate as possible should be abandoned. It also ignores the fact that hypnotized subjects made twice as many errors in response to leading questions than waking subjects, but were no more accurate than the latter in response to nonleading questions (Putnam 1979).

To summarize, suggestions of hypnotic hypermnesia result in the production of moderately more material accompanied by a tendency to confabulate in an effort to comply with the hypnotist's desires. Orne (1979) and Putnam (1979) think that the additional material can be accounted for mainly by the reduction in the subject's standards for acceptable memories. Thus, hypnosis may produce an increase in material recalled at the price of a reduction in accuracy.

Professional versus Police-Officer Hypnotists

The use of hypnosis in police and investigative work has been advocated by both lay and professional hypnotists (Arons 1977). In the past, many law-enforcement agencies employed outside professional hypnotists in their investigations, and some still do. But as the volume of these investigations began to increase, there was pressure to train police officers as hypnotists to develop an in-house capability and thus eliminate the expense and inconvenience of employing outside experts (White, Hogan and Roberts 1979). Martin Reiser of the Los Angeles Police Department (LAPD) was in the forefront of this movement, having initiated a pilot training program at the LAPD in 1975 to train eleven lieutenants and two captains in the techniques of investigative hypnosis (Reiser 1978, 1980). The program was divided into three phases. The first phase was a forty-eight-hour training course given by outside experts. In phase two the investigators worked in pairs with an outside consultant, and in phase three the investigators were assigned to a case with a consultant on call but not necessarily present during the hypnotic interviews (Reiser 1978, 1980; Reiser and Nielson 1980). The program was deemed a success and has been permanently adopted by the LAPD. It was given the American Express/International Association of Chiefs of Police Award in 1977 as the year's outstanding contribution to police science and technology (Anon. 1977c; Reiser 1980).

Reiser founded the Law Enforcement Hypnosis Institute in Los Angeles in 1976 to train investigators from other law-enforcement agencies and, as of 1979, some 450 students had passed the four-day course (Reiser 1978; Wilson 1979). Investigative hypnosis is also taught at the North Central Texas Counsel of Governments' Regional Police Academy in Arlington, Texas (Robinson 1979).

These investigative hypnotists have founded The Society for Investigative and Forensic Hypnosis. Membership in this society requires some training, experience, and adherence to an ethical code (Reiser and Nielson 1980).

The increasing use of lay hypnotists in police investigations has led to considerable controversy and many professional hypnotists oppose the practice vigorously (Burrows 1981; Worthington 1979).

It is necessary at this point to define terms. Some writers refer to hypnotechnicians, or lay hypnotists, who practice hypnosis for a fee as *professional hypnotists* in the same sense that an athlete who competes for money is a professional athlete. As used in this book, the term professional hypnotist refers to a qualified psychologist or psychiatrist trained in hypnosis. Reiser objects to the distinction between professional and police-officer hypnotists and maintains that police officers are professionals (Gravitz 1980). He also points out that being skilled in the clinical usage of hypnosis does not make one skilled in its forensic usage.

The issue of whether policemen are professionals simply hinges on how the term is defined. It can refer to a member of a learned profession or simply to a person who does something to earn a living. Classically, the learned professions were limited to law, medicine, and the clergy. In modern usage the term is generally used to refer to a field that requires graduate education for admission, but it is often extended to fields requiring only a bachelor's degree (especially by the practitioners in such fields). The term will probably lose all meaning within a generation or two because of the increasing number of years of education attained by the average citizen and the tendency to use the term *profession* to refer to any job. Police officers certainly require a good deal of vocational training to do their jobs properly and their status should not be downgraded. But whether or not police are considered professionals, they are clearly not trained as professional psychologists. The issue, therefore, is whether a person not trained in the science of psychology can practice forensic hypnosis without imposing unwarranted risks on both subjects and the integrity of the criminal-justice system (Gravitz 1980).

Critics claim that the use of hypnosis by laymen may endanger subjects and increase the intrinsic risk that hypnosis may produce inaccurate testimony that the subject may believe to be true. Since a police officer is not an impartial expert, he may cue or lead the subject, wittingly or unwittingly (Ault 1980; Gibson 1982; Margolin 1981; Wilson 1979).

Stratton (1977) notes how easy it is to learn to induce hypnosis but how much more training it takes to deal with the innumerable possibilities of side effects and problems. Diamond (1980) believes that police-officer hypnotists are inadequately trained and Teitelbaum (1963b) says that even being a qualified psychiatrist is not sufficient qualification for a forensic hypnotist. He thinks that additional training in both law and hypnosis is necessary. Diamond agrees that even professional hypnotists are naïve concerning the limitations of hypnosis as a truth-telling technique. Although training in law and psychology as well as hypnosis would seem to be the ideal preparation for a forensic hypnotist, there are far too few such dual professionals to satisfy the need for hypnotic investigators.

Advocates of police-officer hypnotists claim that the alleged dangers of lay hypnosis are baseless and that in their experience, these problems do not occur (Gravitz 1980; Reiser and Nielson 1980). They claim that their ethical code makes the welfare of the subject the hypnotist's prime responsibility and that no adverse psychological effects on subjects have been noted (Ault 1980; Gravitz 1980).

With respect to the issue of implanting false memories or generating confabulations and fantasy, Reiser maintains that his department has a policy of corroborating all hypnotically obtained information, which renders this fear a "red herring." He notes that police officers use hypnosis in an investigative not a clinical setting, and work with the same population that they would without the hypnosis (Gravitz 1980). Reiser believes that many of his colleagues in psychology do not trust police or lawyers, and this attitude needs to be reevaluated (Gravitz 1980; Wilson 1979). He believes that the remedy for these dangers is the professionalism of the police. Wilson (1979), however, quotes Margolin's challenge to the claim of adequate corroboration. Margolin claims to have documented twenty cases in which false confessions were elicited under hypnosis.

Distrust of the police and the reluctance to rely on their professionalism as a safeguard is not a new attitude. The framers of our Constitution shared this distrust; it was the principal reason that a Bill of Rights was added to that document.

It is doubtful that the average police officer really understands the fundamental notion that the civil rights and liberties of law-abiding citizens cannot be protected unless the rights of the most antisocial persons are also protected. The idea of relying on the training of the police as a protection against the abuse of police power is as foreign to our legal system as would be the idea that a defense attorney is unnecessary because a prosecutor has an ethical obligation to his profession to avoid convicting innocent people.

This is not to deny that there are many honorable people in the ranks of the police and public-prosecutors' offices. It simply means that the job of a trial lawyer is to win cases, and the primary job of a police officer is to help a prosecutor prove his case, not to protect the rights of a defendant (Warren and Roberts 1980).

The ethical principle that the police hypnotist's first responsibility is to the subject sounds commendable, but if it were really true, why would a witness ever be hypnotized? What benefit is there to a witness who produces evidence to help the *People's* case to balance any risks that he may suffer? The actual risks to a subject from even incompetent, episodic experimental usage of hypnosis appear to be miniscule compared to the risks of clinical hypnosis, but little data exist concerning the effects of forensic hypnosis (Conn 1972; J. Hilgard 1961, 1974; Orne 1965; Udolf 1981; West and Deckert 1965). The fact that police officers report no problems in their experience is not impressive in the absence of data concerning what follow-up procedures were used to detect sequelae and the clinical qualifications of the person doing the follow-up. It is likely that there will be little risk to subjects from investigative hypnosis since their personalities are not being altered. But because considerable anxiety may be aroused by the nature of the material being retrieved, this prediction is uncertain.

Reiser (1978) and Robinson (1979) believe that police officers trained in hypnosis will someday qualify as expert witnesses in court. This is a conclusion that should be heartily contested, unless the area of expertise about which such witnesses are to be questioned is limited to the induction of hypnosis as such, or standard police practices. Judging from the writings of police-officer hypnotists, most of them not only are not knowledgeable about basic concepts in psychology but often suffer from very serious misconceptions concerning the state of the hypnotic art. The major value of an expert witness to a court is his or her ability to enlighten a jury concerning the characteristics of the hypnotic state and its limitations, as well as its capabilities, and to place it in context in the body of psychological knowledge. This is a task well beyond the capacity of any layman no matter how well trained he may be in another field.

As a result of concern about the dangers to subjects and to the criminal-justice system resulting from the limited training of police-officer hypnotists, the Society for Clinical and Experimental Hypnosis (in October 1978), and the International Society of Hypnosis (in August 1979), adopted identical resolutions condemning the use of hypnosis by police officers and declaring it unethical for members of these societies to train laymen in the use of hypnosis or to collaborate with or serve as consultants to them in its use (Holden 1980; Jenkins 1980; Wilson 1979).

The author has mixed feelings concerning this resolution. It is true that police officers are inadequately trained to do hypnotic investigative work on their own. But this is an expanding field, and the dangers might be minimized if police-officer hypnotists were closely supervised by professionals, even though the risks will not disappear simply because mental-health personnel are involved. Moreover, a resolution restricting the right to teach any subject, however well intentioned, seems a far greater danger than any possible misuse of forensic hypnosis.

Techniques of Investigative Hypnosis

An investigative hypnosis session typically consists of a prehypnosis conference, an induction and trance-deepening phase, suggestions aimed at increasing recall, and finally, a termination of the trance.

During the preinduction phase, the witness's apprehensions about being hypnotized are allayed and the nature of hypnosis and the procedures to be employed are explained. Misconceptions, which may affect a subject's ability to be hypnotized, are also corrected. A subject may, in addition, be told some inaccurate things, such as that everything observed about the events in question has been indelibly recorded in the brain and is waiting to be retrieved, if only the proper method is employed.

If a police officer is to be the hypnotist, he or she will generally conduct the entire session. If a professional hypnotist is used, the professional may conduct the entire session or be limited to the induction and awakening, transferring rapport to an investigator for the actual questioning of the witness. This may be done on the theory that the latter is more skilled in eliciting information from witnesses. It is likely that police officers do elicit more information than professional hypnotists, but it is also likely that this information is less accurate. It has been shown previously that the more directive the questioning the more information is obtained, but at a cost of reduced accuracy.

The induction and deepening techniques used will vary with the training and personal preferences of the hypnotist. It is probably not an important variable. There is no evidence that the method of induction has any effect on the phenomena obtainable during the subsequent trance state. The best method of induction, in forensic as in clinical work, is the one that is most acceptable to the subject and his unique personality. It should also be one with which the hypnotist feels comfortable, for hypnosis is an interpersonal relationship involving both subject and hypnotist.

There are three common techniques used for eliciting information once hypnosis is achieved:

1. Suggestions of hypermnesia and improved recall ability;
2. Suggestions of age regression and revivification to the scene of the crime; and
3. Movie or TV-screen techniques. (Haward and Ashworth 1980; Kleinhauz, Horowitz, and Tobin 1977; Kroger and Douce 1980; Reiser 1974, 1978; Robinson 1979)

Age regression is a technique that has the advantage of permitting the subject to describe the events in a narrative form, rather than in response to specific questions, and hence it reduces (but does not eliminate) the possibility of inadvertent leading of the witness (Haward and Ashworth 1980).

The movie or TV-screen technique is a form of age regression. Subjects are told that they can witness the events in question on a giant television or movie screen. Typically, a video recorder is suggested so that subjects can be told that they have controls available for speeding up, slowing down, or reversing the action. They may also be told that they have a zoom control to zero in on parts of the scene, and the ability to freeze the action. The video tape may be described as a documentary of the events in question. This is probably the most common method used by police-officer hypnotists and is one of the most likely to produce false reports.

In the first place, what is being obtained is not a memory but a fantasy. The witness did not view the crime on a television screen but in real life. Second, by being indoctrinated in the erroneous exact-copy theory of memory prior to hypnosis and then having the program that they are to hallucinate described as a "documentary," witnesses are led to believe that whatever they hallucinate must be accurate. Thus, in addition to introducing factual errors, this procedure may also foster in witnesses a false conviction of the reality of these confabulations and fantasies.

One of the theoretical advantages of the TV-screen technique is that since the subject is distanced from the original traumatic events by witnessing them safely on a screen as opposed to reliving them in person, the anxiety that may interfere with memory retrieval is reduced. This is probably true. However, by separating the affect from the event, important psychic connections that might lead to more accurate memories may be interfered with. Police-officer hypnotists probably favor this method because it reduces the likelihood of producing an emotionally distraught subject with whom they are inadequately trained to deal. Also, it would add support to the arguments against the use of investigative hypnosis by police if abreactions were common in investigative work (Orne 1982).

Often police artists are used to make composite sketches from descriptions given by hypnotized witnesses (Kassinger 1979; Reiser 1974). The theory is that the subject can correct the sketch while the image of the criminal is still vivid. The danger, of course, is that he can also be led to believe that the suspect looks like the sketch.

Often, prior to the termination of hypnosis the suggestion will be made to a subject that he or she may remember further information posthypnotically and should contact the investigator if this occurs. Some investigators routinely follow up on such suggestions and contact the witness after a day or two (Stratton 1977). If a witness's recollection appears to be refreshed under hypnosis, but remains impaired posthypnotically, Tietelbaum (1963b) suggests that a transcript of the hypnotic session could be used to refresh recollection. Of course, a video tape could be used for the same purpose. In each case the question is: Has the material elicited under hypnosis refreshed the witness's recollection or has it created it? A posthypnotic suggestion to a hypnotized witness that he will remember everything that occurred while under hypnosis would be the simplest way of having him remember the material posthypnotically. If the investigator is primarily concerned with the welfare of the subject, as is usually claimed, this suggestion should be made permissively, and the subject told that he is free not to remember it if it is too traumatic. Under such circumstances, a refusal to remember is a sign that the subject could profit from some psychotherapy concerning his feelings about the incident. Of course, if investigative hypnosis were properly used, no subject would ever be called as a witness and it would not matter if the subject did not remember in the waking state.

Other hypnotic techniques sometimes used in investigative work include dream induction, automatic writing, and ideomotor questioning (Reiser 1978; Robinson 1979).

Induced dreams can be produced during hypnosis or posthypnotically and their content is readily modifiable by suggestion. As a device to produce memories, it is probably even more dangerous than the TV-camera technique. These dreams could be used to produce a highly symbolic and therefore distorted view of traumatic events that might permit a witness to remember them in this modified way. These dreams could then be interpreted analytically, and such interpretation might suggest leads to be investigated. Under no conditions could such directed fantasies be considered as having any direct probative value as evidence. Furthermore, research on hypnotically generated dreams indicates that they are more fantasylike than dreamlike and have little evidence of the operation of the dream work. Hence, they may not afford the witness as much isolation from anxiety as might be thought (Barber 1962a). A more direct way of lowering a subject's anxiety level is by suggesting structured and tranquil scenes prior to regressing the witness to the events in question (Kroger and Douce 1980).

Automatic writing is a dissociative phenomenon used to get at material that is not readily available to conscious awareness. The subject is told that his hand will write out answers to questions without his being aware of what it is writing or even what it is doing. It is a laborious and time-consuming process that normally requires a very good subject. If this type of approach is to be used, Hilgard's technique of automatic talking by a "hidden observer" seems easier. This is a method used in research to get reports of pain in hypnotic subjects who have been given suggestions for analgesia. Subjects are told than when given a signal, a part of them that knows things that they are consciously unaware of will speak. Pain is often reported under these circumstances that subjects fail to report when asked directly.

Contrary to the classic view of dissociation, however, Hilgard's Neo-Dissociation Theory holds that when a subject is given two tasks to perform simultaneously, one on a conscious and one on an unconscious level, both tasks are performed less, not more, efficiently. In addition to the normal interference between the tasks, the extra effort involved to keep a subject out of conscious awareness also detracts from performance (Hilgard 1973a, 1973b; Stevenson 1976).

It is difficult to see why automatic writing or talking should be of more value in recovering unavailable memories than a direct suggestion to the subject to remember. The attempt is to make the unconscious conscious, not to perform two independent tasks simultaneously. Nor is it desired to compare two different levels of mental operations simultaneously, as in the case of pain research. Perhaps it is the notion of communicating directly with the unconscious that gives the technique its appeal to police hypnotists.

Ideomotor questioning is another method that some writers equate with communicating directly with the unconscious, whatever that expression may mean to them. It is a technique in which the subject responds to questions with an ideomotor signal such as a finger lift or eye blink to indicate a response of "yes," "no," or "I don't know." The response is supposedly made without conscious awareness or intent, and Arons (1977) has even advocated that it be used for lie detection.

Although any ideomotor response can be made voluntarily or involuntarily, and hence offers no assurance against a subject's lying, this is not the major objection to this technique in forensic work. Subjects can lie if they are motivated to, no matter what method of interrogation is used. The principal problem is that most questions that are phrased to elicit a yes or no answer, as they must be with this technique, are leading questions.

The question of the reality of a suggested age regression (or even the presence of hypnosis and its depth) is irrelevant if the material obtained is to be used solely for investigative purposes and not as evidence. It also has little bearing on the likelihood that the facts obtained are true, but may be of importance for purposes of cross-examination.

Forensic Dangers of Hypnotic Investigation

If all police investigators used hypnosis solely as a discovery device on subjects who would never appear in court as witnesses, this section could be labeled "Sources of Error and Inconvenience" in hypnotic investigation rather than "Dangers." However, when hypnotic techniques of investigation are used with potential witnesses, even by well-trained and honest investigators, there is always a danger of creating or destroying evidence. The major dangers will be summarized at this point, for they relate to the standard operating procedures that are employed by various law-enforcement agencies. These procedural guidelines were adopted in an effort to control these sources of error or at least to enable prosecutors to claim that they have not destroyed the value of a potential witness by pretrial hypnosis.

Even under ideal conditions, with an honest and highly competent hypnotist and an honest witness motivated to get at the truth, there are certain distortions that occur in hypnotic (and even nonhypnotic) recall. These include, but are not limited to the following:

1. Errors and distortions introduced into the original perception and recording process. No method of recall can rectify this situation. (Kleinhauz, Horowitz, and Tobin 1977; Spector and Foster 1977)
2. Confabulations, or the filling in of forgotten details, may occur when the subject unintentionally deduces what should have occurred between remembered events and does not recognize that these memories are not factual. These are really forms of secondary elaboration and closure. (Diamond 1980; Dilloff 1977; Kroger and Douce 1980; Reiser and Nielson 1980; Spector and Foster 1977; Warren and Roberts 1980)
3. Pure fantasies, based on wishful thinking and the dynamic needs of the subject, may also occur. These may be quite vivid and are often commingled with factual material. (Diamond 1980; Kleinhauz, Horowitz, and Tobin 1977; Kroger and Douce 1980; Spector and Foster 1977)

4. So-called screen memories may be produced. These are inappropriate memories or fantasies that are used by the subject as a defense to prevent the retrieval of real but traumatic memories (Kroger and Douce 1980).

In addition to the foregoing sources of error, a subject motivated to lie is fully capable of doing so even in the deepest trance (Dilloff 1977; Douce 1979; Graham 1980; Kroger and Douce 1980; McLaughlin 1981; Pelanda 1981; Spector and Foster 1977; Udolf 1981; Warren and Roberts 1980). Furthermore, there is no way to detect this lying without resort to external evidence (Spector and Foster 1977). Even if they are not lying, subjects may be convinced of the truth of their own erroneous recollections. Thus, neither subjects nor the hypnotist (nor the trier of the facts) can separate fact from fantasy in the witness's story without extrinsic evidence. An honest witness may tell a false story with a strong conviction of its truth (Diamond 1980; Dilloff 1977; Haward and Ashworth 1980; Orne 1961; Spiegel 1980; Stratton 1977). Therefore, hypnotically retrieved memories must be regarded as merely the basis for a working hypothesis, not fact, unless independently established (Kleinhauz, Horowitz, and Tobin 1977).

Distortion may also be introduced by the words used to describe even a vivid and accurate memory trace. The same words may produce radically different images in different listeners (Spector and Foster 1977). This problem can be aggravated if the witness is of low intelligence or lacks skill in English.

If a subject is motivated to lie under hypnosis, he may also simulate hypnosis or a deeper state than he is actually experiencing in an effort to add credibility to his story. This may be convincing to people who naïvely believe that hypnosis is a truth-assuring device (Gravitz 1980; Kroger and Douce 1980; Spector and Foster 1977). There is a plethora of research that indicates that experts are usually unable to detect subjects simulating hypnosis. As a demonstration in his graduate hypnosis course, the author usually has someone hypnotize only one of two students in another room. The other is instructed to act as though he were hypnotized and to try to deceive the class. Both are then brought back before the class and subjected to tests to see if the simulating subject can be identified. To date, such identification has been successful at no more than the level of chance (of course, being students of hypnosis, these simulators are highly sophisticated).

Hypnotic memory refreshment, like all hypnotic phenomena, requires a subject who is both willing and highly motivated. Hypnosis is not capable of forcing information from a reluctant or recalcitrant witness (Dilloff 1977).

If the hypnotist's technique is less than perfect, as it always is, additional errors may be produced by the unreliability of these methods. A major characteristic of a hypnotized subject, besides hypersuggestibility, is compliance, or the desire to please the hypnotist. Most subjects tend to tell the hypnotist what they believe he wishes to hear. Any inadvertent cues, however subtle, that the hypnotist may give the subject that tend to apprise him of these wishes, are likely to affect the results obtained (Diamond 1980; Dilloff 1977; Gravitz 1980; Griffin 1980; Haward and Ashworth 1980; Reiser and Nielson 1980; Spector and Foster 1977; Stratton 1977; Teten 1979; Warren and Roberts 1980; Zelig and Beidleman 1981).

The employment of leading questions, a problem even with waking subjects, is much more a danger with hypnotized subjects for at least two reasons. In the first place, the subject's hypersuggestibility and his desire to please the hypnotist make him easier to lead (Gravitz 1980; Holden 1980). More important, perhaps, is the fact that during a trial, leading questions are usually asked on cross-examination in the context of an adversarial relationship. Typically, the witness, feeling himself under attack (as he in fact may be), is on his guard against the suggestions being made. Under hypnosis, he perceives no such attack and this puts the cause of truth in greater jeopardy. More subtle cues, such as the hypnotist's manner, tone of voice, and the direction of questions, even if nonleading, may also have an effect on the witness's story (Warren and Roberts 1980). So, too, can the physical environment in which a hypnotic interview is conducted (Dilloff 1977). Ideally, the setting for the interrogation should be a neutral one, but this is not really possible. Even the office of a doctor employed by the state is not truly neutral, though it is more so than a room in a police station. The presence of third parties and their affiliations can also exert pressure on the witness to conform to their expectations (Gravitz 1980).

Since hypnosis involves an interpersonal relationship between the hypnotist and the subject, the quality of this relationship is one of the most important considerations in determining how accurate the information obtained is likely to be (Dilloff 1977; Warren and Roberts 1980). Ideally the subject should be convinced that the hypnotist is a neutral person who is merely interested in getting at the truth, whatever it may be. Of course, it is impossible for a forensic hypnotist ever to be truly neutral, because some party has to employ him and there is always some degree of pressure on the expert to produce something to justify his fee. This pressure might be reduced if the hypnotist were employed by the court but it is certainly exacerbated when the hypnotist is a police officer.

The notion of Warren and Roberts (1980) that a hypnotized subject surrenders control over some of his ego functions to the hypnotist in the course of their relationship is really a misconception. In reality, the subject generally will accept only those suggestions that are in consonance with his or her own personality and standards. This is why Orne (1972) notes that the hypnotist's power over the subject is illusory. By limiting suggestions to those acceptable to the subject, the hypnotist seems to have more control over the subject than is the actual case. If the hypnotist really had this control, then a witness would indeed be unable to lie under hypnosis.

In addition to failing to recognize the inaccuracies of their own recollections, subjects may also fail to remember the source of posthypnotic suggestions. The literature contains examples too numerous to cite of false testimony produced under hypnosis or of testimony produced by such faulty technique that the results should be viewed with extreme skepticism (see for example Gravitz 1980; Holden 1980).

So far, the possibilities of errors produced by ethical hypnotists have been discussed. It is not inconceivable that a certain number of forensic hypnotists, whether police officers or mental-health professionals, may prove unethical or overreaching, and may deliberately attempt to product evidence that helps their case without regard for the truth (Warren and Roberts 1980). A police officer or prosecutor may take the view that he knows the defendant is guilty, even though he cannot prove it, and rationalize that the end justifies the means. Actually, such an unscrupulous individual may pose less of a danger than an honest but incompetent forensic hypnotist. Unscrupulous actions are more likely to be detected by a review of a video tape of the hypnotic interview than those of an inadvertently leading hypnotist. This is one of the reasons a video tape of all hypnotic sessions should be required. To be of any value, the tape should cover all contact between the subject and hypnotist from the first introduction until their final parting. An audio tape or a transcript of such an interview cannot provide a satisfactory opportunity for review, for it will fail to record nonverbal cues and suggestions. Such a tape is worse than useless; it is misleading, for it purports to provide a means of checking on the reliability of the operator's technique when in fact it does not. The absence of a tape should always cast the gravest suspicion on all hypnotic proceedings and it renders them valueless (see *Emmett* v. *Ricketts*, 1975).

Video tapes should be made routinely of every forensic hypnotic interview even if the information obtained is intended only for investigative purposes, because it can never be determined with assurance that the witness's testimony will not be required in court.

Teitelbaum (1963b) claims that if a hypnotist sets about to deliberately tamper with a witness's recollection, he may, by suggestion, implant new facts, cause an amnesia for the true facts, or implant an amnesia for the very fact that the witness was hypnotized. If the other side knew of this deception, such an amnesia could be broken down by subsequent rehypnosis, or even the ordinary techniques used in psychotherapy. The unethical hypnotist might suggest to the subject that he would not be hypnotizable by anyone else in the future to circumvent these efforts at detection (Diamond 1980; Dilloff 1977; Teitelbaum 1963b). Such a suggestion could probably be overcome by an expert for the opposing side who suspected its employment, but the difficulty would be compounded by the fact that for it to work at all, the subject would have to be willing, at some level, to take part in this deception. Although these methods of suborning perjury would be harder to employ on an honest witness, it has not been demonstrated to be impossible that such a witness could be deceived about the purposes of the suggestions and the hypnotic situation.

As an example of implanting a false belief (in an admittedly trivial context), the author implanted the delusion in a good subject that the textbook used in her course (written by him) was written by a colleague. In the subsequent waking state, she steadfastly argued with her classmates in support of this view, and came up with every imaginable rationalization to support it, even when confronted with conflicting evidence. For example, when shown the book with the author's name on it, she claimed that her classmates had a different book. In all likelihood, she would have been willing to swear to the truth of this false idea. However, it would be naïve in the extreme to conclude that this proves that she could have been as easily induced to commit perjury in a real lawsuit. The reason for her compliant behavior was probably the fact that she had confidence in the hypnotist, based on the student-teacher relationship. Also, she knew that she was in an experimental situation. This subject was confident that the hypnotist was not going to do anything that would cause her harm, much less permit her to perjure herself.

To get a subject to commit perjury, it is probable that such a trusting relationship would have to be developed beforehand, or the subject would have to be willing to commit the crime in any event, and would merely use the hypnosis as a convenient excuse.

Finally, the hypnotist's own countertransferences, induced emotions, or reality-induced fears can affect the results. Some professional hypnotists will refuse to work on a case if they fear personal retaliation against them by the defendant (Gravitz 1980). Under these conditions, they are probably correct in not handling such cases because it is doubtful that they could function effectively. However, it should be pointed out that unless the defendant is irrational, the risk is probably quite small. The hypnotist is in no sense a witness against anybody, and his function could be performed by any other expert. The elimination of a particular expert would in no way affect the *People's* case. Most criminals expect police and other prosecutorial personnel to do their jobs and are more neutral than hostile toward them, unless the officer in question actually manufactures evidence or testifies falsely.

It can be concluded that although hypnosis has been validated experimentally as a phenomenon and demonstrated to be useful in a clinical context, its forensic use as a memory-retrieval device is not so firmly established. It is impossible to separate the fact from the fiction obtained when using hypnotic memory-refreshment techniques, but this in itself demonstrates that some of the material elicited may be accurate. If the hypnotic material is used merely as a starting point for independent investigation, it can be very valuable. If it is accepted at face value, it may prove disastrous (Diamond 1980).

Procedural Safeguards in the Use of Investigative Hypnosis

Many federal and state law-enforcement agencies have established rigid guidelines for the employment of investigative hypnosis. These guidelines, as previously mentioned, are designed to minimize the danger of producing false testimony, or to enable the *People* to contend that their witnesses' hypnotically refreshed memories were not contaminated.

The establishment of these procedures is a tacit recognition of the fact that many witnesses subjected to investigative hypnosis will ultimately be required to testify at a subsequent trial. If this were not the case, these attempts at procedural safeguards would be unnecessary.

FBI Guidelines

FBI policy on investigative hypnosis is based on guidelines set out by the U.S. Department of Justice in 1968 and revised in 1979, to include the use of specially trained Hypnosis Coordinators (Ault 1980).

Ault (1979) says that the FBI does not intend hypnosis to be used as a substitute for ordinary investigation, and recognizes that the information obtained may be untrue. Therefore, such information requires independent verification. No agent may participate in any hypnotic investigation without the written permission of the Assistant Attorney General of the Criminal Division of the Department of Justice. This permission must be obtained after consultation with the local U.S. Attorney (Ault 1980; Teten 1979).

The use of hypnosis by the FBI is limited to certain major crimes such as bank robberies involving force or large amounts of money, kidnapping, extortion, crimes of violence, and possibly some white-collar crimes (Ault 1979, 1980). The fact that a witness was hypnotized must be disclosed to the court in any subsequent proceeding (Teten 1979).

Hypnosis is only employed by the FBI on willing witnesses and victims to obtain additional information. In no event is it permitted on suspects or potential suspects (Ault 1979, 1980; Douce 1979; Teten 1979). The use of hypnosis on key witnesses and victims, of course, makes it almost inevitable that these subjects will be needed to testify later.

The FBI uses only professional hypnotists. The guidelines specify that the hypnotist be licensed or certified as a psychologist, psychiatrist, physician, or dentist who is qualified as a hypnotist (Ault 1979, 1980). Ault says that, as of 1980, no dentists have been used. The standards set by the American Society of Clinical Hypnosis and the Society of Clinical and Experimental Hypnosis for a "qualified hypnotist" are adhered to by the FBI.

It is difficult to see how either a dentist or a physician (other than a psychiatrist) could be adequately trained to do forensic hypnosis, but it is also true that even a well-trained psychotherapist with experience in hypnosis may lack an appreciation of the legal issues involved. As previously noted, the ideal forensic hypnotist would have training in law as well as in hypnosis and psychology or psychiatry, but there are so few of such people that it is not practical to limit the practice of forensic hypnosis to them. Although the elimination of the use of lay hypnotists would seem a step in the right direction, this guideline is more illusory than real. It is FBI policy to permit a hypnosis coordinator to actually conduct the interview of the witness after the professional hypnotist has induced the trance state. The professional is said to be in charge of the entire proceeding, but he generally is limited to inducing the trance and transferring rapport to the hypnosis coordinator, who actually conducts the interview. At the conclusion of the session, the professional terminates the trance. He is required to be present during the entire session and may permit an agent to be present (Ault 1979; Kroger and Douce 1980; Teten 1979).

Kroger and Douce take the position that the hypnosis coordinator is better qualified to conduct the actual interview than the professional hypnotist because he is trained in the art of interrogation. This is exactly where the principal danger lies. Evidence has been cited earlier that skilled examiners will elicit more information than professional mental-health personnel, but at the cost of accuracy. What is needed in forensic hypnosis is not an interrogator skilled in obtaining a large amount of new material, but one skilled in being nondirective.

Hypnotic interviews by the FBI are divided into three segments. First, there is a preinduction discussion with the subject to dispel his fears and misconceptions about hypnosis (that might interfere with the induction), and to detect any contraindications to hypnosis. Then the subject is given an opportunity, prior to hypnosis, to recall as much about the events in question as possible without prompting. When he has run out of material, he is asked further questions based on what he has said. He is then hypnotized, age-regressed to the time of the incident, and asked to recall the events in question. Again, questions are delayed until the witness has finished his narrative and are based on what he has said. Leading questions are prohibited. The interview takes from one to three hours (Ault 1980; Teten

1979). This procedure, though by no means adequate to assure the accuracy of the resulting material, is designed to minimize the leading of the witness and also to make it possible to say what the witness had remembered about the event prior to the induction of hypnosis. This is important should the admissibility of hypnotically refreshed testimony become an issue at a subsequent trial. How closely these guidelines are followed in practice is another matter. The FBI requires all hypnotic interviews to be recorded either on audio or perferably video tape so that the procedures can be reviewed later by defense experts. The tape should record everything that happened from the time the hypnotist was introduced to the subject because prehypnotic suggestions and expectations can affect the material elicited as much as suggestions made under hypnosis or immediately thereafter. FBI policy seems to require the recording of some aspects of the preinduction briefing of the subject such as his consent, the discussion of preconceptions, the qualifications of the hypnotist, a description of the procedures to be used, and so on, but not necessarily everything that transpires. The video tapes are required to be treated as evidence and the chain of custody controlled. A written report of the results obtained must be filed for evaluation (Ault 1979, 1980).

Ault (1980) makes the point that the hypnotist and the hypnosis coordinator should not know any more about the case than necessary (to avoid being in a position to cue the witness inadvertently), but specifies no method of assuring that they will be given no unnecessary information. Obviously, some information is needed to age-regress a subject to a crime scene. Orne (1977) takes the position that the information supplied to a forensic hypnotist should be given in the form of a written memorandum so his knowledge of the crime can be established. Some police-officer hypnotists, however, have contended that the hypnotist should know as much about the case as possible prior to hypnosis, "in order to deal with the subject" (Millwee 1979). Such a view, coupled with the notion of the video-recorder theory of memory that is taught to police-officer hypnotists, is hardly calculated to instill confidence in the understanding of these lay hypnotists of either the legal or the psychological problems of forensic hypnosis.

The U.S. Air Force Office of Special Investigations
(AFOSI) Guidelines

According to Hibler (1979), the procedures followed by the Air Force Office of Special Investigations are quite similar to FBI procedures. Only willing and highly motivated subjects are examined under hypnosis and they are limited to witnesses, victims, or investigators. Suspects are excluded form hypnotic investigations "except in exculpatory considerations," and if a witness or victim incriminates himself, the trance is terminated and the subject is advised of his rights. Permission to do a hypnotic investigation is only granted when conventional investigation has been exhausted or in crisis situations, for example if hostages are involved. One reason for the reluctance of this agency to use hypnosis is the fact that the Manual for Courts Martial makes statements derived from hypnosis inadmissible at a trial.

Like the FBI, the AFOSI uses only professional hypnotists [clinical psychologists, psychiatrists, or psychiatric social workers, who have had specialized training in hypnosis and hold membership in the American Society of Clinical Hypnosis (ASCH) or the Society for Clinical and Experimental Hypnosis (SCEH)]. Also, as in FBI investigations, the professional managing the trance does not generally interrogate the witness. This task is left to a lay forensic-science consultant. The professional simply induces the trance, estimates its depth, and age-regresses the subject to the scene of the crime. Hibler notes that the professional is not given specific details of the crime in question, but it would seem more important that the forensic-science consultant who actually questions the subject be kept in similar ignorance.

Hypnotic interviews are recorded on color video tape with a continuously displayed time and date and the interview is guided by a detailed script. The tape is handled in the same manner as evidence. Following the hypnosis, the subject is requested to repeat the information given under hypnosis "to evidence enhanced memory." This procedure seems pointless, for what is at issue in court is the witness's memory at the time of giving testimony, not at some time in the past. In addition, repeating the testimony just given under hypnosis does not necessarily establish memory for the events testified to. It may merely demonstrate memory for what was said under hypnosis, or a successful memory implant.

Los Angeles County Sheriff's Office Procedures

Stratton (1977) describes a somewhat different procedure used by the Los Angeles County Sheriff's Office. Unlike the Los Angeles Police Department, the sheriff's office has its hypnotic interviews conducted by professionals with training and experience in hypnosis. In the pilot program, volunteer members of ASCH were used as hypnotists. The hypnotic investigation was limited to serious crimes and the investigator was required to get the approval of the department psychologist and the detective division chief or the assistant sheriff prior to using hypnosis.

The investigator familiarized the hypnotist with "certain aspects of the case to set a background." The information given was minimal but evidently was determined by the investigator and was not recorded.

The people present at the interview were the subject, the doctor, and the investigator. All sessions were audio taped. The subject was initially shown a fifteen-minute video tape designed to allay his fears and correct his misconceptions. He was then given an opportunity to ask questions of the doctor. Incredibly, some doctors asked the subject if there were anything he personally wanted to get out of hypnosis, thus placing themselves in the roles of therapists. This well-intentioned bit of role confusion probably did much to increase whatever capacity the hypnotist had to lead the witness inadvertently. It demonstrates that the use of professional therapists as forensic hypnotists does not automatically assure optimal procedure. After hypnosis, the doctor suggested that if the subject remembered anything later, he should contact the investigator, and the investigators were encouraged to do a two-day follow-up in any event. Follow-up reports on all cases were filed and monthly meetings were held by the five volunteer doctors and the department psychologist to discuss cases and evaluate the procedures.

This sample of standard operating procedures used in hypnotic investigations demonstrates the lack of standardization among agencies. It also shows that there are problems even with carefully thought-out attempts at safeguards. There is one virtue shared by all of these programs—the person nominally in charge is a professional with some expertise in hypnosis and its associated phenomena. The safeguards provided by these procedures may be subverted if the hypnosis is undertaken by a marginally trained or a lay hypnotist. This is often the case in programs set up by local police departments. For example, consider the Hypnosis-Unit procedures developed by a police officer trained as a hypnotechnician.

In this case as in the foregoing procedures, hypnosis is limited to witnesses and victims of serious crimes (felonies) and no suspects are to be hypnotized. Internal departmental approval for the use of hypnosis is also needed, but here the lay hypnotist determines if hypnosis is likely to be productive. Hypnotic sessions are tape recorded and the tapes handled as evidence, but there appears to be no requirement for a video tape. The subject is reexamined after the hypnosis "to establish independent memory."

The hypnotist espouses the following beliefs:

The subject should be told that the mind is like a tape recorder, and that all things seen or heard are recorded in the brain.

A subject can lie under hypnosis, "however if the subject is in a *true state* of hypnosis and wants to answer the question the truth will most likely be the outcome . . . "

The hypnotist must have complete knowledge of the case.

He also describes testing trance depth in terms of Arons' (1977) inaccurate notion that trances occur in definite stages, each of which is accompanied by invariant signs. He formerly advocated using age regression as a test of trance depth, but abandoned it because it required the presence of a psychiatrist or psychologist. Interestingly, he does not find it objectionable for a hypnotechnician to age-regress a subject during questioning, only during depth testing. This is not written to be critical of any particular individual but because it illustrates the superficial understanding of hypnosis that is common among lay hypnotists. This makes possible the uncritical accep- tance of intrinsically unbelievable testimony of hypnotized subjects. This is so, no matter how honest and well-intentioned the police-officer hypnotist may be. In effect, lay hypnotists are the victims of training institutes that have led them to believe that forensic hypnosis can be practiced successfully by an operator untrained in the psychology of perception, learning, memory, or psychodynamics. This is simply not true.

Levitt (1981) describes what he calls the *modal setting* of forensic hypnosis as including these characteristics:

The witness is hypnotized by a police officer;

No one is present but law-enforcement agents;

There may be an audio tape record but no video tape from the beginning to the end of the session;

The police-officer hypnotist knows all of the facts of the case developed to the time of the hypnosis;

No effort is made to determine that the subject is actually hypnotized or the depth of the trance.

Levitt (citing Orne) also makes the point that it is well known that most witnesses vary their stories from interrogation to interrogation. If this is so, it may be asked why there should be a problem if a hypnotized witness does the same. He answers that once a hypnotized witness changes a story, he never changes it again, that the normal processes of recall and its associated minor distortions stop. It is as though the witness has become firmly convinced of the accuracy of the account that he gave under hypnosis and he may become unshakeable in his conviction, even if the story is false. He may become what Spiegel (1980) has called an "honest liar." He may also become a very convincing one.

In a 1977 affidavit filed with the U.S. Supreme Court in the case of

Quaglino v. *People*, Orne outlined a set of procedural guidelines recommended to minimize the likelihood of erroneous testimony being generated by hypnotic interviewing and to assure that there would be an adequate record for review by opposing experts.

In this case, a husband's conviction for the murder of his wife in a hit-and-run accident was based on a witness's hypnotically refreshed memory, and was upheld by the state courts. The U.S. Supreme Court denied *certiorari* (Ault 1979; Gold 1980; Jenkins 1980; Levitt 1981; Wilson 1979; Worthington 1979).

Orne recognizes that these procedures are unnecessary if the subject is not to be used as a witness. However, it is not possible to be certain that the testimony of a witness in an investigation will not be needed at the trial, particularly when police agencies freely hypnotize victims as well as other witnesses.

Orne's guidelines include the following:

1. The hypnosis should be carried out only by a psychiatrist or psychologist with special training in hypnosis.
2. The hypnotist should be given whatever information he may need concerning the case by memorandum, not verbally, so that there is a record of exactly what he knew and did not know about the case should the issue of inadvertent cueing arise.
3. The hypnotist should be an independent professional, not associated with the prosecution or the investigators. (This requirement could be met if the subject is a potential witness by having the court appoint a hypnotist, but in preliminary investigative work it would pose a practical problem, since at this stage of the proceedings there is only one party, the *People*, and the court is not yet involved.)
4. *All* contact between the hypnotist and the subject should be video recorded, from their first introduction until their final parting, as preinduction suggestions can influence the material elicited as much as suggestions made in the trance state or thereafter.
5. Prior to trance induction there should be a brief evaluation of the subject. (The court in *People* v. *White* (1979) suggested a mental and a physical examination to protect the subject.)
6. Prior to hypnosis, the hypnotist should elicit a detailed account of the facts as the witness remembers them. (In jurisdictions that hold that hypnosis renders a witness incompetent, memories prior to hypnosis may be admissible, and this will establish what these memories were. If given the chance by a skilled listener, important new information may emerge without the need for hypnosis, with its attendant legal risks.)
7. The hypnotist should strive to avoid adding new material to the witness's description, in other words, leading him.

8. No one should be present during hypnosis except the hypnotist and the subject. If the prosecution or defense wish to witness the procedure, they may do so through a one-way mirror or a video monitor. (Though this requirement may seem more appropriate to an inquisitional proceeding than to our adversary system of justice, it should be noted that this is not like an ordinary examination before trial where counsel is able to object to questions or personally examine the witness. The absence of third parties prevents them from cueing the witness nonverbally or reinforcing his responses by their reactions.)
9. Tape recordings of prior interrogations should also be maintained.

These guidelines, with minor elaboration, were recommended by the court as procedural requirements for the pretrial use of hypnosis in the case of *People* v. *White* (1979) (Conour 1980; Jenkins 1980; Orne 1979; Warner 1979).

They were also adopted in substance, to a greater or lesser degree, in three New York cases: *People* v. *Hughes* (1979), *People* v. *Lewis* (1980), *People* v. *McDowell* (1980), and in New Jersey in *State* v. *Hurd* (1981).

In *People* v. *Lewis*, the proffered expert testimony was excluded because (in addition to other reasons) these standards were not met. In that case there was a video tape of only part of the hypnotic sessions and no record of prehypnotic conversations between the hypnotist and subject. Also, the defendant's attorney was present during the sessions. In *People* v. *McDowell*, however, the court held that these guidelines were substantially met when the hypnotist was a social worker who had used hypnosis extensively in his work for five years and was working under contract for the county sheriff's department. The hypnotist was not notified in writing of the facts, but testified that he was aware only that a murder had occurred and that another individual was involved.

These guidelines, important as they are, do not assure the accuracy of hypnotically refreshed memory. By and large, they are designed to minimize the cueing and leading of a witness inadvertently or otherwise by the hypnotist. They do not protect against other major sources of distortion such as the influence of the physical setting of the interview or the witness's own intrapersonal dynamics and motivation (Dilloff 1977; Gravitz 1980). Even under the best of conditions hypnotic testimony can never be regarded as anything other than a mixture of fact and fantasy that can only be distinguished by independent evidence. In this light, it may seem inconsistent that Orne, who has always recognized the unreliability of hypnotically induced evidence, has set forth guidelines that appear to give such evidence greater legitimacy. It is the author's view that this is simply the pragmatic recognition that hypnotically refreshed testimony is not going to disappear because experts recognize how unreliable it is and wish it would, any more than the courts are likely to stop accepting eyewitness testimony because psychologists recognize it is often in error. There is a great deal of interest in this type of procedure in police departments all over the country, and the trend is for an increase in the introduction of hypnotically influenced testimony. These procedures are designed to minimize the sources of error that can be minimized, and to facilitate their detection and exposure when they occur.

Up to this point the most common use of investigative hypnosis has been considered, namely its employment by the police or prosecutor's offices on witnesses and victims in the preliminary investigation of crimes. Most of what has been said applies as well to the use of hypnosis on witnesses by the defense, although such use is less common. The use of hypnosis by police on defendants in criminal actions is much less common. Such use is prohibited by most departmental procedural guidelines (see chapter 4).

The use of investigative hypnosis on defendants by the defense might be indicated in the case of defendants who either have an amnesia for the events in question, or who are unable to recall important details that might aid their lawyer in preparing a defense or in locating potential witnesses.

On the one hand, if a defendant is not in custody, there is little to prevent the defense from attempting hypnotic memory refreshment (Herman 1964). On the other hand, if he is in custody, court permission is generally required to gain access to him by the hypnotist. In addition, this provides the *People* with notice of the identity of a potential defense witness, which in an adversary system of justice is not always desirable for the defense (Warner 1979). The question of whether a defense attorney has a right to have his client examined privately by a hypnotist, while in police custody, was answered affirmatively by the California Supreme Court in the landmark case of *Cornell* v. *Superior Court* (1959).

Cornell was an attorney defending a client charged with murder, a client who because of "shock, intoxication or otherwise" was unable to remember his whereabouts on the night of the murder. Cornell had asked the sheriff to permit him to examine his client with the aid of a hypnotist and was refused. The Superior Court of San Diego County then denied a motion to compel the sheriff to grant the request and Cornell brought a petition for a Writ of Mandamus in the Supreme Court of California, to compel the Superior Court to order the sheriff to permit the examination.

Cornell alleged that lost memory may sometimes be regained by the use of hypnosis, that the proposed hypnotist had a great deal of success in such cases in his fourteen years of experience with hypnosis, and Cornell believed that the technique might help his client recall important facts.

The *People* opposed the writ on the grounds that it could not help the defense, since such an examination would not be admissible at the trial. They cited cases upholding a trial court's refusal to admit statements made by a defendant while under hypnosis (*People* v. *Ebanks*, 1897) and, by analogy, cases rejecting truth-serum and lie-detection results.

Justice Peters writing for the court held that the cases relating to the admissibility of evidence given under hypnosis had no application to this matter as the issue was one of discovery, not evidence. What Cornell was hoping to get from the interview was not testimony but information about a possible bona fide defense of alibi, which might be provable by independent means.

The court then discussed the meaning of the right to counsel and cited authority that an attorney not only had a right to the assistance of a psychiatrist when examining his client, but to other kinds of experts. It held that the right to counsel would be a sham if counsel were not given the opportunity to ascertain the facts about an alleged crime so that he could prepare a defense properly. The court held that there was no legal difference between the right of counsel to use a hypnotist to attempt to probe his client's subconscious recollections and the right to use a psychiatrist to determine his sanity. It also held that the failure of the lower court to grant the hypnotic examination was an abuse of discretion.

Lastly, in the motion filed in the Superior Court, Cornell had asked that the hypnotic examination be conducted under the surveillance of officers from the sheriff's office. The application for the Writ of Mandamus contained no such restriction, and Justice Peters said that in the absence of a waiver of his right to confer privately with counsel, by the defendant, no such limit was proper. He held that a lawyer does not have to confer with a client charged with a crime in the presence of representatives of the prosecution, and the same right of privacy is required for experts that he retains to help him prepare his case (Davis 1960; Dilloff 1977; Herman 1964; McLaughlin 1981; Palmer and Sims 1970; Reiser 1978; Robinson 1979; Spector and Foster 1977; W. S. 1969; Warner 1979; Warren and Roberts 1980; Wilson 1979).

The use of hypnosis evidently proved helpful to the defense in this case, for the defendant had been charged originally with first-degree murder following a rape, but when his memory had been restored he denied the rape and claimed that the killing was accidental. The jury was persuaded by his story and convicted him only of second-degree manslaughter (Anon. 1969).

In a contrary decision, the Supreme Court of Ohio (*Sheppard* v. *Koblentz* 1962) refused a Writ of Mandamus to permit a postconviction hypnotic examination of a defendant, on the theory that a prisoner has only those rights conferred on him by law. This case is distinguishable from *Cornell* in that it involved postconviction procedures. However, in another California case (*In Re Ketchel* 1968), involving a request for a hypnotic examination of a prisoner, the court allowed it, holding that it would do no harm to prison safety or orderly administration and there was no reason to prohibit it if counsel thought it might be useful.

This chapter has considered the uses of hypnosis as a discovery tool for the development of leads to new and independent evidence and some of the dangers that result if witnesses or victims, subjected to hypnotic interviewing, are later called as witnesses in a trial. If hypnosis is used solely to discover new evidence, by a competent expert who is aware of the potential value and the limitations of hypnosis, it may prove very useful. If used by an inadequately trained person unfamiliar with the psychology of memory, it can generate many false leads. If used on a witness under such circumstances it may generate false testimony. The next chapter covers the legal status of hypnotically influenced testimony as evidence in a trial.

3 The Admissibility of Hypnotically Influenced Testimony

In the previous chapter the advantages and disadvantages of hypnosis as a psychological discovery technique were considered. In this chapter the legal consequences of using hypnosis on witnesses will be discussed. The use of hypnosis to break an amnesia or enhance the memory for details of a nonamnesiac trial witness is very different from its use as a discovery device on a subject who, in theory at least, is not likely to be a witness in a subsequent trial.

In order to understand the judicial decisions concerning the admissibility of hypnotically influenced testimony, it is necessary to be familiar with some of the basic rules of evidence.

The Relevant Rules of Evidence

The *facts in issue* in any trial are those facts that are in dispute between the parties, and that the party with the burden of proof is required to establish. In a civil case, the facts in issue are defined by the pleadings, or the preliminary papers that the parties are required to serve on each other (such as complaint, answer, and reply). These facts must be established by a preponderance of the evidence by the party with the burden of proof. In a criminal case, they are defined in the allegations of the information or indictment, and the *People* are required to prove them beyond a reasonable doubt.

Evidence is anything that tends to prove or disprove a fact in issue. The rules of evidence are exclusionary. In other words, anything that is probative or tends to prove or disprove a fact in issue is admissible in evidence unless there is some rule precluding it. In general, the rules of evidence are designed to:

1. Avoid the introduction of collateral matters and keep the evidence confined to the operative issues of the case;
2. Limit evidence to material whose probative value is not outweighed by the prejudice it may produce; and
3. Protect the constitutional rights of parties.

This discussion will be limited to those rules of evidence that are directly applicable to situations involving the introduction of hypnotically influenced testimony. (For a broader introduction to the rules of evidence and procedures in criminal cases appropriate for the non-legally trained reader see Cohn and Udolf 1979.)

Any time inadmissible evidence is offered, the opposing party must object to it or the objection is deemed waived, and the admission of such evidence cannot be claimed as an error on appeal. However, the trial judge always has the discretion to refuse to admit evidence on his own motion. Similarly, if opposing counsel stipulates to the admission of what would ordinarily be inadmissible evidence, such as the results of a polygraph or lie-detector test, such stipulation may be honored, subject to the trial court's discretion (*State v. Valdez* 1962). [For bibliographic information on cases, see the Table of Cases and Case Index.] The stipulation must not be contrary to public policy nor adversely affect the rights of a third party (Palmer and Sims 1970).

Ordinary witnesses (as opposed to expert witnesses) are required to testify to what they have directly observed. Except in certain limited and commonplace matters they are not permitted to testify to opinions or conclusions. Furthermore, they must testify about their observations from present memory. They may not read notes concerning an event in issue into evidence, but may be permitted to read them for the purpose of refreshing their recollections so that they can testify from "present recollection refreshed." The courts may permit a variety of memory-jogging devices to be used, ranging from notes to newspaper articles to hypnosis and even leading questions, but in every case witnesses must state prior to testifying that they are doing so from present memory.

Hearsay evidence is inadmissible unless it falls under some recognized exception to the rule against it. Hearsay is the evidence that results when a witness testifies that he heard someone else say something and this is offered to establish the truth of what was said. If the fact in issue is what the other party said, as for example, in a defamation action, then the evidence is not hearsay but direct testimony.

The reason that hearsay is objectionable relates to the Sixth Amendment right of confrontation. This means the right to cross-examine opposing witnesses. Every witness at a trial, after testifying in response to questions asked by the party calling him, must be subject to cross-examination by the adverse party. In this situation, unlike in direct examination, the cross-examining party is permitted to ask leading questions, that is, questions that suggest an answer. The purposes of cross-examination are to impeach the witness by showing that he was not able to observe, remember, or relate accurately, or that he had some motive for distorting his testimony; or to bring out the whole truth, not just the part that helps the proponent's case.

Hearsay is objectionable because it destroys the adversary's right to cross-examine the witness and thus undermines a very important safeguard for assuring the truthfullness of testimony. If a witness testifies to what somebody else said as evidence of the truth of this statement, then the declarant who is not on the stand and not the witness would have to be cross-examined to determine the truth of the statement. It is impossible to cross-examine an absent declarant. Any time there is no person on the witness stand who can be cross-examined, the evidence amounts to hearsay. This is the reason that a witness cannot ordinarily read notes into evidence: notes cannot be cross-examined. Of course, if the fact in issue is not the truth of a letter or notes but what they contain, then they are not hearsay and may be admitted as documentary evidence.

Notes may also be admitted as "past recollection recorded" if the witness can testify that they were made soon after the events described and remembers that they were accurate when made although the witness has no present recollection of the event.

There are a myriad of exceptions to the hearsay rule. Evidence that would normally be excluded as hearsay may be introduced under such exceptions. In all such cases, there is some special reason to assume that this evidence is likely to be true and this replaces the safeguard normally achieved by cross-examination. For example, contemporaneous records kept in the regular course of a business (such as hospital records) are admissible as exceptions to the hearsay rule. This is because the business purpose of these records assures their accuracy.

A dying declaration of the victim of a homicide who has given up all hope of recovery is admissible to establish the identity of the slayer, provided that the victim would have been a competent witness had he or she lived. Here the safeguard of truth, if any, is the supposed imminence of a final judgment of the declarant by the Almighty.

Another exception to the hearsay rule is the *res gestae* (a verbal act). Declarations made by a party to an action, which are spontaneous and occur before there is time to think, are admissible under this doctrine. An admission is another important exception to the hearsay rule. This is an act or statement by a party to an action that is contrary to the position that the party takes at the trial. A declaration against interest is also admissible as an exception to the hearsay rule, but it need not involve a party to an action. Some jurisdictions and all federal courts recognize statements against penal interest as well as statements against financial or proprietary interest as admissible; others limit the exception to the latter. These are all admissible because such acts or statements are contrary to the interest of the declarant, and they would be unlikely to have been made if untrue.

A self-serving statement, however, is not admissible in evidence. A party or a witness will not be permitted to bolster or corroborate his own testimony by the introduction of evidence that he said the same thing on a prior occasion unless the claim is made that the story told is of recent origin (Fed. Rules of Evid. 801 [d] [1]; Warren and Roberts 1980).

Statements made to a physician for the purposes of treatment are generally regarded as exceptions to the hearsay rule because the motivation of the patient to be treated properly is an assurance of the truthfulness of his statements (Fed. Rules of Evid. 803[4]; Spector and Foster 1977).

The results of most scientific tests are essentially hearsay. It is possible to cross-examine experts concerning the procedures they used and the basis for their conclusions, but these may ultimately come down to the results of blood tests or polygraph readings that cannot be cross-examined.

The most common rule to determine whether or not the results of a scientific procedure should be admissible in evidence was laid down in *Frye* v. *United States* (1923) and is known as the *Frye* Rule. In substance, this holds that for the results of a scientific test to be admissible in evidence, the test must be generally recognized as reliable for the purpose used by experts in the appropriate scientific community (Herman 1964; Warner 1979; Worthington 1979).

Under this rule, the usual testimony of an expert for the proponent of hypnotic evidence, that he considers hypnosis to be reliable for the purpose for which it was used, is really irrelevant. What the expert should testify to is the status of opinion in the scientific community concerning the reliability of hypnosis.

Polygraph or lie-detector tests and so-called truth-serum tests are scientific tests that have been generally regarded by the courts as failing to meet the *Frye* standards, and hence are inadmissible in evidence, in the absence of a stipulation between the parties (Boyd 1973; *State* v. *Classen* 1979). Tests that generally meet these standards are blood tests, fingerprints, and x-rays (Boyd 1973). [For a discussion of standards for scientific evidence see *Reed* v. *Maryland* (1978). For a discussion of polygraph and truth-serum evidence see *Cain* v. *State* (1977); *Cullin* v. *State* (1977); *People* v. *Barbara* (1977); and *United States* v. *DeBetham* (1972).]

The majority of the appropriate scientific community does not regard hypnosis as a reliable truth-assuring device (Pelanda 1981; Swain 1961). If hypnosis is used, however, not to assure truth but to help form an opinion concerning the defendant's mental state at the time of a crime, capacity to stand trial, or motivation, it is generally recognized as valid (Spector and Foster 1979).

Both the American Psychiatric Association (1958) and the American Psychological Association (1958) have recognized hypnosis as a valid clinical tool. The term *reliability* as used in the *Frye* decision and by the courts relates more to what a psychologist would call *validity* than to the psychological meaning of the term reliability. In any event, this is not an all or none situation in clinical diagnosis. Rarely will hypnosis alone be able to establish a diagnosis with a high degree of certainty. Most often it will be one of many tests available to form some basis for a diagnostic impression.

In considering the admissibility of hypnotically influenced testimony, it is necessary to consider the time of the induction of the hypnosis, the purpose for which the evidence is offered, and the jurisdiction involved, since the rules are not uniform among jurisdictions. In many states, the admissibility of hypnotically influenced testimony is still a matter of original impression, although some jurisdictions like California and the Federal Courts of Appeal (particularly the Ninth Circuit), have a well-developed body of case law in this regard. As of mid-1982, a search of the reports of the highest courts of all 50 states and all of the federal courts disclosed a total of 399 cases in which hypnosis was mentioned. Of these, only about a quarter of the decisions were directly concerned with hypnotic issues to any significant extent. Thirty-one states were represented in these decisions, so the issue is novel in about two-fifths of the states.

Testimony under Hypnosis Offered as Substantive Proof

No cases have been found to date in which a witness was permitted to testify while under hypnosis before the trier of the facts, although in two cases a witness was hypnotized in court. In the usual method of trying to introduce evidence of what a witness or party said while under hypnosis, the proponent of the testimony offers tapes or a transcript of the interview, or the expert who conducted it testifies to what the witness said (Pelanda 1981). The courts have been consistent in refusing to admit such proffered evidence, when offered as proof of the truth of the statements made under hypnosis.

The earliest American case involving this issue was *People* v. *Ebanks* (1897). The defendant was charged with murdering two elderly people while he was drunk. The defense offered to call as a witness one B.F. Stephens who would testify that he was an expert hypnotist who had hypnotized the defendant and that, while hypnotized, the defendant had denied his guilt. The trial court sustained the *People's* objection to the testimony and declared, "The law of the United States does not recognize hypnotism. It would be an illegal defense and I cannot admit it." The defendant was convicted of murder in the first degree and sentenced to death. Commissioner Searls of the California Supreme Court affirmed the trial judge's ruling without comment (Anon. 1969; Bodine and Lavine 1980; Dilloff 1977; Douce 1979; Herman 1964; Lehan 1970; Levy 1955; Reiser 1978; Sarno 1979; Solomon 1952; Swain 1961; Warner 1979; Warren and Roberts 1980; Worthington 1979).

In *State* v. *Pusch* (1950), the defendant appealed a conviction of murder in the first degree. The North Dakota Supreme Court affirmed the refusal of the trial court to admit the testimony of a psychologist who had hypnotized the defendant and offered to testify that Pusch had denied his guilt while under hypnosis and that, in the expert's opinion, he was telling the truth, since a hypnotized person "loses all control of the conscious mind and is governed entirely by the subconscious mind." The attorneys for the state were invited to participate in one of the several hypnotic sessions but they declined. The court noted that no case was cited by either side relating to the admissibility of the hypnotic evidence and no case was found by it. It held without further discussion that the evidence was "clearly inadmissible." It also rejected an offer of polygraph results by the defense (Dilloff 1977; Gold 1980; Herman 1964; Sarno 1979; Solomon 1952; Swain 1961).

In the course of a *habeas corpus* proceeding in *Cantrell* v. *Maxwell* (1962), the defendant made a motion that he be hypnotized to prove his innocence. This was denied, without a discussion of the reliability of such a procedure, on the grounds that *habeas corpus* is not an alternative form of appeal nor a substitute for one and deals only with matters that would render the original conviction void. Thus, guilt or innocence is not an issue in a *habeas corpus* procedure.

In *Rucker* v. *Wabash Railroad Co.* (1969), the U.S. Court of Appeals for the Seventh Circuit sustained the trial court's exclusion of a taped hypnotic statement of one of the plaintiffs, which was submitted on redirect examination. The court did not discuss the reason for its decision beyond noting that the statement did not clarify or explain any elements of the witness's testimony, but merely tended to corroborate it.

The New York Court of Appeals, in *People* v. *Halpern* (1970), affirmed without opinion a trial court's rejection of an offer of testimony by a psychiatrist, that he had hypnotized the defendant who had described his activities and whereabouts on the day of the crime and had never admitted being at the scene of the crime or having had anything to do with the rape complainant or any other woman. The doctor also offered to testify that a person under hypnosis cannot lie without being detected and must tell the truth, and that in his opinion the defendant was incapable of committing the acts charged. The trial judge found that there was insufficient professional acceptance of the infallibility of statements made under hypnosis to admit such testimony.

In *State* v. *Taggart* (1973), an Oregon court concluded that statements made under hypnosis by defendants were not admissible, because the value of such hearsay was outweighed by the danger that it would confuse the jury on other issues of the case (Scott 1977).

An Oklahoma court, in *Jones* v. *State* (1975), permitted a physician specializing in hypnosis who had hypnotized a murder defendant prior to trial to testify that the defendant's statements made during hypnosis were similar to those made at the trial. The witness was not permitted to testify as to the defendant's specific replies nor to his own opinion concerning their accuracy.

The trial court was found to have properly rejected this offer of proof because its validity rested solely on the reliability of hypnosis, which had not been established, and receiving it would have been tantamount to the acceptance of self-serving hearsay declarations (Sarno 1979; Warner 1979).

The Court of Appeals of Michigan, in *People* v. *Hangsleben* (1978), held, as a matter of first impression, that evidence of what a defendant said under hypnosis was not admissible. The court found that in the instant case the testimony could have been offered for only one of two purposes: either to establish the truth of what was said under hypnosis or to bolster the credibility of what the defendant testified to at the trial, by arguing that the pretrial hypnosis had a "mind-jogging effect." It noted that courts in other jurisdictions had universally disallowed the use of hypnotic evidence for the first purpose on the grounds that it is unreliable.

Although the court believed that the mention of pretrial hypnosis would be more likely to impeach than support the testimony of a witness, since the physical evidence in the case equally supported both stories that the defendant told (before and after the hypnosis), the court thought that it might have the "abnormal" effect of enhancing his testimony. However, the judge refused to permit any mention of the hypnosis, since the only foundation for it was the assertion that the hypnotist was a qualified psychiatrist. In order to permit the mention of the prior hypnosis, it was necessary, the court held, to show by the testimony of other experts or subjects that hypnosis had been successful in restoring the memories of others.

In all of these cases, the testimony of the defendant or a party was offered as proof of the truthfulness of the facts asserted. Even though two of the courts did not give reasons for their rulings, such evidence is clearly self-serving hearsay. In order to be admissible as an exception to the hearsay rule, as a scientific test, it would have to be established, under the Frye doctrine, that hypnosis was generally recognized by the scientific community as a reliable truth-finding device. Without this consensus, the evidence is, and should be, inadmissible.

The next group of cases involves the attempt to introduce into evidence statements made under hypnosis by witnesses other than the defendant. Though these statements are not necessarily self-serving, they are all vulnerable to the objection of being hearsay, and may involve the objectionable bolstering of the testimony of a witness with a prior consistent statement.

In *Shockey* v. *State* (1976), a Florida court affirmed a murder conviction and denied an appeal that was based on the grounds that a codefendant's lawyer refused to waive a physician-patient privilege and permit a hypnotist to testify to what the codefendant said under hypnosis. The court held the testimony would have been inadmissible (Millwee 1979; Sarno 1979).

The Supreme Court of California, in *People* v. *Blair* (1979), upheld the trial court's exclusion of tapes of hypnotic testimony, which were offered by the defense. The tapes described two men leaving the scene of a murder. The defense, on appeal, conceded that the tapes offered were hearsay and did not come within any exception to the hearsay rule, but argued that due process of law is not always compatible with technical adherence to the Rules of Evidence. In view of the importance of the evidence to the defense, counsel argued it should have been admitted. The case of *Chambers* v. *Mississippi* (1973) was cited in support of this position. In that case, the United States Supreme Court held that the rule in Mississippi, that a declaration against penal interest is not admissible as an exception to the hearsay rule, coupled with the voucher rule (that a party calling a witness vouches for his integrity and hence cannot impeach him), prevented the defendant from getting the fact before the jury that another person had confessed to the crime for which he was charged, and hence denied him due process of law (Spector and Foster 1977). The court distinguished the *Chambers* case from the instant one and pointed out that in the present case there was no compelling reason to believe that the hearsay evidence offered was reliable, even though the witness was a neutral person with no motive to lie. It cited expert testimony to the effect that there is no way to determine if a person under hypnosis is relating actual facts. Finally, the court, citing *People* v. *Cartier* (1959), *People* v. *Hiser* (1968), *People* v. *Johnson* (1973), *People* v. *Jones* (1953), *People* v. *Modesto* (1963), and *People* v. *Morse* (1964) said that under California law statements made under hypnosis or truth serum may be admissible to establish the basis of an expert's opinion, but they are not admissible to establish the truth of the facts related (Worthington 1979).

Courts generally exclude tapes or transcripts of testimony given under hypnosis on the grounds that they are hearsay. But why should it be objectionable if the witness testifies while under hypnosis?

There are several objections to such proffered testimony. In the first place, such a witness cannot be cross-examined effectively. His literality in understanding questions requires that they be carefully phrased by an expert, rather than framed by a lawyer. Furthermore, because of the hypersuggestibility of a hypnotized witness, a cross-examiner permitted to ask leading questions could get a witness to say almost anything. In addition, the dramatic circumstances of a hypnotic induction could unduly impress lay jurors who might erroneously conclude that hypnosis assures the production of the truth. Although no cases could be found where a court permitted a witness to testify while under hypnosis, there have been at least two in which a defendant was hypnotized in court, one in the presence of the jury.

In the unreported case of *State* v. *Nebb* (1962), the defendant was hypnotized in court, in the absence of the jury, as a result of a stipulation between the prosecution and the defense. The defendant was charged with the first-degree murder of his wife's lover. His testimony under hypnosis showed that there was no premeditation of the crime. This was the same story that he previously told on the witness stand. The hypnotist testified that he believed that statements made under hypnosis were reliable, and that a hypnotic subject would probably tell the truth if he was a good subject and deeply hypnotized. This view is not in accord with prevailing expert opinion, and seems somewhat surprising coming from a psychiatrist qualified as an expert in hypnosis, but evidently the prosecutor was convinced. He amended the charges, reducing them from first-degree murder to manslaughter and assault. The defendant thereupon entered a plea of guilty to both reduced charges and was given concurrent prison terms, thus eliminating the necessity for the court to rule on the admissibility of the statements made under hypnosis (Anon. 1969; Diamond 1980; Dilloff 1977; Herman 1964; Reiser 1978; Teitelbaum 1963a; Teten 1979; W., S. 1969; Warner 1979).

Unless the prosecution and the defense stipulate that the testimony elicited should be admissible as evidence, there is no reason for such evidence to be any more admissible than other statements made under hypnosis. Such a stipulation would seem unlikely, as neither party would know in advance what the witness would testify to, and the stipulation would involve a substantial risk to their cases.

In *Regina* v. *Pitt* (1967), the Supreme Court of British Columbia permitted a defendant to be hypnotized in court in the presence of the jury. The defendant had been previously hypnotized to refresh her recollection, but was again unable to recall after a few minutes of testifying. Rather than argue for the admissibility of the tapes of the prior hypnosis, the defense asked for permission to hypnotize the witness in court to refresh her recollection. After hearing the testimony of two psychiatrists who regarded hypnosis as a useful way of dispelling a functional amnesia, the court decided it would be unfair to deny the defense the assistance of this procedure and permitted the hypnosis—provided that no questions were to be asked under it. The witness would simply be given the posthypnotic suggestion that her memory would be restored in the subsequent waking state. On awakening, the defendant was able to remember and testified in a manner that convinced the jury of her lack of intent (W., S. 1969; Warner 1979).

This case should be contrasted with *Greenfield* v. *Commonwealth* (1974). There the Supreme Court of Virginia held that is was not error for the trial judge, after being told that a hypnotic session conducted during a trial recess had failed to jog the defendant's memory, to order a defense psychiatrist not to attempt to hypnotize him again (Warner 1979). It is not clear from the decision what the objective of this order was. It appears to have impeded the efforts of the defendant to participate in his own defense and seems contrary to the spirit of the *Pitt* and *Cornell* cases.

The Supreme Court of Arizona, in *State* v. *Austin* (1979), held that newly discovered evidence that a defense witness had given under hypnosis was insufficient as a basis for granting a new trial following a conviction for first-degree murder. This decision was predicated on the finding that the new evidence would have been unlikely to have changed the verdict had it been available at the trial rather than on considerations of hypnotic issues.

Testimony under Hypnosis Offered as the Basis of Expert Opinion

The foregoing cases all held that the testimony of witnesses or parties under hypnosis is inadmissible for the purpose of establishing the truth of the facts testified to, but this does not mean that such evidence is inadmissible for any purpose. There is a substantial body of case law holding that tapes or other evidence of what a defendant said under hypnosis are admissible for the purpose of showing the basis of an expert's opinion concerning the subject's mental capacity or state of mind (Packer 1981). The same is true for statements made under truth serum (see *People* v. *Cartier* 1959, and *Eaton* v. *State* 1978).

The theory behind having an expert witness testify is that often juries, composed of laymen, are required to render decisions involving technical questions that they lack the specialized knowledge to decide. Hence, an expert is called to help them in their task. Unlike an ordinary witness, one qualified as an expert is not limited to testifying to facts personally observed, but may give his opinion on matters within his area of expertise. Since the responsibility for the ultimate decision rests with the jury, and not the expert, they must be able to evaluate the facts on which his decision is based. Hence, it is improper for an expert to give an opinion based on "all the evidence in the case." He must disclose all of the facts that entered into his opinion so that, if the jury regards them as inadequately established, they may appropriately evaluate the opinion. Usually the facts that an expert's opinion is based on are included in a hypothetical question. However, if an expert has personal knowledge of the facts he or she may testify to both the facts and an opinion based on them. (*State* v. *Galloway* 1979).

An expert witness should not only state the factual assumptions upon which his opinion is based, he should also explain the scientific principles and logic that entered into it. Expert testimony that simply states conclusions without explaining how they were arrived at has little value. Additionally, if the conclusions reached are conclusions of the law rather than professional opinion, they may usurp the function of the jury (*People* v. *Bassett* 1968; *People* v. *Lewis* 1980; Bazelon 1974).

The problem with expert testimony regarding a prior hypnotic interview is that although it is a legitimate source of the expert's opinion concerning the defendant's mental capacity or state of mind, a jury may, in spite of the court's cautionary instructions, be overly impressed by the drama intrinsic in the procedure and regard such evidence as substantive proof.

To resolve this dilemma, trial courts, even in jurisdictions admitting such testimony, are generally given discretion to determine whether the value of the hypnotic evidence in establishing the basis of an expert's opinion is outweighed by the danger of misleading the jury. The trial court must exercise this discretion on a case-by-case basis. Failure to exercise discretion is an abuse of discretion and will constitute reversible error.

In *People* v. *Busch* (1961), the hypnotist, a general practitioner with one year's experience with hypnosis, was not permitted to testify to his opinion based on a series of hypnotic interviews, that at the time of a sexual murder the defendant lacked the capacity to form an intent. The hypnotist did not qualify as an expert and an inadequate foundation, concerning the reliability of hypnosis, was established (Anon. 1969; Dilloff 1977; Herman 1964; Reiser 1978; Sarno 1979; Warner 1979). This decision should be contrasted with an earlier one (*State* v. *Donovan*, 1905) that held that a witness could be qualified as an expert in hypnosis on the basis of merely reading a book. The *Busch* case indicates that police officers and other lay hypnotists are unlikely to be accepted as expert witnesses.

The trial court in *People* v. *Modesto* (1963), permitted a defense psychiatrist to testify as to her opinion, based on her hypnotic examination of the defendant, concerning the defendant's state of mind at the time of the murder of two young girls. However, it excluded both her proffered explanation of the use of hypnosis as an analytic tool and the tapes of the hypnotic session. The Supreme Court of California ruled that it was error to exclude the explanation of hypnosis as an analytic tool, since this was admissible to explain the basis for her opinion. The court also noted that the trial court could have excluded the tapes in its discretion but in this case it failed to exercise any discretion and erroneously assumed that the *Busch* case required their exclusion. This was error, for here the witness was qualified as an expert psychiatrist. Thus, the court should have listened to the tapes, in the absence of the jury, and then determined in its sound discretion if the tapes' value for establishing the basis of the expert's opinion was outweighed by the danger that the jury would confuse the purpose of their admission into evidence (Anon. 1969; Dilloff 1977; Reiser 1978; Sarno 1979; Spector and Foster 1977; Warner 1979).

In *State* v. *Harris* (1965), the Supreme Court of Oregon upheld the trial court which, in the exercise of its discretion, excluded tapes of the defendant's hypnotic interview that were offered to establish the basis of an expert opinion that the defendant suffered from amnesia. The exclusion was because the court believed that there was no way to prevent a jury that heard these tapes from regarding them as proof of the statements made under hypnosis (Dilloff 1977; Sarno 1979; Scott 1977; Warner 1979).

Similarly, in *People* v. *Hiser* (1968), a California trial court was upheld in excluding a tape of a hypnotic interview offered to show the basis of an expert's opinion concerning the mental state of a defendant convicted of voluntary manslaughter in a child-abuse case. The appellate court held that the trial judge had exercised his discretion in excluding the tapes (Dilloff 1977; Sarno 1979; Warner 1979).

In *People* v. *Thomas* (1969), however, a California trial judge allowed a film of the defendant under hypnosis to be viewed by the jury to help it evaluate the testimony of the defense psychiatrist that at the time of the killing the defendant was incapable of forming the intent to murder her child (Anon. 1969; Warner 1979). In light of the fear expressed by many that a jury may be overimpressed by hypnotic evidence or regard it as substantive proof of the facts related under hypnosis, it is interesting to note that in this unreported case the jury found the defendant guilty of first-degree murder, in spite of the admission of the film. [See also *State* v. *Turner* (1970), in which a doctor testified, by stipulation, that he believed the defendant's exculpatory statements made under hypnosis to be true, and the jury nevertheless voted to convict (Warner 1979).]

In the murder prosecution of Sirhan Sirhan (*People* v. *Sirhan* 1972) a defense psychiatrist related how Sirhan was hypnotized in his cell and how he had reenacted the murder in a manner indicating that he was psychotic. A defense application to reenact this interview by hypnotizing the defendant in court was denied. It was found that such a reenactment could serve no purpose in establishing the basis of the expert's opinion and would simply serve to influence the jury unduly (Warner 1979).

The Supreme Court of South Carolina in *State* v. *Pierce* (1974) upheld a trial court that permitted a hypnotist to testify to what the defendant said under hypnosis, which aided a psychiatrist to form his opinion of the defendant's mental state, but excluded statements concerning the defendant's whereabouts on certain dates or his guilt or innocence. The trial judge heard the hypnotist's proffered testimony in the absence of the jury, and properly exercised discretion about which portions of the testimony should be admitted. The reviewing court noted that the material testified to under hypnosis was not admissible for purposes of proving its truth (Sarno 1979).

In all of the foregoing cases involving the introduction of hypnotically induced statements used as evidence of the basis of an expert's opinion concerning the mental condition, motivation, or specific intent of a defendant, the courts have held that these statements were admissible for this purpose only, not as proof of the facts stated. Whether or not the court actually admitted the evidence, in whole or part, was simply a matter of how it exercised discretion in striking a balance between the value of the evidence for the purpose stated, and the possibility that the jury would regard it as substantive proof of what was said.

Following a discussion of the general unreliability of hypnotic evidence, however, the Supreme Court of Virginia in *Greenfield* v. *Commonwealth* (1974) held that despite the fact that "a few jurisdictions have permitted hypnotic evidence to be admitted under limited circumstances," hypnotic evidence, whether in the form of the subject testifying in court under hypnosis or another's relating what he said, is inadmissible (Reiser 1978; Sarno 1979; Spector and Foster 1977; Warner 1979).

In *Rodriguez* v. *State* (1976), a Florida conviction of second-degree murder was affirmed after the trial court excluded testimony of a psychiatrist-hypnotist regarding statements made by the accused while under hypnosis. The appellate court ruled that the trial court did not abuse its discretion in ruling out such testimony as unreliable (Millwee 1979; Sarno 1979).

In a similar ruling, the Supreme Court of Pennsylvania (*Commonwealth* v. *Luzasky* 1976) affirmed a sentence, when a psychiatrist's opinion concerning the state of mind of the defendant at the time of the shooting was excluded. Justice Manderino dissented and said that once it was established that the psychiatrist was properly qualified, the issue of the value of his testimony should have been submitted to the collective wisdom of the jury.

To summarize the cases presented to this point, all are in essential agreement that statements made under pretrial hypnosis are inadmissible as hearsay when offered substantively, and in the case of exculpatory statements made by a defendant, as self-serving as well. There is no reason why, if a statement made under hypnosis falls within one of the recognized exceptions to the hearsay rule, it should not be admissible. But most of them do not.

Statements made under hypnosis are often compared by legal commentators with truth-serum or lie-detector tests. This comparison results from confusing hypnosis with a truth-assuring device. If looked upon in this light, however, hypnosis, like polygraph and truth-serum results, fails the *Frye* test and is not admissible in evidence because there is no acceptance of hypnosis by the scientific community as a reliable method for purposes of detecting the truth.

However, hypnosis is a recognized method of clinical investigation and diagnosis. Hence statements made under hypnosis may be admissible to show the basis for an expert's opinion, providing that the trial judge does not believe the risk that the statements will be treated by the jury as substantive evidence of the facts stated outweighs its value in helping the jury evaluate expert opinion.

An illustration of the value of knowing the basis of an expert's opinion is found in the decision of the Appellate Division of the New York Supreme Court in *People* v. *Wofford* (1977). A nonjury conviction in a murder case was reversed on the basis of the evaluation of conflicting psychiatric and psychological testimony concerning the sanity of the defendant (some of which testimony involved hypnotic interviewing). Without knowledge of what the experts' conclusions were based on, such a review would be impossible.

The majority of the cases support the admissibility of hypnotically induced statements to show the basis of an expert's opinion, but Virginia does not even allow this use of hypnotic statements. No case has been found in which a court permitted an in-court hypnotic examination of a witness in the presence of a jury. Whether or not such hypnotic testimony should be regarded as hearsay because of the practical difficulty it would impose on cross-examination, it is usually excluded because it would be unduly impressive to the jury, and hypnosis has not been demonstrated to be a reliable method of getting at the truth. If anything, the problems discussed in chapter 2 indicate that testimony under hypnosis is not only not more reliable than waking testimony; it may often be even less reliable.

Pretrial Hypnosis to Refresh the Memory of Witnesses

There is another line of cases that deal not with the admissibility of statements made by a hypnotized subject, but with statements made by waking subjects after pretrial hypnosis to break an amnesia or refresh memory. As in the previous decisions, these cases have been resolved in accordance with established rules of evidence. The law permits a wide range of devices to be used to jog the memory of witnesses and, as long as the witnesses testify that their memories have been restored and they are now testifying from present memory, they are permitted to do so. However, because the courts recognize the danger that hypnosis can produce memory distortions and even alter the ability of subjects to recognize these distortions, some courts impose limits on how the hypnosis must be documented to minimize these risks. Some courts do not permit witnesses to testify from hypnotically refreshed memory under any circumstances.

Harding v. *State* (1968) was one of the first cases to deal with the issue of hypnotically refreshed testimony given by a waking witness. The defendant appealed convictions for assault with intent to rape and assault with intent to murder on the grounds that the trial court had admitted into evidence the testimony of the victim following the use of hypnosis to refresh her recollection of facts that she was previously unable to recall.

The Court of Special Appeals of Maryland held that since the witness stated that she was testifying from present memory, the facts of the hypnotic procedure were fully disclosed, the hypnotist was a professional psychologist with a master's degree and four years of experience in hypnosis, and there was sufficient corroboration of the witness's testimony, the trial court was correct in admitting the evidence and the conviction was upheld. The court also found that the fact that the witness told an inconsistent story prior to the hypnosis related to the credibility and weight of her testimony, not to its admissibility, and this was a matter for the jury to decide. The trial court cautioned the jury not to give the hypnotically refreshed testimony any more credibility than any other testimony. The U.S. Supreme Court declined to review the case (Bodine and Lavine 1980; Diamond 1980; Dilloff 1977; McLaughlin 1981; Palmer and Sims 1970; Reiser 1978; Robinson 1979; Sarno 1979; Teten 1979; Warren and Roberts 1980; Worthington 1979).

The court in the *Harding* case, in concluding that a master's-level psychologist (with some additional work toward the doctorate) who did not graduate from any "school of hypnotism" was qualified as an expert based on professional experience in hypnosis, found that formal training was unnecessary as long as the record demonstrates that the expert is "possessed of any knowledge or information which would elevate his opinion above the level of conjecture . . . " (*Hewitt* v. *Maryland State Board of Censors* 1966).

Dilloff (1977) criticizes this decision on a variety of grounds. He believes that the court assumed that because the hypnotist expressed the opinion that the recollections obtained under hypnosis were reliable, this demonstrated that hypnosis was acceptable to the scientific community in accordance with the *Frye* test. Dilloff points out that the hypnotist had a vested interest in vouching for the reliability of his own procedures. This author doubts that the court was that gullible, but agrees that there were many procedural errors in the hypnotic interview. The location of the interview was a police barracks rather than a more neutral office, the hypnotist was hired by the state, and two police officers were present and interviewed the witness immediately after hypnosis. Dilloff claims that it was obvious to the witness that all present had a strong desire to have her identify Harding, and that her story prior to the hypnosis (which had been changed as well as augmented by hypnosis) was probably the more accurate. However, the defense in this case did not call its own experts to question these procedures.

In *People* v. *Harper* (1969) a rape victim who was unable to identify her assailant was subjected to hypnosis and sodium amobarbital. The hypnotic interview produced no information but under sodium amytal she identified the defendant as her attacker. The defense sought to admit her statements made under the drug in order to show the basis of her initial failure to identify the defendant. The *Harding* case was cited by analogy to justify the use of the drug to unlock the witness's memory. The Appellate Court of Illinois held that in this case, the evidence of what was said under the influence of the drug was clearly being offered to establish the truth of the matters asserted and hence was inadmissible hearsay.

With respect to the analogy made to hypnosis, the court saw no reason to equate an examination by hypnosis with an examination under a drug, except to note that neither technique is scientifically reliable enough to permit the results of such tests to be admitted in evidence in "the serious business of criminal prosecution." The court, paraphrasing Lincoln, said, "Calling a drug Truth Serum does not make it so" (Worthington 1979).

In *State v. Jorgensen* (1971), the Court of Appeals of Oregon, following the *Harding* case, held that it was not error for the trial court to permit an eighteen-year-old girl who was a witness to a homicide and rape to testify from present memory previously refreshed by hypnosis and sodium amytal, providing the facts concerning the prior hypnosis and drug treatment were fully disclosed and the witness was subjected to prolonged and rigorous cross-examination. Tapes of the hypnotic interview were played to the jury at the request of the defense. Defense objections that the witness had told different stories at prior times were held to go to the weight of the testimony (which was within the jury's province to determine) and not to its admissibility. The defense never raised the issue, through its own experts, that the prior hypnosis may have precluded an adequate cross-examination, by convincing the witness of the accuracy of her recollections (Conour 1980; Dilloff 1977; McLaughlin 1981; Reiser 1978; Sarno 1979; Scott 1977; Teten 1979; Warren and Roberts 1980; Worthington 1979). (See also *State v. Brom* 1972.)

The U.S. Court of Appeals for the Fifth Circuit, in *Connolly* v. *Farmer* (1973), upheld the trial court's exclusion of tapes of a hypnotic session and expert testimony concerning the hypnosis during which the plaintiff stated that his speed at the time of an accident was fifty-five miles per hour and not the ninety miles per hour claimed by the defense witnesses. The plaintiff had been denied recovery in the trial court on the theory of contributory negligence. The tapes and testimony were offered as a foundation for the expert's opinion that the plaintiff's amnesia for the accident was genuine, under an exception to the hearsay rule governing statements made by patient to doctor for the purpose of treatment. The trial court ruled that the evidence was not admissible substantively and excluded the tapes in the exercise of its discretion, believing that cautionary instructions to the jury concerning the purpose for which the evidence was admitted would be insufficient to prevent them from regarding the tapes as substantive evidence of the plaintiff's speed.

The circuit court found that if there was an error it did not prejudice the plaintiff since he was later able to testify to his speed, from present memory refreshed by hypnosis, and give his version of the accident. Under cross-examination by the defense the plaintiff informed the jury of the hypnosis. It should be pointed out that the possible error the court referred to was the exclusion of the evidence because it was not found to be an exception to the hearsay rule, which it felt unnecessary to discuss. The exercise of the court's discretion was patently not an error.

Wyller et al. v. Fairchild Hiller Corporation (1974) was a civil action for negligence, strict product liability, and breach of implied warranty, brought by a survivor and the estates of two victims of a helicopter crash against the manufacturer of the aircraft. The U.S. Circuit Court of Appeals for the Ninth Circuit held that it was not error for the trial court to deny the motion of the defense to limit the plaintiff's testimony to matters testified to at his deposition (prior to the use of hypnosis to refresh his recollection, four years after the events in question), or in the alternative, to require the hypnotist to establish the reliability of hypnosis prior to the admission of hypnotically refreshed testimony. The court refused to accept the argument that the use of hypnosis rendered Wyller's testimony inherently untrustworthy. In accordance with the *Harding* decision, it held that his credibility and the weight to be given to his testimony were matters for the jury to decide. It noted that the hypnotist had fully elucidated the procedures employed and the defense had tested both the reliability of the remembered facts and the hypnotic procedure itself by extensive and thorough cross-examination of both Wyller and the hypnotist. Thus, the jury was in a position to evaluate the risks of the use of hypnosis. The court made no cautionary instructions to the jury and admitted some portions of the tapes of the hypnotic interview into evidence, but since the defense did not object to these rulings at the time, these objections were deemed waived on the appeal. The defense also failed to have its own expert witness examine the tapes, and did not object to the reliability of the procedures used (Dilloff 1977; McLaughlin 1981; Reiser 1978; Warren and Roberts 1980; Worthington 1979).

People v. Peters (1974) involved a police officer who was ambushed, and later hypnotized to refresh his memory. The California court, in dicta, said that California law does not preclude hypnosis to establish state of mind, and hypnotic evidence would have been admissible if a foundation had been laid (Reiser 1978; Teten 1979).

Kline v. Ford Motor Co., Inc. (1975) was a consolidated action in strict tort liability brought by the driver and passenger in a car against the manufacturer for injuries received in a single-car accident alleged to be caused by faulty design of the car. The driver died of her injuries and her mother was substituted as administratrix of her estate.

At the time the passenger's deposition was taken, she had a retrograde amnesia and was unable to recall the events of the crash or those shortly before. After this she was hypnotized by a psychologist at the University of California Medical Center and her memory revived. The trial court, after hearing the testimony of the hypnotist concerning the procedures used and listening to the tape recordings of the hypnotic session, sustained Ford's objection to her testimony and ruled that the hypnosis had rendered her incompetent to testify to the facts recalled under hypnosis. The Ninth Circuit U.S. Court of Appeals held that this was error. It ruled that competency refers to the condition of a witness at the time of giving testimony. At this time the witness was fully capable of expressing herself and understanding her duty to tell the truth. She had been present and personally observed the facts testified to. That her memory at the time of testifying was claimed to be hypnotically refreshed was held to go to the credibility of her testimony and the weight it was entitled to, not its admissibility or her competence as a witness. Although the method of memory refreshment was unusual, legally it was no different than permitting a witness to revive his memory by inspecting a document. As in the Wyller case, the weight and credibility of her testimony were found to be matters for the jury to determine (Spector and Foster 1977; Warren and Roberts 1980; Worthington 1979).

In *United States* v. *Andrews* (1975), a sailor was shot by an assailant he was unable to identify. Two months later he was taken to a naval psychiatric ward and under hypnosis by a psychiatrist holding the rank of commander, was ordered to remember the details of the incident and to fix in his mind a picture of the assailant. On awakening, the victim was shown a photograph of the suspect, Andrews, and he was able to identify him in spite of two previous failures to do so.

At the court martial the military judge sustained the defense objection to the testimony on the grounds that hypnosis as a memory-refreshing technique was unreliable and untrustworthy (Monrose 1978; Pelanda 1981). Dilloff (1977) believes that this ruling was based on the previous failures of the victim to identify Andrews, the coercive nature of the hypnotic interview (a military superior commanding a petty officer to remember), and the fact that the victim was given the idea that the naval authorities believed that they had the right man and were anxious to get an identification. He notes that the fact that defense counsel was present during hypnosis may have suggested that the accused needed a lawyer.

The presence of defense counsel is an interesting problem, for if he is present, the proceedings may be criticized on the grounds that they are suggestive. If he is not present, then the criticism may be raised that the rights of the accused were not adequately protected.

Evidently the trial judge in the *Andrews* case was correct in his ruling, for Orne (1977, 1979) reports that Andrews's alibi was subsequently corroborated and this case seems to be an instance of an honest witness misled in his testimony by hypnotic influence. Although the professional judgment of the hypnotist may be questionable, there appears to be no reason to doubt his integrity or that of the other naval authorities involved. This case illustrates that the dangers of the forensic use of hypnosis are not limited to its use on disreputable witnesses or by overzealous or unethical law-enforcement personnel.

Although the federal rules of evidence do not deal specifically with the admissibility of hypnotically influenced testimony, it would be covered under the rule for other scientific evidence, which is essentially a restatement of the *Frye* test (Dilloff 1977). The Federal Rules of Evidence (FRE 703) allow an expert to base an opinion on hypnotically induced statements (Spector and Foster 1977, 1979).

The manual for Courts-Martial (142e, 1969), in contrast, specifically covers hypnosis-induced interviews, classifying them with polygraph tests and interviews in which drugs are employed. It says that conclusions based upon and statements made during interviews under drugs or hypnosis are inadmissible in evidence in a trial by court-martial (Day 1980).

This would appear to mean that not only are statements made under hypnosis inadmissible to prove the truth of the facts stated, they are also inadmissible to show the basis of an expert's opinion. It appears that the basis of the decision in the *Andrews* case, and in a variety of other court-martial cases cited by Dilloff (1977), in which military judges limited witnesses' testimony to facts they could remember prior to hypnotic refreshment, were based on considerations of the general unreliability of hypnotically refreshed testimony rather than the rule of evidence cited, which does not seem to apply to a waking witness testifying from present memory refreshed.

United States v. *Narciso* (1977) involved two Veteran's Administration hospital nurses charged with five counts of murder, ten counts of poisoning, and conspiracy, in a highly publicized case. The defendant's motion for a new trial was granted by the United States District Court on grounds unrelated to hypnosis, but the court considered the admissibility of an identification of one of the defendants by a patient (following the patient's hypnosis by a psychiatrist working with the FBI) as the person near his bed just prior to his cardiac arrest.

On two occasions prior to hypnosis the witness said he could not remember the person in his room at the time in question. Following two hypnotic sessions the witness (Neely) identified the defendant (Perez) as one of his nurses, but did not say that she was in his room at the time of the incident. Almost a month later he spontaneously told the FBI that he remembered who had been in his room and identified the defendant Perez from a photograph. In his deposition, Mr. Neely said that he had known the identity of the defendant from the time of her arrest, but he did not tell the FBI "to protect her."

A defense psychiatrist, Dr. Dennis Walsh, found that the witness was a terminally ill, chronic alcoholic with memory deficits for recent events and a borderline personality. On the one hand, Dr. Martin Orne testified for the defense, after reviewing the tapes of the hypnosis, that Neely's testimony could have been influenced by suggestions made during the session. On the other hand, Dr. Herbert Spiegel testified for the government that Mr. Neely was a person of low susceptibility to hypnosis who did not have a rich fantasy life and was not unduly subject to hypnotic suggestions. Spiegel said he was greatly impressed by the skill of the FBI agents in maintaining neutrality during the interview. The court, on reviewing these expert opinions, concluded that the defense had failed to meet the substantial burden imposed by the United States Supreme Court in *Simmons* v. *United States* (1968) on a party seeking to exclude an identification. Such party must show that the procedures used created a "very substantial likelihood of irreparable misidentification." The court then went on to consider whether the identification should be excluded on the grounds that the evidence was such that it "cannot possibly be true, is inherently unbelievable or is opposed to natural laws," and concluded that such was not the case. It held that, in the absence of the impossibility of correct identification, the credibility of hypnotically refreshed memory under our system of law is for the jury and not the court to decide (Diamond 1980; Warner 1979).

Diamond (1980) states that the *Narciso* case shows how far the courts will go in following the doctrine of the *Harding* case in admitting hypnotically refreshed testimony even when the validity of the testimony is extremely suspect. This view seems to miss the legal point made by the court in *Narciso*. The court did not hold that the evidence was very probative. It simply said that if it is not impossible on its face for the evidence to be true then the issue of its believability is one of fact and, under our legal system, this decision is within the province of a jury, not the court. Hypnotic evidence is not the only weak or unbelievable evidence routinely presented in court and these matters have always been resolved by juries. This is the function of a jury. Indeed, it would amount to the usurpation of the role of the jury for a judge to decide to exclude testimony that violates no rule of evidence simply because he did not believe it.

In *State* v. *McQueen* (1978), a conviction on two counts of first-degree murder, based on hypnotically refreshed testimony of a prostitute five years after the event, was upheld by the Supreme Court of North Carolina. The court, citing *Kline* v. *Ford Motor Company, Inc.*; *Wyller* v. *Fairchild Hiller Corp.*; *State* v. *Jorgensen*, and *Harding* v. *State*, held that since the witness was testifying from present memory, it was immaterial how that memory was refreshed and the effect of the prior hypnosis on its credibility was for the jury to decide. The issue of hypnosis related to the weight of the evidence, not its admissibility. The court distinguished the case of *State* v. *Pierce* from the present case in which there was no attempt to admit evidence of what the witness said while under hypnosis. The court also noted that the defense had access to a tape recording of the hypnotic session and raised no objections to the procedures used as being unduly suggestive. It also chose not to cross-examine the witness on the role that hypnosis played in her testimony, nor did it seek to examine the hypnotist, who was available to be called as a witness. Hence any objections to the procedures used were deemed waived on appeal (Anon. 1978c; Bodine and Lavine 1980; Sarno 1979; Worthington 1979).

People v. *Smrekar* (1979) was a case of novel impression for the Illinois courts. Following hypnosis for memory refreshment, the sister of one of two murder victims identified the defendant as the man she had observed outside of the victims' house for some thirty to forty seconds on the night of the murders. The victims had been potential witnesses against the defendant in a misdemeanor case. The witness had identified the defendant following a chance meeting at the courthouse, after having just selected his picture and that of another man from a group of six, as resembling the man she saw on the night of the murders. On appeal from a conviction and two consecutive sentences of from 100 to 300 years, the defendant argued that the prior hypnosis suggested his identification to the witness and deprived him of his right of cross-examination. The court distinguished the present case from *People* v. *Harper* and noted that no evidence was offered concerning what the defendant said under hypnosis. The court, going along with the line of cases *supra*, also held that the testimony of the witness and her identification of the defendant was not rendered inadmissible by her prior hypnosis when:

1. The hypnotist was shown to be competent (he was a general practitioner but had been using hypnosis regularly in his practice for ten or fifteen years);
2. The evidence indicated that the hypnosis was not unduly suggestive;
3. The identification was corroborated by other substantial evidence unknown to the witness at the time of the identification; and
4. The witness had ample time to view the defendant at the scene of the crime.

Not only did the court hold that the effect of pretrial hypnosis relates to the credibility and not the admissibility of the evidence, but it also discussed the possibility that the use of pretrial hypnosis could make cross-examination less effective. The court dismissed this argument by agreeing that it might, but added that many other factors may render even witnesses who were *not* subjected to hypnosis less amenable to cross-examination (Anon. 1981b; Conour 1980; Sannito and Mueller 1980; Spector and Foster 1979; Thigpen 1981).

In a dissenting opinion, Justice Craven noted the absence of any foundation in the trial record concerning the nature of hypnosis, its scientific basis, or its value as an aid in the truth-seeking process. He believed that objections that the defense should have made were not made and that, had the court decided the issues raised on the basis of waiver by the defense rather than on the merits, serious questions concerning the competence of counsel would be raised. He held that it is "incumbent upon one who tenders testimony retrieved, enhanced or obtained by hypnosis to establish what the procedure is, what its limitations are and what such tinkering amounts to." The defendant was obviously not viewed very sympathetically by the court, as evidenced by the sentence imposed, and Justice Craven felt that this decision was an example of the old legal adage that "Hard cases make bad law."

A New York County Court in *People* v. *Hughes* (1979), ruled on a pretrial omnibus motion that a rape victim was not rendered incompetent to testify as a result of pretrial hypnosis to refresh her recollection and assist in an identification, when a proper foundation was presented showing that the hypnotic procedures used contained procedural safeguards to assure reliability, that the use of hypnosis had been disclosed to the defense, and its general acceptance in the scientific community was established (evidently to the court's satisfaction).

The court also held that the hypnosis was clearly an identification procedure within the meaning of New York Criminal Procedure Law Sections 710.20 and 710.30 which entitled the defendant to a pretrial hearing to determine if, under the totality of the circumstances, the procedure was so impermissively suggestive as to raise a substantial likelihood of an irreparable misidentification.

Finally, the court held that the hypnotic sessions conducted by the *People* were not a critical stage of the proceedings requiring the presence of defense counsel under the Sixth Amendment. It noted that the availability of recordings of the session for review by the defense safeguarded the defendant's right to the effective assistance of counsel.

The Appellate Division of the New York Supreme Court evidently agreed with the trial court's opinion that the *Frye* standards were applicable to hypnotically refreshed testimony but disagreed with its conclusion that these standards had been met. Hence, it reversed the conviction and remanded the case for retrial.

In *People* v. *McDowell* (1980), another New York trial court held that although great care must be taken to avoid tainting a witness's testimony by pretrial hypnosis, the use of hypnosis itself did not render her incompetent to testify as a matter of law nor did it deprive the defense of its right of cross-examination. In its motion, the defense had argued that the hypnosis may have led the witness to believe in the accuracy of his hypnotically induced confabulations and hence prevented effective cross-examination. The trial court, after reviewing the tapes of the hypnotic session, was satisfied that the procedures were not suggestive and held that it was not enough for the objecting party to show that hypnosis can produce errors in testimony. The party seeking to suppress hypnotic evidence must show that the dangers alleged have in fact been realized in the instant case.

The court was of the opinion that if hypnosis was used on a witness by either the *People* or the defense, the other side was entitled to notice within a reasonable time prior to trial so that it could properly prepare any appropriate motions relative to such testimony.

In *Merrifield* v. *State* (1980) the Supreme Court of Indiana held that the use of hypnosis could not have tainted an identification of the defendant by the rape victim because she had recognized him when he came into the restaurant where she worked on the day of the crime, as having made a sexual proposition to her a few months earlier. Also she had picked the defendant's picture out of a photographic display two days prior to the hypnosis. Furthermore, at the time of the in-court identification, the defense did not object and hence waived the issue on appeal. The court noted that no evidence was admitted or offered at the trial concerning testimony elicited during hypnosis and the court stated it was therefore expressing no opinion on those matters (Conour 1980).

In *Pavone* v. *State* (1980), the same court heard an appeal from a conviction for felony murder. The defense made a motion to suppress any testimony by an accomplice who had been hypnotized and turned state's evidence, on the grounds that all of the witness's memories had been tainted by hypnosis or, in the alternative, that the witness be barred from testifying to anything he was unable to recall prior to the hypnosis. The defense also moved to exclude any tape recordings or transcripts of what was said by the witness while under hypnosis. The trial court granted only the last motion and the defendant assigned error to the denial of the first two.

The appellate court noted that the defendant did not object to the introduction of prior written statements of the witness when offered at the trial and hence waived his objections to them. In addition, the defendant in his motion did not establish how the witness's testimony was influenced by the hypnosis; he simply speculated that it was tainted. It appeared from the record that, through the court's discovery order, all statements of the witness including the video tape of his hypnosis were available to the defense and could have been used to demonstrate any evidence of taint or prejudice to the defendant. This was not done. Thus, the court held that an objection to the use of hypnotically refreshed testimony must allege some factual basis for the abuse claimed and since in this case the motion made no such allegation, the trial court did not abuse its discretion in denying it (Conour 1980).

All of the foregoing cases (except *Hughes*) hold that evidence of what was said under hypnosis is not admissible except under certain circumstances, but that the evidence given by a previously hypnotized, awake witness who is testifying from hypnotically refreshed present memory is admissible. The fact of the hypnosis was held to relate to the weight and credibility of the testimony, not to its admissibility; and weight and credibility are matters for the jury to determine. The admissibility of hypnotically refreshed memory was implicitly or explicitly held to be subject to the sound discretion of the trial judge, who has the authority to exclude the testimony if the circumstances of the hypnotic interview make it likely that the testimony was tainted by incompetent or unduly suggestive procedures.

However, the courts have not been unanimous in considering pretrial hypnosis as acceptable as any other common method of refreshing the recollection of a witness. In several recent cases, the supreme courts of Arizona and of Minnesota have rejected the use of pretrial hypnosis to jog the memory of a witness in criminal cases.

The Supreme Court of Arizona in *State* v. *LaMountain* (1980), held that although it was error to admit the hypnosis-induced identification of a witness, it was not reversible error since the remaining evidence was sufficient to sustain the conviction for rape and related crimes. The court noted that there was no expert testimony regarding the effect of hypnosis on memory and it had no way of knowing how an identification in a photographic lineup made under hypnosis (induced by a sheriff's deputy with a year's experience in hypnosis) could have affected the witness's in-court identification of the defendant (Bodine and Lavine 1980; Conour 1980).

State v. *Mack* (1980) involved a matter of novel impression for the courts of Minnesota, and the lower court certified the question of the use of hypnotically refreshed testimony in a criminal trial to the Supreme Court of Minnesota. Justice Wahl, after reviewing the testimony of five experts (Drs. Carl Malmquist, Allan Roberts, Charles Mutter, Leo Alexander, and Martin T. Orne), concluded that the testimony was inadmissible. The court reviewed the psychological testimony and correctly concluded that hypnotically induced memory would not meet the standards of the *Frye* rule which it held applicable. The court also acknowledged the value of hypnosis in overcoming an emotional memory block but recognized the dangers of confabulation on the part of subjects and their desire to please the hypnotist as well as the inability of either the witness or an expert to separate confabulation from accurate recall. The court found that hypnosis makes it impossible to cross-examine a witness in a meaningful way, that it produces a witness who is both convincing and convinced, regardless of the accuracy of his testimony (Anon. 1980b; Manolis 1982; Thigpen 1981; Zeichner 1982). It is difficult to quarrel with these psychologically sound conclusions.

The legal conclusions of the court, particularly its view that there are two lines of cases—one excluding the exculpatory hypnotically induced testimony of criminal defendants and one admitting the hypnotically adduced statements of prosecution witnesses—are much harder to accept. The court ignored all distinctions between self-serving hearsay statements made under hypnosis and pretrial hypnosis designed to jog the memory of a witness who testifies in a waking state. No case has been found to date that would prevent a defense witness from testifying after hypnotic memory refreshment in a jurisdiction that permits a prosecution witness to so testify. Further, no case has been found that has permitted a prosecution witness's statement made under hypnosis to be admitted in evidence as proof of the facts stated.

Although *State* v. *Mack* is sound from a psychological viewpoint, the problem with this decision from a legal point of view is that essentially it holds that evidence of questionable reliability that violates no existing rules of evidence is inadmissible at a trial. This is a novel legal concept that would exclude a great deal of evidence routinely presented in both civil and criminal cases. It would, for example, exclude the testimony of an accomplice granted immunity from prosecution in exchange for his testimony. If it were not for the questionable reliability of much evidence, there would be no purpose for having a jury decide contested issues of fact. This is not to deny that pretrial hypnosis may render a witness less susceptible to cross-examination, but the same problem exists with many honest but mistaken eyewitnesses who are convinced of the accuracy of their erroneous perceptions and memories.

Because of the dangers intrinsic in forensic hypnosis, there are sound arguments for barring hypnotically refreshed testimony. There are also sound arguments for permitting it, for example, to aid a defendant with amnesia to participate in his own defense. However, if hypnotically refreshed memory is to be outlawed or restricted this should be done by statute and not by a court usurping the proper function of a jury. As Judge Pratt (in *United States* v. *Narciso*) quoted from the United States Supreme Court,

> The trial judge cannot arrogate to himself this power of the jury simply because he finds a witness unbelievable. Under our system of jurisprudence a properly instructed jury of citizens decides whether witnesses are credible.

In the *Mack* case defects in the hypnotic procedures were sufficient to permit the court to have held that under these circumstances the hypnotically refreshed testimony should not have been admitted, without enunciating a general ban against such testimony. For if hypnotically refreshed testimony may be false, it may also be true, in part or whole. Perhaps the best way of ascertaining its status is by evaluating how well it fits into the other evidence in the case.

The court noted in *Mack* that hypnosis was not needed to aid in an identification. The hypnotist was a layman with neither formal training in nor scientific understanding of human memory and the operation of suggestion in hypnosis. He was hired by the police, who were present at the hypnotic session, in the absence of representatives of the defense, and there was no independent corroboration of any of the facts recalled under hypnosis.

The court did not rule out the use of hypnosis as a discovery device to investigate a crime, but stated that safeguards for such usage should be established in the event that the witness is later needed to testify to his or her recollections prior to the hypnosis (Ashman 1980; Bodine and Lavine 1980; Conour 1980).

A Canadian provincial court, in a case of first impression, refused to allow hypnotically refreshed testimony against a defendant charged as a juvenile delinquent. The court noted that a trial judge has a measure of discretion to reject admissible evidence on the broad principle that an accused has a constitutional right to a fair trial. The court was persuaded by the arguments of defense counsel that hypnosis was not infallible and there were difficulties in getting the truth from a hypnotized subject (*Regina* v. *K* 1979).

The Supreme Court of Arizona, in *State* v. *Mena* (1981), citing its decision in *State* v. *La Mountain*, reversed a conviction for aggravated assault because of the admission of hypnotically refreshed testimony by a prosecution witness. As in the *Mack* case, the court did not rule out the purely investigative use of hypnosis, but it did discuss in detail the possibility of hypnotic distortion of memories and confusion of real prehypnotic memories with distortions produced under hypnosis. In particular, the court was concerned about the danger that by convincing a witness of the truth of his distorted testimony, hypnosis would render cross-examination ineffective, and hence deprive the defendant of his constitutional right of confrontation. Hence, it held that until hypnosis gains general acceptance in medicine and psychiatry as a method of reliable memory enhancement, without undue danger of distortion, delusion, or fantasy, the testimony of witnesses examined under hypnosis regarding the subject of their proffered testimony, is inadmissible in criminal trials from the time of the hypnosis (Anon. 1982a, 1981f, 1981j; Bailey and Shapiro 1982; Brooks 1981).

In connection with this decision three observations should be made. One is that the language of the court seemed to imply that this decision might be changed when hypnotic memory enhancement becomes a more reliable procedure. This, of course, will probably never happen. The sources of error that the court correctly refers to are intrinsic in the nature of hypnotic phenomona. It is possible by the use of competent technique to reduce their likelihood but they are unlikely ever to be eliminated.

Second, while it is gratifying that the results of psychological research are beginning to be recognized by the courts in their decisions, it must be pointed out that if the same standards employed in this case to rule out the testimony of hypnotically influenced witnesses were to be applied to ordinary witnesses, most of them (as noted by Justice Kaus in his dissent in *People* v. *Shirley*, Calif., 1982), would be unable to testify in a criminal trial.

Third, although hypnosis may render subsequent cross-examination more difficult, it does not necessarily make it ineffective. In general, anything that can be done with hypnosis can be undone by it, or done without it, by the exercise of greater effort and skill. Hence the effect of hypnosis in making the witness unduly confident of the accuracy of his hypnotically refreshed or created memories can probably be undone by a skillful cross-examination conducted by an attorney knowledgeable in hypnosis and its characteristics.

In *State* v. *Hurd* (1981), the Supreme Court of New Jersey, in a thoughtful and well-researched opinion, surveyed the decisions supporting the view that hypnotically refreshed testimony is admissible, subject to the discretion of the court, as well as the newer decisions holding it inadmissible as unreliable. The court also reviewed the psychological evidence relevant to this issue. It concluded that:

1. Hypnotically refreshed testimony must meet the most recent New Jersey formulation for admissibility of scientific evidence in a criminal case, which is that it must have "sufficient scientific basis to produce uniform and reasonably reliable results and will contribute materially to the ascertainment of the truth" (*State* v. *Cary* 1967). However, the standard of general acceptance is also germane.
2. The credibility of the results depends on the reliability of the scientific procedures used.
3. If the procedures used are not capable of yielding reasonably accurate results, then its probative value may be outweighed by its risks, which include prejudice, confusion of the jury, and waste of time and trial resources.
4. Hypnosis is not a method of assuring truth as a polygraph or truth serum is supposed to be. Its purpose is to overcome amnesia and restore the memory of a witness.
5. In the light of this purpose it can be considered reasonably reliable if it is able to produce recollections as accurate as those of unhypnotized witnesses.

Therefore, the court held that hypnotically enhanced testimony is admissible in a criminal trial if the trial court finds that the recall produced is comparable in accuracy to normal human memory (which it recognized has considerable shortcomings). If the testimony is admitted the opponent may challenge the reliability of the particular procedures used but may not try to prove the unreliability of hypnosis as a memory-refresher in general. The court also held that the party seeking to introduce hypnotically refreshed testimony must inform his opponent of his intention to do so and furnish him with a recording of the hypnotic session.

Orne's procedural standards for the conduct of a forensic hypnotic session (chapter 2) were specifically adopted by this court to assure the reliability of the evidence. The proponent of hypnotically influenced testimony must show compliance with these standards and any other facts necessary to establish that the witness's memory is likely to meet the aforementioned standards by "clear and convincing evidence" (Anon. 1981c, 1981k, 1980c; Bailey and Shapiro 1982; Berger 1982; Brooks 1981; Feldman 1981; Thigpen 1981; Zeichner 1980).

The *Hurd* case makes it unnecessary in New Jersey for the proponent of hypnotically influenced testimony to establish the general reliability of hypnosis as a memory-refreshing device. All he need establish by such testimony is that the technique used was proper and the standards were complied with. In applying these principles to the facts of this case, which involved a woman who was able to identify her former husband as her assailant only after hypnotic memory refreshment, the court sustained the trial court's exclusion of her identification testimony because of the failure of the hypnotist to observe the procedural standards and because of pressure exerted by a police officer and the hypnotist on the witness to make the identification, both under and after hypnosis.

The latter was the major reason for the exclusion of the testimony, for the court noted that since this was a case of first impression, the *People* had no way of knowing what hypnotic procedures the court would require. However, not only was a police officer present during the interrogation, but also she was permitted to question the subject and did so in a leading manner. The *Hurd* test was adopted by the New Mexico courts in *State* v. *Beachum* (1981).

In *State* v. *Koehler* (1981), the Supreme Court of Minnesota, citing its decision in *State* v. *Mack*, held it reversible error to admit into evidence the hypnotically refreshed testimony of a witness whose recollection of the defendant's car was incomplete and inaccurate prior to hypnosis but permitted a positive identification after hypnosis. The court directed that on retrial the witness could not testify to anything that he had not disclosed to the authorities prior to the hypnosis. It noted that the hypnotist was not only not impartial but was in fact one of the police officers investigating the subject murder. He had taken a course in hypnosis only two weeks earlier. However, instead of refusing to admit the evidence on the grounds that the circumstances of the hypnosis rendered the results unreliable, the court chose to rely on the broader principle it enunciated in the *Mack* case that all hypnotically refreshed testimony is inadmissible.

A similar result was found by the Supreme Court of Nebraska in *State* v. *Palmer* (1981). After reviewing the psychological evidence of hypnotic memory distortion and many of the foregoing cases, the court decided that the present murder and robbery conviction had to be set aside, either under the *Mack* and *Mena* rule or the *Hurd* rule, although it elected to follow the former doctrine, believing that the latter would be impossible to achieve in practice. It is certainly true that few if any courts, even in jurisdictions without guidelines for hypnotic procedures, would admit hypnotic evidence when the two hypnotists (who worked for the *People*) had recently taken a four-day course in hypnosis. One of the hypnotists had hypnotized about twenty subjects, mostly his classmates in the course, and the other had hypnotized seventy subjects, nearly all classmates.

The court specifically found no objection to purely investigative hypnosis and said that the holding would not exclude otherwise admissible evidence derived from leads obtained under hypnosis.

The Wyoming Supreme Court in *Chapman* v. *State* (1982) upheld a burglary conviction based on the hypnotically refreshed testimony of a witness who was twice hypnotized by a city police officer. Video tapes were made but they were for the most part inaudible. The majority opinion held that the judgment of whether the hypnosis refreshed the witness's own recollection or taught him additional facts was properly one for the fact finder, as are all issues related to the credibility of a witness. It refused to treat the matter as a question of the competence of the witness and rejected the standards set in *State* v. *Hurd* for hypnotically refreshed testimony. The majority further found that though it might be wise for the proponent of hypnotically refreshed testimony to adhere to some or all of those standards to increase the credibility of the witness, there were too many variables in hypnosis to justify mandating such requirements (Anon. 1982b, 1981k).

A dissenting opinion criticized the lack of expertise of the hypnotist, and the majority's failure even to consider the potential of hypnosis for producing unreliable testimony. It also objected to the admission of hypnotically enhanced testimony with such a total lack of foundation.

The most cogent objection to the admissibility of this testimony was the fact that an adequate recording of the hypnotic session was not available. This made it impossible for the defense to attack the specific procedures used or to demonstrate any specific sources of error. In effect, the defense was not able to bring out all of the facts concerning the hypnosis as the majority opinion contended, and its ability to cross-examine the witness was seriously impaired. The fact that the hypnotist was a layman was all the defense really had on which to base its cross-examination.

The Supreme Court of Minnesota in *State* v. *Blanchard* (1982), while recognizing that other jurisdictions have recently found hypnotically in-fluenced testimony admissible under certain conditions, and noting recent law-journal comments on the subject, chose to hold to its decisions in the *Mack* and *Koehler* cases. It ruled that it was error to admit the hypnotically refreshed testimony of a prosecution witness in a first-degree murder case because such evidence fails to meet the standards set forth in *Frye* v. *United States* (1923).

Although in *Blanchard* the court found that the admission of such evidence was error, it also found that it did not amount to reversible error, because there was other "overwhelming" evidence of the defendant's guilt. This included prehypnotic recollections of the hypnotized witness.

The Court of Special Appeals of Maryland, in *Polk* v. *State* (1981) reviewed a conviction for sexual offenses committed against an eight-year-old boy by a forty-year-old man. The defense had fought to exclude the hypnotically refreshed testimony of the child-victim on the grounds that such testimony was the product of "an inexact and unproven science," that the police-officer hypnotist was not an expert, and that the questions asked under hypnosis were improperly leading. It argued that its motion to exclude this testimony was erroneously denied.

The court noted that ten years after its decision in *Harding* v. *State* the Court of Appeals of Maryland had adopted for the first time the "general acceptance rule" set forth in *Frye* v. *United States*, which had not been employed in the *Harding* case. Hence the court reversed the judgment. The case was remanded to the trial court with instructions to hear evidence to resolve the issue of whether the requirement of general acceptability in the relevant scientific community is met by the employment of hypnosis for the purpose of memory refreshment.

The court noted that even if the *Frye* standards were found to be met by hypnotic memory refreshment, the trial court could still exclude such evidence it it were not convinced that the hypnotist was qualified (which in this case he admittedly was not) or if the test had not been conducted under the proper conditions (Anon. 1981e). The incomplete record of the hypnotic session reveals several improperly leading questions and it seems doubtful that this testimony should be admissible, even under the *Harding* rule.

In *Commonwealth* v. *Nazarovitch* (1981), the Supreme Court of Pennsylvania, in spite of strong leanings towards the *Frye* standard, declined to establish the rule that hypnotically refreshed testimony was inadmissible. However, it affirmed the trial court's suppression of the hypnotically refreshed testimony of a murder witness, under circumstances where one of the two hypnotists involved was unqualified and police officers were permitted to participate in the questioning of the witness while he was under hypnosis. There was also no record of the witness's prehypnotic recollections and both hypnotists had been secured by the prosecution. In addition to the procedural shortcomings, the witness had been under the influence of drugs at the time of her original observations three years prior to the hypnosis, and the court recognized that this fact cast serious doubt on the accuracy of her initial perceptions. (Anon. 1981 a).

The Supreme Court of California in *People* v. *Shirley* (1982) reversed a rape conviction based on the hypnotically refreshed testimony of the alleged victim. In reaching its decision the court made an extensive review of the recent line of cases dealing with the issue of the admissibility of hypnotically refreshed testimony, and considered some of the literature on memory as well. It found that there was no scientific support for a video-recorder theory of memory.

The court concluded that the *Frye* test was applicable to hypnotically refreshed testimony and that it failed the test, since it was not generally accepted by the appropriate scientific community for the purpose of memory refreshment. In view of the danger that hypnosis could produce false testimony, the court held that a previously hypnotized witness was incompetent to testify to all matters recalled from the time of the hypnosis forward.

However, since a previously hypnotized witness does not lack the general ability to perceive, remember, and relate, he may be questioned on matters subsequent to the hypnosis if they are wholly unrelated to issues addressed under hypnosis. Lastly, the court ruled that the admission of hypnotically refreshed testimony is not reversible error in the absence of a demonstration that it prejudiced the rights of the opposing party.

To summarize, the majority view holds that hypnotically refreshed testimony given by a waking witness claiming to be testifying from present memory is admissible, subject to the discretion of the court to exclude it if the circumstances of the hypnosis appear unduly suggestive or unreliable. Jurisdictions vary in what guidelines, if any, they set for the conduct of pretrial hypnotic interviews. In the following jurisdictions the fact of hypnosis goes to the weight or credibility of the evidence, not to its admissibility, and hence is a matter for the trier of fact to decide: Illinois, Indiana, New Jersey, New Mexico, North Carolina, Oregon, Wyoming, and the federal courts.

The minority view, which has rapidly developed from recent decisions of courts of last resort in six states, holds that the fact of pretrial hypnosis renders a witness incompetent to testify to anything not remembered prior to the hypnosis. These six states are: Arizona, California, Maryland, Michigan, Minnesota, and Nebraska. This is close to the position advocated by Diamond (1980) although the witness is not rendered totally incompetent to testify, since he or she can still testify to memories reported prior to the hypnosis. These memories, of course, are also subject to modification by the subsequent hypnosis. If the witness were rendered totally incompetent, it would rule out the use of hypnosis as an investigative technique by law-enforcement agencies, since by using hypnosis they would be compromising their own witnesses. None of the courts following this view wanted to go to that extreme.

Pretrial Hypnosis: Abuses, Safeguards, and the Discretion of the Court

In an early North Carolina case, *State* v. *Exum* (1905), the supreme court of that state upheld the trial judge at a murder trial who permitted the wife of the defendant (and the mother of the victim) to be asked by the state about her being hypnotized by the defendant. She replied "Yes, three times." This evidence was allowed to impeach the witness, called by the defense to support his claim of self-defense, by showing that the defendant had a greater influence over her than would be expected from the marital relationship alone.

In this case, the content of the hypnotic sessions was completely irrelevant to the issues of the case, but in line with popular misconceptions, the court evidently believed that hypnotizing a subject gave a hypnotist a degree of power or control over her. It is interesting that the court seemed to believe that three hypnotic sessions provided an influence over a subject comparable in magnitude to a marital relationship (Dilloff 1977; Sarno 1979; Solomon 1952; Swain 1961).

In *United States* v. *Miller* (1969), the defendant appealed to the Second Circuit U.S. Court of Appeals from a number of posttrial orders denying his motion for a new trial following conviction for conspiring to import heroin. In May of 1968 (following the conviction of the defendant), at the request of the defense the government's key witness was brought to the office of a New York psychiatrist for an examination under hypnosis. In the presence of lawyers for the defense and prosecution, and just prior to being hypnotized, the witness disclosed that he had been hypnotized by the prosecution while in custody. This was a surprise to the defense, which had never been informed of the pretrial hypnosis. It developed that this witness, whose identification of the defendant was extremely damaging to the defense, had not only been subjected to hypnotic questioning, but in some cases the attorney who prosecuted the case was the hypnotist!

The court did not discuss the issue of how likely it was that the prosecution-dominated hypnosis sessions shaped the witness's testimony, although it briefly mentioned the possibility that this might have rendered cross-examination and the sanctity of an oath less effective. Instead, the court based its decision to order a new trial on the prosecution's breach of its duty to inform the defense of the hypnosis of a key witness. The court held that this duty existed whether or not it was covered by the discovery provision of the Jencks Act (18 U.S.C. 3500e) (notes made by government attorneys while interviewing their witnesses are discoverable if they are truly the statement of the witness, *Goldberg* v. *United States* 1976) because of the importance of this information to the defense's case in cross-examining a key government witness. In effect, withholding this information deprived the defense of its Sixth-Amendment right to effectively confront an opposing witness. The court did not find (as it might have) that the facts demonstrated bad faith on the part of the prosecutor in not informing the defense, in spite of defense requests for information concerning the prosecution's interviews of the witness. It held that the good faith of the prosecution was immaterial. Had the defense been given this information, it "would have added another arrow to the rather large quiver trial counsel for the defense shot" at the witness. The court conceded that this additional bit of defense ammunition might not have changed the verdict, but it held that in the hands of skillful trial counsel it might have, or at least it might have produced a hung jury. Hence, a new trial was ordered (Dilloff 1977; McLaughlin 1981; Palmer and Sims 1970; Sarno 1979; Warner 1979; Warren and Roberts 1980).

The case of *Emmett* v. *Ricketts* (1975) was a combined case of *habeas corpus* petitions in the United States District Court in Atlanta, on behalf of two petitioners who were tried separately and convicted on murder and felony-murder charges in a widely publicized double murder of two Marietta, Georgia pathologists.

The cases against the defendants were almost entirely based on the testimony of "a self admitted former habitual and prolific user of amphetamines, prostitute and shoplifter," who originally told investigators that she could not remember many details of the crime because "she was 'full of pills' during its commission." After her first two interviews, an agent of the Georgia Bureau of Investigation (GBI) summarized her testimony by noting that most aspects of it were wholly inconsistent with the physical evidence and her subsequent testimony. It contained a "world of discrepancies" and some "weird stuff." For roughly two weeks the witness was quartered in the apartment of a detective on the case, with whom she had sexual relations and whom she claimed to love. During this time she was maintained on her drug habit by the police, who supplied her with amphetamines.

The district court noted that the report of the agent of the GBI was "utterly devastating to [the witness's] credibility," but the prosecution never furnished the defense a copy of it. When the defense learned of its existence and demanded a copy, another agent claimed that the report was missing from the file. The witness was brought to the office of a clinical psychologist and hypnotist for the avowed purpose of getting her off drugs, although the

U.S. District Court found that the dominant if not the sole reason was to shore up her story, which was riddled with inconsistencies, implausibilities, and gaps.

The defense claimed that during hypnosis the witness was programmed with the facts of the case, and the witness told the court that she had been instructed by the hypnotist to scan the newspapers and collect clippings about the case! According to the psychologist he had twelve sessions with her lasting a total of thirty-six hours. During the Emmett trial he testified that from ten to fourteen hours of these were taped. He also represented that he had with him all such tapes and transcripts.

Counsel for Emmett moved that the court take the tapes in custody and perform an *in camera* inspection of them to see if they contained exculpatory material that the defense was entitled to be informed of, pursuant to the requirements of the Brady decision (*Brady* v. *Maryland* 1963). The court took the tapes into custody but refused to perform the inspection, citing the psychologist-patient privilege. (The Georgia Supreme Court subsequently upheld the trial judge in this ruling, on the theory that since the tapes contained nothing except recordings made while the witness was under hypnosis, these would not be admissible in evidence, and, therefore, the defense was not entitled to this information under the *Brady* doctrine.)

The federal district court noted that the tapes submitted, although represented as containing age-regression sessions, actually contained non-hypnotic and non-age-regression sessions. The psychologist testified that the other tapes were possibly erased by reuse. The court specifically found that the psychologist "knew and appreciated the value of these tapes" and further found his "explanation of the destruction to be incredible." It held that the "unavoidable conclusion" to be drawn was that an agent of the state had either unlawfully obstructed justice or committed perjury.

The district court further found that the trial court's denial of defense access to the tapes, and its refusal to review them *in camera*, was error. It held that no privilege ever existed, because the real purpose of the hypnosis was to improve the witness's testimony. There was no real intent to treat the witness and the claim of privilege was a "sham and a facade." Furthermore, the court found that the Georgia Supreme Court was in error in sustaining the actions of the trial court on the grounds that the material sought to be learned from the tape would be inadmissible as evidence. The district court said that, " . . . this Court has never considered admissibility to be a factor under *Brady*" (McLaughlin 1981).

The district court excoriated the prosecution and said that the clear presumption was that the tapes that were "deliberately destroyed" would not have reflected favorably on the witness (who represented the prosecution's whole case), the psychologist, or the prosecution. It held that both the district attorney's office and the psychologist were duty-bound under *Brady* to produce the entire hypnosis file. It further said that "the prosecutorial suppression of nearly all evidence concerning [the witness] resulted in a criminal proceeding that bordered on the Kafkaesque . . . ."

Accordingly, the court ordered the discharge of the prisoners from custody as a consequence of the subject convictions, unless they were to be retried within 120 days. As a parting expression of its outrage, the court retained jurisdiction over the case until "it is given final repose in order to assure that the commands of the United States Constitution are observed" (Diamond 1980; McLaughlin 1981; Sarno 1979; Warner 1979; Warren and Roberts 1980; Worthington 1979).

Both the *Miller* case and the *Emmett* case turned on the issue of the prosecution's duty to advise the defense of the fact of hypnosis and to make available the tapes of the hypnotic sessions so that the defense could effectively exercise its right of cross-examination under the confrontation clause of the United States Constitution. Diamond (1980) calls the *Emmett* case a "veritable nightmare" of abuse and Warner (1979) finds it incredible that the defendants' convictions were sustained throughout the entire Georgia Appellate system. But perhaps the real importance of this case is that it is an answer to those who urge that the professionalism of the police be accepted as a safeguard against hypnotic or other abuses of prosecutorial power. This case illustrates that when a prosecutor's office receives enough pressure from the press, some prosecutors seeking a quick conviction that will take the public pressure off them, respond by forgetting their professional responsibilities to the court and constitutional niceties.

The *Miller* and *Emmett* cases should be contrasted with *Lawson* v. *State* (1979). Here a prosecution witness in a murder case was hypnotized on at least three occasions by a neighbor, who was also a prosecution witness, for the ostensible purpose of calming her nerves so that she could face the ordeal of testifying. This was done without the knowledge of either the prosecution or the defense. On learning of this, the defense made a postconviction motion for a new trial. The Supreme Court of Iowa held that since the prosecutor did not violate his duty to disclose information about the hypnosis of his witness, the *Miller* and *Emmett* cases did not apply. Instead, the court treated the issue as a case of newly discovered evidence, and held that the defense failed to show that this new evidence was other than cumulative or impeaching, and hence upheld the trial court's dismissal of the postconviction petition.

Miller and *Emmett* must also be distinguished from *Shockey* v. *State* (1976), in which a Florida court denied a motion for a new trial made by a defendant convicted of first-degree murder, on the grounds that his codefendant's attorney refused to waive a physician-patient privilege and permit a psychiatrist to testify to what the codefendant had said under hypnosis concerning his role in the killing. The appellant claimed that the testimony would show that he was guilty only of a lesser crime. The court affirmed the conviction, holding that the evidence excluded would be inadmissible since it involved a statement made under hypnosis. The court added that even if the evidence were admissible, it was unlikely to produce an opposite result on a second trial (Millwee 1979; Sarno 1979).

In *United States* v. *Adams* (1978), two defendants appealed their convictions for conspiracy, assault, robbery, and murder in connection with a series of postal robberies. At the trial, Adams unsuccessfully moved to have the testimony of an eyewitness to the murder limited to statements he made prior to pretrial hypnosis to refresh his memory. Actually, Adams called the witness and the *People* impeached him with his posthypnotic statements. The U.S. Court of Appeals for the Ninth Circuit applied the rule that it had invoked in the civil cases of *Kline* v. *Ford Motor Co., Inc.* and *Wyller* v. *Fairchild Hiller Corp.* for the first time to a criminal case, and held that pretrial hypnosis affects the credibility, not the admissibility, of evidence. The court noted that other jurisdictions had followed this rule in criminal cases and saw no reason for a different standard to apply in criminal cases than in civil matters.

The court said that it was mindful that the investigative use of hypnosis carried with it the dangerous potential for abuse and that great care was necessary to assure that posthypnotic statements were the product of the witness's memory rather than of recall tainted by suggestions. The court also said that it did not approve of the hypnosis methods used in this case because an uncertified hypnotist conducted the interview, and no record was made of the identity of those present nor of the questions asked and the responses given. It said that, as a minimum, stenographic records should have been maintained.

However, in this case Adams did not raise an objection to the adequacy of the foundation laid for the hypnotically refreshed testimony. Instead, he argued that no testimony from any witness who had been hypnotized could be reliable, and the use of previously hypnotized witnesses would deny him his constitutional right of confrontation and cross-examination. This is a premise that the court rejected in the *Kline* case and it rejected it again in this case (Anon. 1978b; Conour 1980; Diamond 1980; Mutter 1980; Sannito and Mueller 1980; Warner 1979; Warren and Roberts 1980; Worthington 1979).

The case of *United States* v. *Awkard* (1979) involved five prisoners convicted of murdering a fellow inmate. A government witness, Hackney, was one of the inmates who stabbed the decedent, and after being granted immunity he began to recall the names of other inmates involved. His memory was aided by hypnosis. At the trial the government called Dr. Willian Kroger, who had hypnotized and interrogated Hackney. Kroger, an international authority on medical hypnosis, explained the techniques that he used and stated his opinion about the reliability of hypnosis as a memory aid and about the accuracy of Hackney's recollections in particular.

The defendant objected to the use of hypnosis to refresh the witness's recollection. The Ninth Circuit U.S. Court of Appeals found this objection to be without merit, since pretrial hypnosis to refresh a witness's recollection is permitted in this circuit in both civil and criminal cases. The fact of hypnosis, if disclosed to the jury, goes to the credibility of the evidence not its admissibility.

The defendants also objected to the trial court's refusal to exercise discretion in regard to the testimony of Dr. Kroger, which was received out of sequence before the testimony of Hackney, and in the absence of any attempt by the defense to impeach him by reference to hypnosis. The defense claimed that this amounted to an improper buttressing of Hackney's testimony. The court found this objection more troublesome.

It said that in jurisdictions where the admissibility of hypnotically refreshed testimony is still an open issue, a foundation regarding the reliability of hypnosis is necessary. However, in the federal courts of the Ninth Circuit, this issue has been settled since *Wyller* and thus there is no need for a foundation concerning the nature and effects of hypnosis. The government argued that the use of expert testimony is within the discretion of the trial court. In this instance, however, the circuit court found that the trial court did not exercise any discretion but read the decisions in *Kline* and *Wyller* as requiring expert testimony to establish admissibility.

Moreover, the Federal Rules of Evidence limit a trial judge's discretion when the expert testimony concerns only the ability of a witness to recall details. The court noted that Federal Rules of Evidence 801 (d)(1) prevents the introduction of prior consistent statements of a witness, unless the adversary charges the witness with recent fabrication or improper influence or motivation. Also, Federal Rules of Evidence 608 (a) permits evidence of truthful character only when the truthfulness of the witness has been attacked.

In this case, as a matter of trial strategy, given the eminence of the expert witness, the defense did not want to impeach the witness on the issue of hypnosis or even mention it on cross-examination. It was therefore error for the court to permit Dr. Kroger to testify at the time and in the manner that he did. Also, it would have been improper under any circumstances to permit an expert to express an opinion about the truthfulness of the witness. The court, quoting from *United States* v. *Barnard* (1974) said, "Credibility . . . is for the jury—the jury is the lie detector in the courtroom."

However, while the court held that there was error in these decisions, it also held that it was not reversible error, since there was ample other evidence to sustain the convictions, and it was more probable than not that the jury would have convicted the defendants without Dr. Kroger's testimony (Warren and Roberts 1980).

People v. *Tait* (1980) was reminiscent of the *Miller* case. Here a deputy sheriff, who was the prosecution's main witness against the defendant in a case involving an assault with intent to murder, had his recollection for a significant detail in his testimony hypnotically refreshed by the prosecutor, who was an amateur hypnotist. The defense was given no notice of this hypnosis until after the testimony of the witness, and the trial court refused to permit the defense to refer to the hypnosis in the presence of the jury. It also refused to charge the jury with respect to the unreliability of hypnosis and the capacity of a witness under hypnosis to fantasize. The appellate court held that the action of the *People* was prosecutorial misconduct and noted that even in jurisdictions permitting hypnotically refreshed testimony, this would be grounds for setting aside a conviction. However, it additionally held that the requirements for the admission of hypnotic evidence were the same as for the admission of lie-detector or voicewriter evidence, namely that general scientific recognition be established by the evidence of disinterested professionals.

In the instant case, the conviction was reversed and remanded for a new trial, but the court found that the testimony of the deputy sheriff had been so damaged by the hypnosis that it prohibited the prosecution from calling him as a witness at the retrial (Anon. 1980a).

In *People* v. *Bicknell* (1981), the California Court of Appeals for the First District held that the introduction of the testimony of a prosecution witness, whose memory was refreshed by hypnosis in a pretrial interview conducted without prior notice to the defense, was error because it denied the defendants their Sixth-Amendment right to confront and cross-examine their accuser. Therefore, the witness was rendered incompetent to testify. The court held, however, that the error was not a reversible one in this case, and affirmed the defendants' convictions for first- and second-degree murder. Justice Poche said "Effective cross examination is simply not possible if the witness has no recollection of the subject matter." In a concurring decision, Justice Christian disagreed with the majority on the hypnosis issue. He said that an intermediate appellate court should be reluctant to issue a new rule of evidence. He also noted that is was unnecessary, since California Courts are empowered to exclude otherwise relevant evidence that is unreliable or prejudicial (Anon. 1981g; Lieber 1981).

It seems settled that the prosecution is required to advise the defense of the use of pretrial hypnosis on one of its witnesses and to make available to the defense a record of the proceeding, so that the issue of unreliable or suggestive procedures may be fought out during cross-examination. But it is not so clear whether the defense has a corresponding duty to the *People*.

There have been two decisions found where this issue has been expressly recognized, and these courts have said that either side in a criminal prosecution which uses hypnosis on a witness must inform the other (*People v. McDowell* 1980; *State v. Hurd* 1981). However, as a public official charged with the administration of justice, a prosecutor has an ethical and a legal duty to inform the defense of any exculpatory evidence he discovers. A defense attorney has no such dual role and is generally not permitted, much less required, to inform the *People* of any incriminating evidence he uncovers. This suggests on the one hand that it may not be sound to require him to disclose the use of hypnosis on a defense witness. On the other hand, the *People* have a right to cross-examine defense witnesses, and information about pretrial hypnosis is certainly important for this purpose. If, as seems likely, the use of hypnotic investigations by defense attorneys expands, the courts will have to consider this issue more closely.

In Oregon, a statute requires the prosecution or the defense, if it intends to offer the testimony of any witness who has been subject to hypnosis, (including the defendant) to make a video or other tape of the entire procedure and make the tape available to the other party as a condition of the use of such testimony (Or. Rev. Stat. 136.675, 1977). However, Oregon Revised Statute 136.685 (1977) places some restrictions on the use of hypnosis by law-enforcement agents only. Prior to using hypnosis in an investigation such agent must advise the subject that:

1. He is free to refuse to be a subject;
2. There is a risk of psychological side-effects from the process;
3. If he agrees he may reveal emotions or information of which he is not aware and may desire to keep private;
4. He may request that the procedure be conducted by a medical doctor or psychologist at no cost to himself (McLaughlin 1981; Warren and Roberts 1980; Wilson 1979).

Wilson (1979) claims that this legislation was pushed through the Oregon legislature by the American Civil Liberties Union, which was concerned about the increasing use of hypnosis by the police, but had no national policy on the matter. If so, it is a classic example of poorly thought-out legislation which may well create more problems than it corrects. The wording of Oregon Revised Statute 136.675, which was intended to preserve the adversarial right of cross-examination, may by implication be held to mandate the admission of hearsay evidence obtained under hypnosis if the conditions of recording and disclosure are complied with. Yet the statute was totally unnecessary to compel the *People* to disclose the fact of hypnosis to the defense. There has been a whole line of cases (cited *supra*) as well as the Sixth Amendment to the Constitution that have accomplished this.

It is not clear what, if any, abuses Oregon Revised Statute 136.685 was intended to remedy. It certainly does little to lessen the danger of unreliable or manufactured hypnotic testimony. Nor does it lessen the risk that pretrial hypnosis will render a potential witness less susceptible to cross-examination. It does not even do anything to prevent the employment of lay hypnotists in forensic investigations, although it gives the illusion of restricting this practice. In short, it seems to have been enacted for the purpose of doing someting, but reflects little understanding of the problems of forensic hypnosis.

United States v. *Kimberlin* (1981) is unique in that it involved the hypnosis of a juror instead of a witness. Here a United States District Court held that without a demonstration by the defense that it was actually prejudiced thereby, the denial or nondisclosure of a juror during a *voir dire* of the fact that he had undergone prior hypnosis was not grounds to support a motion for a new trial.

4 Hypnotic Confessions, Statements, and Admissions

A *statement* is an out-of-court declaration concerning the facts in issue, or relevant to the issues, in a lawsuit or criminal trial. A statement made by a party to an action that is inconsistent with the position that he takes at the trial is called an *admission* and is admissible in evidence as an exception to the rule against hearsay evidence.

A prior statement consistent with the position taken by a declarant party at a trial is called a *self-serving statement* and is not admissible as an exception to the hearsay rule, since there is no special reason to believe it is likely to be accurate. Indeed, its self-serving character provides reason to believe that it is likely not to be. Even if the declarant were a witness and not a party to an action, such a prior statement consistent with his in-court testimony would not be admissible, because it tends to bolster the witness's testimony in an unreliable manner. In effect, it would permit the witness to corroborate his own testimony. However, if the story told on the witness stand has been attacked as a recent fabrication, then such prior consistent statements are admissible in rebuttal. Also, if the prior statement is inconsistent with the present testimony of the witness, it is admissible by the adverse party for the purpose of impeaching the witness's credibility.

A statement made by a defendant in a criminal case that admits all of the allegations that the *People* must prove to secure a conviction of a crime is called a confession.

A statement may admit some elements of the prosecution's case and deny others or remain silent with respect to them. Statements made by criminal defendants to law-enforcement agencies are generally reduced to writing and signed by the defendant, but even if they are not, the party to whom the statement was made may testify to the contents of the statement.

It is not correct to say that an admission of a fact in issue by the defendant makes it unnecessary for the *People* to prove this fact, but such an admission is evidence that can be used to meet the *People's* burden of proof. The credibility of the witness establishing the admission is still a question for the jury to decide.

If a defendant has made a statement that amounts to a confession, this is still not enough to sustain a conviction in most jurisdictions. In addition to the confession, there may be a requirement of some degree of corroboration. In New York, for example, there must be some independent evidence that the crime confessed to has, in fact, been committed. This requirement has been necessitated because some mentally disturbed people have so great a need for punishment or attention that they confess to crimes that they could not possibly have committed (Teten 1979). This behavior of individuals who, subject to no pressure by the police to confess, nonetheless come forward voluntarily to admit crimes, demonstrates that confessions, particularly under the circumstances of a police interrogation, are not always reliable.

In order for a confession, or any statement made by a defendant, to be admissible in evidence over objection, the *People* must establish that the statement is voluntary. The defense is often entitled to a notice, prior to trial, if the *People* intend to introduce certain kinds of evidence such as statements or confessions. The defense is always entitled to make a pretrial motion to suppress such evidence if its use is illegal (Warner 1979). The major ground for objecting to the use of statements or confessions is that they were not made voluntarily.

At the time of this motion, or when the statement is offered into evidence over objection, the trial court must make a preliminary finding of fact concerning whether or not the statement was voluntarily made. A statement may be involuntary as a matter of law even if it is in fact voluntary, if it was procured in violation of the rights of the defendant. The courts have decided to exclude statements obtained in this manner to discourage law-enforcement agencies from resorting to proscribed practices.

For example, under the rule established in *Miranda* v. *Arizona* (1966), when defendants are arrested they must immediately be informed by the authorities that:

1. They have a right to remain silent;
2. Anything they say may and will be used against them;
3. They have a right to consult with a lawyer prior to making any statement or to have one present during any interrogation and that one will be appointed if they cannot afford one.

Defendants must then be asked if they understand the warning and if they want to consult a lawyer. They may not be questioned unless they reply that they understand. If defendants say they want a lawyer, they may not be questioned until they have consulted with a lawyer and then only in the lawyer's presence. Finally, if defendants say they understand the warnings and do not want a lawyer, they may still not be questioned until asked if they desire to make a statement and answer in the affirmative.

Mr. Chief Justice Warren, in the *Miranda* case, did an extensive review of the police literature concerning psychological methods of coercing and tricking defendants into making confessions, and discussed the isolation and vulnerability of the suspect under such circumstances. He then held that any statement obtained in violation of these requirements is involuntary as a matter of law and inadmissible in evidence.

Miranda warnings are only required when a suspect is taken into custody. They need not be given if the suspect "voluntarily" comes to a police station and consents to be questioned (*Alderman* v. *State* 1978; *Barfield* v. *State* 1977; *State* v. *Brom* 1972). A confession produced by tricking the defendant may still be admissible providing the trick is not such as is likely to produce a false confession (*Commonwealth* v. *Baity* 1968).

Prior to *Miranda*, these warnings were not required in American courts although they have long been required in England. Contrary to the predictions of law-enforcement opponents of the rule these warnings did not render the American criminal-justice system ineffective, nor have they had such an effect in England. Like most court decisions, *Miranda* does not apply to cases adjudicated prior to it.

Even before *Miranda*, American courts recognized that confessions and statements could be psychologically as well as physically coerced (*In Re Cameron* 1968; *People* v. *Ubbes* 1965). Indeed, if the police failed to bring an arrestee before a court for arraignment within a reasonable time, the voluntariness of any confession obtained became suspect, and unreasonable delays have resulted in their exclusion (see, for example, *Darwin* v. *Connecticut* 1968).

If the trial court finds that a statement is involuntary as a matter of law or was obtained in violation of a constitutional right, it must suppress it. If the court finds that the statement is not voluntary as a matter of fact, the statement is also excluded. Even if the court finds a confession or statement voluntary, the jury may still reject it as involuntary. A statement is voluntary if the defendant was free to choose whether or not to make the statement, without undue physical or psychological pressure, and was not under the influence of any promises or representations by the *People* that would tend to make the defendant falsely incriminate himself or herself (N.Y.P.L. Sect. 60.45). The former practice of the New York courts, in which the trial judge determined that it was possible for a confession to be voluntary and left it to the jury to decide the issue, was rejected by the United States Supreme Court in *Jackson* v. *Denno* (1964).

In *Jackson* v. *Denno*, the Court stated that "It is now axiomatic that a defendant in a criminal case is deprived of due process of law if his conviction is founded in whole or in part upon an involuntary confession without regard for the truth or falsity of the confession . . . even though there is ample evidence aside from the confession to support the conviction."

There are two distinct reasons that involuntary confessions are inadmissible. Historically, they have been rejected because they are not probative. A confession made in response to physical torture, sleep deprivation, psychological pressure, or threats is not believable evidence of anything. More recently such confessions have been struck down because they violate the defendant's right to due process of law under the Fifth and Fourteenth Amendments to the U.S. Constitution, because of the basic unfairness of the procedure (Herman 1964; Spector and Foster 1977). In addition to the Fifth-Amendment guarantee to a criminal defendant of due process of law against the federal government, and the Fourteenth-Amendment guarantee of such due process against the states, the Fifth-Amendment protection against self-incrimination is often cited as a bar against the use of hypnotic confessions (Solomon 1952; Swain 1961).

Whether this objection is well taken would appear to depend on the circumstances of the hypnosis. The protection against self-incrimination has been held to be a protection against testimonial compulsion only. It is permissible to require a defendant to take part in a lineup and to take fingerprints for identification. It has also been held permissible to subpoena the books and records of a defendant. It is obvious that a defendant may voluntarily choose to testify in his or her own defense. Hence the use of hypnosis to obtain a statement from a defendant would probably only be barred by the constitutional protection against self-incrimination if the hypnotic interview were involuntary. Even in the absence of a Fifth-Amendment bar, such statements would not be admitted as an exception to the hearsay rule because the courts have uniformly ruled that statements made under hypnosis are not reliable and hence not probative.

In view of the fact that the induction of hypnosis requires the cooperation of the subject, the question arises how it could ever be considered to be involuntary. The answer is that *involuntary* does not mean *against the will of* but *without the consent of* the subject. It would appear to be impossible to hypnotize a subject who actively resists hypnosis; however, it is quite possible to induce hypnosis and get the subject's cooperation in a setting that he does not recognize as hypnosis. Examples of this would be describing the procedure as relaxation or the use of the chaperone technique mentioned in chapter 1.

Thus hypnotic statements or confessions resulting from involuntary hypnosis are subject to attack on the basis of being oppressive and violative of due process of law, and on the grounds of self-incrimination. These statements may also be attacked on the basis that they are unreliable regardless of whether the hypnosis was voluntary or involuntary. The same is true of statements made shortly after hypnosis (Haward and Ashworth 1980; Herman 1964). Confessions made under conditions analogous to hypnosis (such as sleep or narcosynthesis) have also been excluded as not being probative (Levy 1955; Spector and Foster 1977).

The courts have been uniform in excluding hypnotic confessions on the foregoing grounds. Thus most law-enforcement agencies employing hypnotic investigations have established the policy of not using hypnosis on suspects (Kleinhauz, Horowitz, and Tobin 1977; Levy 1955; Solomon 1952; Teten 1979).

For a variety of psychological reasons as well as legal ones, hypnosis has no legitimate use in the interrogation of suspects or in obtaining confessions. It is generally recognized that hypnosis is not capable of preventing a subject motivated to lie from doing so. Hence, it is of no value to a prosecutor in getting at the truth. Even proponents of its use on suspects admit that it cannot compel a guilty defendant to confess if he is determined not to do so (Arons 1972). If it could, such a confession, even if true, would violate both the Fifth and Fourteenth Amendments. If the goal of the criminal justice system were simply to get defendants to confess to crimes, there are other more effective ways of doing this than hypnosis. All that need be done is to bring back the rack and the thumb screw. The lure of hypnosis, to the uninformed, is that it seems to be a means of selectively compelling the guilty, but not the innocent, to confess. Hypnosis does not have this ability. There is no way to protect the rights of innocent citizens unless society is prepared to extend the same rights to the guilty (*Stevenson* v. *Boles* 1963). This notion is the cornerstone of our legal system and, even if hypnosis could be demonstrated to compel only the guilty to confess, its use for such purpose would still violate the proscription against self-incrimination and the requirements for due process of law.

Palmer and Sims (1970) express the view that since a hypnotic subject cannot be compelled to act against his "primary self-interests," if he would decline to confess in the waking state he would usually "decline with equal resolve under hypnosis." They claim, however, that hypnosis would permit a subject inwardly inclined to confess to do so by breaking down some of his "restrictive inhibitions." Neither the first premise nor the conclusion based on it have been demonstrated to be correct and both are very likely not to be. The second notion could just as logically be used to support the position of permitting any kind of mental coercion to be used to get a confession and then justifying the procedure by saying that if the suspect were not inwardly inclined to confess he would not have.

What hypnosis actually can accomplish is to render a subject hyper-suggestible and compliant. Subjects are easier to lead under hypnosis, and even honest examiners may cue them in a manner that significantly affects their responses. A dishonest examiner can subtly get a good subject to say almost anything and to believe in the truth of what he or she has been led to say (Solomon 1952). This is the real reason that hypnotic confessions are not and should not be admissible. They are not reliable or probative of the facts in issue. In addition to procuring a false confession, hypnotic suggestions may convince a defendant that it is to his advantage to confess because he is not morally guilty, or because he will feel better, or because somehow it will help him. A true confession produced in such a manner is just as objectionable as a false one, and is not voluntary. It is produced by deception and psychological coercion and should not be admitted into evidence.

Herman (1964) argues that if a defendant is hypnotized by the defense and his testimony under hypnosis is exculpatory, then as a condition of admissibility he should be required to be hypnotized in the presence of the prosecutor, and different rules of admissibility should be invoked depending on whether the second hypnotic session is inculpatory or exculpatory and whether it is deemed reliable or unreliable by experts. Such a scheme seems to be both unnecessary and impractical. In the first place, the only reason for a defendant to be hypnotized by the defense would be to break an amnesia or to fill in missing memories of details. If this is successfully accomplished the hypnotic interview need not be offered in evidence and he can testify from present memory refreshed. In the second place, if the jurisdiction involved does not permit hypnotic memory refreshment, then a constitutional issue is involved in applying such a rule against a defendant, for it would effectively bar him from participation in his own defense.

The notion that an expert can determine the reliability of a hypnotic statement places too much credence in the ability of an expert. Without independent evidence, no expert can ever know whether a statement made under hypnosis is accurate in any particular detail. What an expert can say is that a procedure was defective and likely to produce distortion, but that is very different from saying that it *has* done so. Finally, even if a procedure were done perfectly, this is no assurance that the statements elicited are factually correct. Errors can come from the internal needs, motives, fantasies, and other dynamics of the subject.

The voluntary submission to hypnosis by a defendant endeavoring to prove his innocence, with the results to be admitted in evidence by stipulation, is possible, but there is little to recommend it. From the *People's* point of view, exculpatory statements made under such conditions carry no assurance of accuracy, unless established by independent evidence. From the defendant's point of view, there is a risk of giving the *People* additional information that may hurt the defense. Unless the *People* stipulate in advance to permit the introduction into evidence of what the defendant says under hypnosis, any exculpatory statements made would be inadmissible as self-serving. As in the *Nebb* case, such arrangements have resulted in favorable plea bargains but this was more from the lack of sophistication concerning hypnosis on the part of the *People* than the ability of hypnosis to establish the truth.

As in the case of lie-detection and truth-serum tests, it is improper to permit a jury to draw any inference concerning the defendant's guilt or innocence from his request for or refusal to be hypnotized (Haward and Ashworth 1980; *State* v. *Levitt* 1961).

Although hypnosis used as an inquisitorial device is capable of producing inaccurate statements, it may also produce some accurate ones that can be independently verified. Although constitutional considerations preclude the involuntary or covert use of hypnosis on defendants in criminal cases, it might be productive as a means of interrogating prisoners of war were it not outlawed by the International Rules for Land Warfare (Antitch 1967; Solomon 1952).

It would seem that if a criminal defendant voluntarily submitted to investigative hypnosis by the *People* for the purpose of clearing himself, and produced inculpatory statements, these should not be excluded because of considerations of due process of law or self-incrimination. They should, however, be excluded because they are not reliable and not voluntarily made because of the hypnotic influence.

The courts have uniformly rejected confessions obtained under hypnosis whether voluntarily induced or not. Sometimes, however, the issue is whether or not a police interrogation of a defendant involved the use of hypnosis. In general, if a confession was procured by hypnotic means it will be inadmissible, regardless of whether the agents of the state intended to employ hypnosis, it resulted inadvertently, or even as the result of a spontaneous trance. In all such cases hypnosis interferes with the ability of the defendant to freely choose whether to make a statement (Haward and Ashworth 1980).

Cases

Rex v. *Booher* (1928) was a Canadian case involving the application of the Crown to admit a confession of the defendant into evidence. The Crown had employed as its agent a Dr. Langsner, who claimed to be a criminologist who could obtain information by means not used by ordinary investigators. He said he could exercise "hypnotic effects" upon a subject by "feeling" his thoughts. After being present as a spectator at a preliminary inquiry he visited the defendant in a guard room on the next day. Following the interview, during which Dr. Langsner said he had no conversation with the defendant, he went to the murder scene with a police sergeant and they found the murder weapon, a rifle, in less than half an hour. An extensive search for the weapon by the police and neighbors had previously proved fruitless.

Dr. Langsner made subsequent visits to the defendant for the purpose of obtaining a confession, and again alleged that there was no conversation with the suspect. On the last occasion, he left the prisoner and went to the guard room and told the officers that they might expect a confession in a short time. In a few minutes, the defendant asked to see a Detective Leslie and made the confession.

Chief Justice Simmons of the Alberta Supreme Court held that under these circumstances the Crown should clearly establish that the defendant's mentality was not affected by Dr. Langsner's visits. In view of the circumstances of the finding of the rifle, and the doctor's admission that "he can practice magnetism," the court said that his denial of the use of hypnosis should be viewed with suspicion. Though ordinarily the confession obtained would have been admissible, the court excluded it because the Crown failed to discharge the onus placed on it to establish that it was not the product of mental suggestion exercised by Dr. Langsner (Herman 1964; Levy 1955; Solomon 1952; Spector and Foster 1977; Swain 1961; Warner 1979).

In the case of *People* v. *Leyra* (1951) the New York Court of Appeals was confronted with a situation "on all fours" with the Booher case. The defendant had been convicted and sentenced to death for the hammer murders of his mother and father. The convictions rested largely on the confession of the defendant received in evidence by the trial court. The defense claimed that the confession was obtained by hypnosis and it was reversible error to admit it.

The circumstances surrounding the confession were reviewed by the court and were uncontested by the *People*. The suspect had been subjected to prolonged questioning by a Captain Meenahan without opportunity to sleep from about 2 P.M. Thursday until about 9 A.M. Friday. During this period he made some damaging admissions. He was then taken by detectives to the funeral of his parents and was returned to the police station. He signed a consent to remain in police custody and was then taken to lunch and allowed to sleep for an hour and a half before being rturned to the police station. The defendant had been suffering from an acutely painful sinus attack and Captain Meenahan had agreed to get a physician to help him. Instead, at about 7 P.M. that evening, he introduced the defendant to a Dr. Helfand, who was not a medical practitioner but a psychiatrist. Unknown to the defendant, this doctor was not employed to help him with his pain but to help the police investigation and had been briefed by them as to the facts in the case.

The doctor agreed to see the defendant on the condition that no one else be present, but he knew that the interview room had been bugged and his conversation with the defendant was being recorded. The doctor talked with the defendant for about an hour and a half. Based on the recording of this conversation, the court found that in the course of this interview the doctor had misrepresented himself as being present to help the defendant and as being his doctor. On at least forty occasions, in one way or another, he promised to help the defendant.

Judge Froessel quoted passages from the transcript where the doctor commanded the defendant to remember and told him it was to his advantage to do so. The doctor also pressed the suspect's forehead and told him that it would bring back memories. Promises of help by such statements as "We'll help...," "Everybody will help you...," "We're with you 100 percent...," and so on were found to run throughout the transcript.

The doctor, in a manner reminiscent of a hypnotic induction by the Flower method, commanded the sleepy and exhausted prisoner to open and close his eyes. He also made numerous suggestions as to what the defendant should say. He threatened to give him an injection to make him speak truly. He told him things such as, "You have a much better chance to play ball [noise] than if you say you don't remember. If you tell me that you were in a fit of anger, that you were angry, that you just swung the hammer, but if you tell me that you don't remember, then you will be working against yourself..." and "These people are going to throw the book at you unless you can show that in a fit of temper you got so angry that you did it. Otherwise they toss premeditation in and it's premeditation. See?".

After this interview the defendant asked to see Captain Meenahan and confessed to him. Thereafter, in the same evening, the defendant made additional statements to a police officer, to a trusted friend, and to two representatives of the district attorney's office.

At the trial, the defense raised the issue that the confessions were obtained by hypnosis and were involuntary and untrue. The defendant denied that he had killed his parents and claimed that he did not know what had happened after talking to the doctor for the first few minutes. He testified that the doctor had made gestures with his hands and with some object, after which he recalled nothing. One of two defense psychiatrists called testified that the doctor's actions could have been nothing but hypnotism.

The Court of Appeals found that the issue of the hypnotic nature of the procedure had been fully and impartially submitted to the jury and that they had chosen to believe Dr. Helfand rather than the defendant. Thus there was no reason to interfere with that finding. However, it did not necessarily follow from this that the confessions obtained were voluntary, within the meaning of the New York Code of Criminal procedure.

The court found that the undisputed facts of this case—the defendant's mental and physical condition and the psychiatrist's pretense of being his doctor and playing on his fears and hopes, pressing the prisoner's head while making commands and suggestions, persistent and unceasing questions, and deceptive offers of friendship and promises made in a pseudo-confidential atmosphere of a doctor-patient relationship—all added up to the equivalent of mental coercion.

The court held that a trial court should reject a confession, as a matter of law, if it would have to set aside a verdict based on such confession as against the weight of the evidence. It asked, "If a physician may be thus used, then why not a lawyer or a clergyman?" It added, "We have held that an involuntary confession is by its very nature evidence of nothing... Moreover our Federal Constitution (14th Amendt.) is a bar to the conviction of any individual in our courts of justice by means of a coerced confession..." (Dilloff 1977; Herman 1964; Levy 1955; Solomon 1952; Spector and Foster 1977).

After the original conviction was vacated by the New York Court of Appeals, the defendant was retried and convicted on the basis of the subsequent confessions only. The defendant's claim that these later confessions, made on the same evening as the invalidated one, were also involuntary, was submitted to and rejected by the jury. The New York Court of Appeals upheld the subsequent convictions and the United States Supreme Court denied *certiorari*. Thereupon, the defense brought a *habeas corpus* proceeding in the U.S. District Court alleging that the confession had been coerced (*Leyra* v. *Denno* 1953). The district court considered and denied the petition and the U.S. Circuit Court affirmed with Judge Frank dissenting. This time, the United States Supreme Court granted *certiorari* because the constitutional question involved appeared substantial.

Mr. Justice Black wrote the opinion of the Court and held that the Fourteenth Amendment prohibited the use in a state criminal trial of a defendant's confession obtained by coercion, whether physical or mental. Therefore, the court examined the circumstances surrounding the procurement of the confessions in question. It found that "the undisputed facts in this case are irreconcilable with petitioner's mental freedom 'to confess to or deny a suspected participation in a crime'". All of the confessions were found to be obtained as part of one continuous process, within a period of five hours. They were all found to be obtained by mental coercion and violation of due process of Law (Levy 1955; Spector and Foster 1977; Spiegel 1980; Swain 1961; Worthington 1979).

Mr. Justice Minton dissented, largely on the issue of the submission of the question of the voluntary nature of the confession to the jury. It was his view that submitting contested issues of fact to a properly instructed jury is not a denial of due process of law.

Portions of the transcript of the interview between the doctor and the prisoner were published as an appendix to the decision of the Court. The record strongly suggests that the defendant was probably hypnotized to some extent, either by the covert efforts of the doctor, or as a result of a spontaneous trance state produced by the stress of his circumstances (a lack of sleep and incessant questioning). In any event, there is little question that the doctor was putting words into the prisoner's mouth, not only by the use of leading questions, but by repeating and rewording his answers. The transcript appears to justify the court's decision that the resulting confessions were mentally coerced and probative of nothing.

This case dramatically illustrates the dangers intrinsic in the use of hypnosis and other psychological techniques in obtaining confessions. It also suggests that mental-health professionals who work in the context of the criminal-justice system require special training in basic legal concepts so that they can appreciate some of the constraints imposed upon the party whose cause they seek to aid.

In *State* v. *Walker* (1967) the Supreme Court of Missouri found no basis in the record to support the claim of the defendant that his confession was involuntary and that a state's interrogator had attempted to hypnotize him. Indeed, the appellant's description of the attempted hypnosis clearly indicated that it had been unsuccessful even if the alleged attempt had been made.

In *Parker* v. *Sigler* (1969) the U.S. Circuit Court held that the totality of circumstances under which a confession was obtained, which included patting the defendant on the shoulder, stroking his hair, lifting his chin, and forcing him to maintain eye contact with the interrogator, (as well as subjecting him to a lie-detector test and saying that it indicated that he was lying, and then accusing him of murdering his wife), went beyond approved standards and rendered the confession involuntary. The court also found that the submission to the jury of the issue of the voluntariness of the confession was contrary to the doctrine of *Jackson* v. *Denno*, which was held by the United States Supreme Court to be retroactively applicable (*Desist* v. *United States* 1969).

However, in *People* v. *Norcutt* (1970) the Supreme Court of Illinois found nothing in the record to support the claim of the appellant, convicted of arson and felony murder, that his confession was psychologically coerced and that a police officer had hypnotized him. The officer in question had denied knowledge of hypnotic technique.

The unreported case of *People* v. *Shelly* (1973) involved a defendant who was amnesic for the circumstances of a double murder, as well as for his confession to the crime. A court order was obtained permitting his counsel to have him hypnotized in jail to break the amnesia. While the hypnosis did not restore any memories concerning the facts of the murders, it did enable the defendant to recall the events incident to his confession. It developed that he had been subjected to "exceptionally coercive tactics" including the infliction of pain and the denial of medical assistance. As a result of this information the defense was able to obtain what Warner (1979) calls a favorable plea bargain. It is not clear from Warner's report what evidence other than the defendant's coerced confession the *People* had, but unless this was substantial, it is hard to understand how a plea bargain made on behalf of a defendant who could not remember the events of a crime charged can be deemed advisable, much less favorable.

Schneck (1967) reports another case in an extralegal context in which hypnosis detected the probable falsity of a confession made while the accused was not hypnotized. The case involved a college student who was expelled after confessing and later denying a theft in a college fraternity. Hypnoanalysis disclosed a pattern in which the subject falsely accepted blame as a way of expressing hostility toward his father.

A New York trial court in *People* v. *Baldi* (1974) found the defendant guilty of murder in a nonjury trial. One of the issues at the trial concerned the voluntary nature of the statements he had made. At the trial, the defendant denied the murder and claimed no recollection of any admissions made or reenactments performed. Under cross-examination the defendant admitted that he had learned self-hypnosis. Two psychiatrists testified that the defendant had a high trance capacity and under certain circumstances might go into a trancelike state spontaneously. The court found that there was no evidence that the detective interrogating the defendant, either by accident or design, sought to hypnotize him and it doubted that he had the requisite training to do so. If there was a trance state during questioning, (as the court concluded that there was), it was held to be self-induced. Drawing an analogy with self-induced intoxication, the court decided that this trance would not be enough to render the admissions inadmissible, unless the defendant was intoxicated "to the degree of mania or of being unable to understand the meaning of his statements."

By failing to recognize that a spontaneous trance produced in a susceptible subject by stress is not the same as one intentionally induced by self-hypnosis, the court avoided the necessity of dealing with the effect of such a situation on a confession. Identical objective situations may represent very different levels of stress to different individuals. If a subject perceives the circumstances of an interrogation as stressful enough to seek unconsciously to escape it by entering into a spontaneous trance, as suggested by Spiegel (1980), then counsel might argue that, with respect to this suspect at least, the circumstances amounted to psychological coercion.

In *Coon* v. *State* (1980) the Supreme Court of Alabama upheld a decision of the Alabama Court of Criminal Appeals that found that a hypnotic interview of a defendant, conducted by a police officer a week prior to the making of a confession, did not invalidate the confession where it was not shown that the confession resulted from the hypnosis [Anon. 1981(l)].

Derivative Evidence

Haward and Ashworth (1980) say that there is a small danger that a suspect may be hypnotized without his consent and that although a confession resulting from such hypnosis would be excluded, English law would permit the introduction of evidence discovered as a result of such a confession.

Levy (1955) cited the law in The Netherlands, that a prisoner may be subjected to hypnosis to get information which, while not admissible against him, may lead to other evidence that is admissible. He found no constitutional difficulty with such use of hypnosis in the United States, and citing Ladd (1902), suggested that the unfairness of such a procedure is no greater than that of other detection methods that are either sanctioned or "winked at" by the courts.

The first problem with this view is the unacceptable notion that law-enforcement agents should be permitted to "wink at" the requirements of the law, and then use the fact that such reprehensible practices are commonplace to argue for a proposed new rule of law. The second problem is that the law has developed a more realistic viewpoint since 1955. Prior to *Mapp* v. *Ohio* (1961), a state court was not constitutionally required to exclude illegally obtained evidence (*Wolf* v. *Colorado* 1949). The federal courts, however, having inherent supervisory powers over federal law-enforcement agents, were required to exclude such evidence (*Weeks* v. *United States* 1914). In the federal courts evidence seized as a result of an illegal search was excluded if obtained by a federal officer, but was admitted if seized by a state officer, unless the latter was working in conjunction with a federal agent (the "silver platter" doctrine).

An exception to the rule for state courts was provided in the case of *Rochin* v. *California* (1952), in which the forced use of a stomach pump on a defendant to obtain evidence shocked "the conscience of the court" and caused it to hold that in certain limited cases (involving coercion, violence, or brutality) state courts had to exclude illegally obtained evidence.

Mapp v. *Ohio* (1961) specifically overruled the *Wolf* case and held that the Fourth Amendment, as incorporated by the Fourteenth Amendment, required state courts to exclude evidence obtained by an unlawful search and seizure, as well as any derivative material that flowed from such illegally obtained evidence.

Although this line of cases deals primarily with illegal searches, it reflects the belief of the courts that if a law-enforcement agent is permitted to violate the law and use illegally obtained evidence to prove his case, constitutional guarantees become meaningless.

Applying this philosophy to derivative evidence based on the involuntary hypnosis of defendants, one would expect it to be inadmissible. Herman (1964) states, however, that state case law fails to support this expectation. He advances as the reason for this state of affairs the fact that hypnotic confessions were originally excluded on the grounds that they were unreliable rather than coercive. Following this reasoning, if the derivative evidence that resulted from leads obtained while the defendant was hypnotized were shown to be reliable, it would be admitted. In the last forty-five years, the emphasis has shifted from issues of reliability to issues of due process. Today such evidence would probably be excluded, to discourage law-enforcement agents from utilizing such practices. However, if the hypnosis were undergone voluntarily by the defendant, and if the derivative evidence obtained was independent and reliable, there appears to be no reason why it should not be admissible.

Polygraph and Truth Serum versus Hypnosis

A polygraph, or lie detector is a device that purports to tell when a subject is lying. A truth serum is a drug that is supposed to prevent lying and cause a subject to tell the truth. Neither device is related to hypnosis, since there is no evidence at all that hypnosis has the ability either to detect lies or compel the truth. However, many judges and lawyers, naïve concerning the abilities and limitations of hypnosis, suppose otherwise, and hypnotic evidence has often been dealt with by drawing analogies to lie detection or truth-serum evidence. If misused as a truth-seeking device rather than as a lead-generator hypnosis does share the unreliability that the courts have ascribed to polygraphs and truth serums (Boyd 1973).

Polygraphs

A polygraph is essentially a device for recording certain autonomic nervous system (ANS) responses over time such as pulse rate, blood pressure, respiration rate, and galvanic skin response (GSR). It is an excellent research tool in studies in which the dependent variable is some such physiological response. However, its use as a lie detector is based on the theory that lying affects these responses in a reliable and detectable way that can be recognized by an expert. Since some people have more labile ANS responses than others, each subject must first have his responses calibrated when responding to neutral questions and then when instructed to lie. Following this, he is asked a series of filler questions interspaced with key questions. His responses to the key questions are then compared to his responses to known lies. Proponents claim that these results are from 73 to 90 percent accurate, when interpreted by an expert. Just what constitutes expertise is unclear. Often lie-detector operators are former police officers with little or no formal training in either psychology or physiology. There are some schools that train polygraph operators, but no such school has been found that operates under the supervision of a university. In a normal subject, it would not be surprising if lying could occasionally be detected by such a device, but to say that it is capable of obtaining accurate results uniformly, or with a psychopath or a severely mentally disturbed subject, requires more evidence than is currently available.

Mutter (1979) reported the combined use of hypnosis and a polygraph in an actual murder case. The subject was a witness and accomplice in a double murder. She was anxious to testify against her boyfriend because she feared he would kill her. Also the district attorney promised her immunity in exchange for her testimony, provided that she could prove that she was not the slayer.

She had failed two previous lie-detector tests, the second involving the additional use of hypnosis, when Mutter was called into the case. He hypnotized her, dissociated her left hand, and gave her an ideomotor signal to indicate lying. She was then age-regressed to the scene of the crime for hypnotic lie detection and a simultaneous polygraph examination. When asked if she killed the victim she said, "No." The polygraph indicated a lie; the ideomotor signal did not. Mutter accounted for the conflicting results by theorizing that the subject unconsciously believed that she had killed the girl because she had been the one that discovered her at the scene of the first murder. When asked if she pulled the trigger she said "No" and both measures indicated that she was telling the truth.

It is interesting to note that when the two measures yielded different results, Mutter developed a theory to account for it, instead of simply assuming that neither method is reliable, but when they agreed he interpreted this to indicate that one test had confirmed the other. It is known that hypnotically induced feelings of guilt can cause a polygraph to yield a positive response erroneously. If guilt feelings produce this result with a lie detector why do they not do so with an ideomotor response?

Weinstein, Abrams, and Gibbons (1970) tested the validity of the polygraph by hypnotically inducing guilt about taking money in three subjects and "repressing" guilt in another three. The polygraph operator was completely misled by the three "guilty" subjects. The authors asserted that this demonstrates that a polygraph would not be useful in detecting false confessions induced by unrelated guilt feelings. The three subjects who repressed guilt feelings only partially deceived the operator. He thought that they probably were guilty, but he would not be able to swear to this in court. The authors concluded that, to the extent that a polygraph works, it detects subjective factors, not objective truth. They also suggest, without specifying how, that hypnosis might be used with a polygraph to "amplify" the findings. This seems odd, for if anything their study showed how hypnosis could distort not enhance polygraph results. It is difficult to see how combining two poor devices for lie detection is likely to produce a good one. The view is often expressed that hypnosis can calm a subject so that the polygraph test is more accurate. It would seem that such calming might make it even less accurate, if it attenuates the emotional response to lying that the machine is supposed to detect.

Even if the claims of accuracy made by proponents of the device could be demonstrated to be true, it is still not suitable for use in a courtroom. The issue in a lawsuit, civil or criminal, is not whether the machine is likely to be accurate 90 percent of the time, but whether a specific assertion made by a particular witness is true or not. Juries do not assess the probability of guilt. They must find a defendant guilty or not guilty. It is true that they do not always do this without error, but if they are to be replaced with a machine, the machine should be demonstrably better than they are at this task. This is particularly so, since jurors have attributes that no machine can replace, such as common sense and compassion. [See Abrams (1973) for a bibliography on the validity of the polygraph.]

Truth Serum

Danto (1979), a physician and police officer, reviewed the use of sodium amytal in psychiatry as a device to overcome catatonic muteness and to make it easier for patients to talk and answer questions. He described its early use in exploring the unconscious through narcoanalysis and its use during World War II in treating combat fatigue and interrogating enemy prisoners. He compared sodium brevital with sodium amytal and concluded that it was essentially the same drug but sodium brevital had fewer side effects and contraindications.

Danto also described the techniques used in police interrogations with sodium brevital and claims that unlike hypnosis, susceptibility to the drug is universal. He claims that in his experience even "known liars" are more likely to tell the truth under the drug and can be "interrogated closely" by persons familiar with the facts. The effect of the drug is claimed to be the inhibition of the "censor portion of the mind." Patients are said to be unable to discriminate what they are saying and their responses are spontaneous, yet they are aware that they are being questioned and can follow directions. Danto says that it is easier to overcome "unconscious resistance" under sodium brevital because subjects do not retain control of the interview, as they would under hypnosis.

Danto tries to make a case for the police use of brevital in the interrogation of suspects. His statement that under brevital the subject is not in control of the interview should prove fatal to this goal, for if true it would demonstrate that any statement made cannot be voluntary within the legal meaning of that term. As a matter of logic, if a drug could really prevent a subject from lying, then it must take away his freedom of choice and make his statement involuntary, which would render it inadmissible whether reliable or not.

The procedure that Danto outlines for a brevital investigation leaves much to be desired, from both the legal and psychological points of view. Prior to the test, the subject is reassured and informed of his right to refuse the test or to have his attorney present if he desires. (If a defendant is represented by an attorney, he cannot consent to such a test without his attorney's permission.) It is unclear why an attorney would agree to let his client be given such an unreliable test by the *People*, unless he believed that it would convince the prosecution of his client's innocence and result in the dropping of charges. If this does not happen the results are not admissible in evidence, absent a stipulation, and the *People* cannot even mention that the test was given. However, there is no reason why reliable derivative evidence flowing from such a test would not be admissible, and this is a real danger for the defense.

Danto tells his subjects that the tape of the interview is his property but that a copy will be given to the police. No mention is made of giving a copy to the defense. The questioning techniques used are similar to those employed under hypnosis, such as the suggestion of an imagined TV screen and age regression, and the same opportunities for leading the witness are present, especially since Danto advises having personnel familiar with the facts of the case present.

Although so-called truth serums may make it easier for some patients to verbalize material, this in no way demonstrates that these verbalizations are factually accurate. As in the case of a hypnotic interview, the accuracy of the material is totally irrelevant in therapeutic work, but it is vital in forensic investigations. There is no reason to suppose that making a subject more verbal is any more likely to result in the truth when accomplished by a truth serum than it is if the same result were to be obtained by getting him drunk. Furthermore, the accuracy of verbalizations elicited under a truth serum needs to be established in carefully controlled experiments, not in actual legal cases in which the facts are always in dispute.

Zonana (1979) reports a case of a seventeen-year-old defendant who killed his grandmother and aunt while high on drugs and who had no memory of the crime. He developed the psychotic defense of hallucinations. His memory for the crime was not restored by sodium amytal, but it was restored by hypnosis, and his insanity plea was uncontested. Zonana cited the case as evidence that hypnosis and truth serum are different devices and one can succeed when the other has failed. Following hypnosis, the subject's hallucinations diminished, the implication being that the material elicited was accurate, but this in no way established this. It simply means that these verbalizations, true or false, probably had a therapeutic effect. The most interesting thing about this report is the lack of support for the idea that somehow truth serum, like hypnosis, has the ability to increase recall. If anything, to the extent that it alters the normal operation of the brain, it ought to be expected to impair recall. The function of a truth serum (or alcohol) seems to be to relieve inhibitions and lower the defenses of a subject, not to sharpen memory.

Lastly, the recall under hypnosis of any events that were forgotten as a result of an intoxication by drugs or alcohol ought to be viewed with extreme skepticism. It is likely that this condition has interfered with the process of memory formation, and the enhanced recall may well be more fantasy than memory.

Even though lie detectors, truth serums, and hypnosis are different devices with different theories, modes of operation, capabilities, and limitations, the courts tend to treat their results similarly because as truth-obtaining devices they all fail to meet the *Frye* standards of general acceptance as reliable by the appropriate scientific community (Boyd 1973). The principle advocates of the forensic use of polygraphs or truth serums are those who have a financial interest in their employment, attorneys whose cause may be aided by the results in a particular case, and those who believe that the law should utilize scientific advances and technology but are untrained in the methods and standards of science.

However, there is no reason why polygraphs and truth serum should not be used as investigative and lead-generating devices in a manner similar to hypnosis, provided that the results are not intended to be used as evidence. Unlike hypnosis, a lie-detector test is unlikely to contaminate a prospective witness or render him resistant to future cross-examination. In this respect, it is safer than hypnosis, but it also has little potential to recover repressed memories. Truth serum may well contaminate a witness and may lower repression at a cost of reduced accuracy. Like hypnosis, its investigative use is best restricted to individuals unlikely to be future witnesses.

5 The Role of the Expert Witness

It is the function of an expert witness to aid the jury in its deliberations by giving an opinion concerning the technical issues of the case within his or her area of expertise. The factual or assumed basis of this opinion must also be given since the expert should not usurp the jury's function as the finder of the facts but aid them in discharging that duty. The jury is free to disregard an expert's opinion and substitute its own. The courts have always been wary of the tendency of many psychiatric experts to testify to conclusions of law, such as that a defendant is legally insane, when their proper function is to describe the defendant's mental condition, leaving it to the jury to apply the law to this fact (Bazelon 1974).

Before permitting a witness to testify as an expert the court must make preliminary findings that:

1. The area to be testified in is one in which the jury requires the help of an expert; and
2. The witness is qualified as an expert.

Expert testimony is not admissible on a matter about which the jury could reach a conclusion as well as an expert (*People* v. *Lewis* 1980). Thus, the English Court of Appeals upheld the exclusion of psychiatric testimony to establish the defendant's mental state at the time of an alleged crime when mental illness was not claimed, because the jury could determine this as well as an expert (Haward and Ashworth 1980).

Similarly, it is improper for an expert in hypnosis to testify that in his opinion a witness told the truth under hypnosis, because it is the function of the jury (not an expert) to determine the credibility of a witness. Such a conclusion is also unwarranted psychologically, for no expert can ever be sure of whether the material elicited under hypnosis is fact or fiction without independent verification. In spite of these principles, some American courts have permitted experts to state their opinion on the veracity of statements made under hypnosis, as long as they were properly qualified.

The issue of whether a defendant is competent to stand trial relates to mental illness, even though the test used to determine this issue is different than the ones used to determine criminal responsibility. Expert testimony is admissible on this issue. As in the defense of insanity, hypnosis is a recognized and valid method of making such diagnosis (Kline 1979).

To have the capacity to stand trial the defendant must generally be able to understand the nature of the charges against him; and be able to cooperate with counsel (see *South* v. *Slayton* 1972; *State* v. *McClendon* 1966). If the defendant could be tried without the ability to cooperate in a meaningful way with his lawyer, the latter would be unable to represent him properly and the constitutional right to counsel would be a mere sham.

A witness's qualification as an expert is a preliminary matter of fact to be determined by the trial judge. The court will take into consideration such factors as formal education and degrees, special training, professional experience, authorship of books and journal articles, teaching experience, licensure, board certification, professional-society memberships, and reputation. None of these factors is controlling. It is possible to be considered an expert in a field, based on professional experience, without a degree, but the days should be past when reading a book on hypnosis would qualify one as an expert (as in the *Donovan* case, chapter 3). The court must find that the expert has some level of special knowledge beyond that of a well-informed layman. An expert must have sufficient skill, knowledge, and experience to aid the jury, and the state of the art must permit rendering of a valid opinion (Boyd 1973). Merely being a physician or a psychologist is not enough to qualify a witness as an expert in hypnosis (see *People* v. *Busch*, chapter 3). However, a master's-level psychologist with professional experience in hypnosis was held to be qualified (*Harding* v. *State*, chapter 3). The court in the *Mack* case (chapter 3) held that a lay hypnotist with no scientific understanding of memory or hypnotic suggestion would not qualify as an expert in hypnotic memory refreshment.

In some jurisdictions (for example New York) an adversary cannot prevent the jury from hearing the credentials of an expert witness by conceding that the witness is qualified. However, if a party desires to contest the qualifications of a proffered expert, he will do so by objecting to the first question that seeks to elicit the witness's opinion, on the grounds that he is not qualified.

An expert witness can only be asked his opinion concerning matters within the area of expertise in which he has been qualified. In other matters he must testify, as any other witness, only to facts that he has personally observed.

Herman (1964) states that an expert in hypnosis should be a psychiatrist who uses hypnosis frequently in his practice. It is interesting that Herman does not consider a clinical psychologist an expert in hypnosis, but for some reason thinks that a polygraph operator should be a psychologist. It is widely recognized that a clinical psychologist is an expert in mental status (Bazelon 1974; *People* v. *Pennington* 1967).

The executive council of the Society of Clinical and Experimental Hypnosis has established an American Board of Clinical Hypnosis which certifies candidates as competent in medical, dental, or psychological hypnosis. Diplomates in psychological hypnosis are certified either in clinical or experimental hypnosis.

However, neither the American Medical Association nor the American Dental Association has a specialty board in hypnosis. A New York trial court in *Bakal* v. *New York Telephone Co.* (1978) saw no reason to interfere with the telephone company's policy of limiting specialty notations in their directory to those recognized by the American Medical Association and refusing to list the plaintiff under the separate caption *Medical Hypnosis.*

An expert witness who has no personal knowledge of the facts in issue in a case cannot be subpoenaed like an ordinary witness, but comes into court as a result of an agreement with the attorney who calls him. Part of that agreement will include a fee to be paid to the witness for his time. Even if an expert has personal knowledge of a case and is subpoenaed, he is entitled to a fee, if he is qualified as an expert and is asked for an opinion on the issues.

Following his direct testimony, an expert witness is subject to cross-examination by the opposing party as is any other witness. All of the ordinary methods used to impeach a witness may be used against an expert. In addition, there are special techniques that can be used against experts. A common method is asking questions concerning the amount of the fee paid for the expert's testimony, to imply that he has a motive to testify to what the proponent of his testimony desires. A proper answer to such a question is that the witness is being paid nothing for his testimony, because it is not for sale. He is, however, being paid a certain amount for his time (Cohn and Udolf 1979). This is a dangerous kind of question to ask on cross-examination, since jurors are likely to think that the per-diem fee of the average expert witness is outrageously high, and it may convince them that the witness must be very eminent indeed to command so large a fee. An expert may also be attacked by demonstrating that in fact he is not an expert, impressive credentials notwithstanding. One way of doing this is to quote passages from a book that the witness has admitted is authoritative, but that contradicts him, and ask him to explain the difference between his testimony and the book. An expert must be careful about what books he admits are authoritative. But this kind of question can also backfire on counsel, for if the witness is able to explain an apparent discrepancy satisfactorily, his credibility will be greatly increased (Cohn and Udolf 1979). Part of this risk can be minimized by adequate pretrial consultation between the lawyer and his own experts.

It is the lawyer's responsibility to brief the witness on all aspects of his courtroom appearance. The lawyer will generally go over the witness's direct testimony so that he knows what to expect from him in court and will instruct him on how to behave under cross-examination. In general, these instructions will include an admonition to limit responses to the questions asked, to avoid volunteering information or sparring with opposing counsel, to pause before answering questions under cross-examination (so that the lawyer calling him can object before his answer is given), and to avoid losing his composure, whatever the provocation (Cohn and Udolf 1979).

The witness in turn should candidly advise the lawyer concerning what admissions he will have to make under cross-examination, and help the lawyer frame not only the questions designed to elicit his own opinion on the case, but also those to be used in cross-examining the adversary's expert. In short, the lawyer must be given a briefing in the technical issues of the case if he is to function effectively.

One of the problems in using an expert witness in our adversarial system of justice, unless he is experienced in his courtroom role, is that he is suddenly shifted from his customary role of a respected authority to the unfamiliar position of having his integrity and professional ability under attack. This makes some witnesses act defensively. Some begin to assume the role of an adversary instead of that of a disinterested professional. Such a posture will prove more of a hindrance than an aid to the cause of the party calling an expert witness. An expert's opinion will carry more weight with the jurors if they see him as a neutral professional with no interest at all in the outcome of the case. To the extent that he is seen as a partisan he loses credibility. That, of course, is what the cross-examining lawyer is trying to accomplish.

Some experts are so concerned about their feelings of vulnerability on the witness stand that they often do things in hypnotic interviews for the sake of bolstering their testimony rather than for their value to the procedure. For example, Mutter (in Gravitz 1980) recognizes that hypnotic depth is unimportant in hypnotic memory retrieval, but advocates measuring trance depth because opposing counsel will ask about it. There is no great harm in making such an estimate, but if it is neglected or if the trance proved to be very light, there is no reason why the witness should not freely admit this and leave it for the lawyer who called him (and has been briefed by him) to bring out, under redirect examination, why this measure is unimportant. Since no court has admitted testimony given under hypnosis into evidence the depth or even the fact of hypnosis is really not in issue. If hypnotically refreshed testimony is admitted, it is admitted because the witness now claims to be testifying from present memory refreshed. It is irrelevant in many states whether this refreshment was produced by hypnosis or any other means. The only important fact is that somehow memory has been restored. Indeed, if the trance depth was light, it may make it harder for the adversarial party to impeach the witness on the grounds that his testimony was influenced by hypnotic suggestion. It is axiomatic that an expert witness should always testify to his candid opinion in the case without regard to whether such an opinion helps or hurts the party calling him. If the honest opinion of the witness seems likely to harm his proponent's case, he ought to advise him of this prior to his courtroom appearance so that the party can reconsider calling the witness. Once in court, an expert should not be concerned about the effect of his testimony; that is the lawyer's responsibility. If, in spite of himself, the witness begins to assume an adversary stance, he ought to remember the truism that if candor will not help a case it is beyond saving. A witness who becomes an adversary, and slants his testimony accordingly, renders himself vulnerable to cross-examination and is more of a liability than an asset to the party calling him.

In cases involving the use of hypnotically influenced testimony the employment of expert testimony is indispensable to both parties. From the point of view of the proponent of the evidence, an expert is needed to lay a foundation for the admission of the evidence and to explain and justify the procedures used and the inferences that may be drawn from the results.

The question of what foundation need be laid for the introduction of hypnotically influenced evidence is complex, for it depends on the purposes for which the evidence is offered, the nature of the evidence, and the jurisdiction involved. If counsel seeks to have evidence of statements made under hypnosis admitted to establish their truth, in a jurisdiction where the matter is still one of original impression, or if counsel seeks to get a court to reverse the unanimous rule against such evidence, he would have to demonstrate that:

1. Hypnosis is generally recognized and accepted among psychologists and other mental-health professionals as a reliable method of recovering repressed or otherwise forgotten memories.
2. The procedures used in the case at bar are generally recognized as reliable and appropriate under the unique circumstances of the case; in other words, that a reliable procedure was used in a reliable and competent manner. This would necessarily include the demonstration that the hypnotist was an expert (Boyd 1973).

Spector and Foster (1979) assert that a foundation for the introduction of hypnotically refreshed testimony should include:

1. Evidence of the hypnotist's qualifications and experience;
2. An explanation of the role of hypnosis in the treatment of amnesia and memory retrieval;
3. The expert's opinion about the reliability of hypnosis as a memory-refreshing device;
4. The etiology and dynamics of the memory problem of the witness hypnotized;

5. The procedures used to induce the trance and an estimate of its depth;
6. A film or transcript of the hypnotic session;
7. The hypnotist's testimony that no suggestions were made that tainted the results; and
8. The hypnotist's opinion of the effectiveness of the technique in dispelling the amnesia.

Certainly the qualifications of the hypnotist are necessary to qualify him to testify as an expert and to establish that the procedures were likely to have been competently conducted. Yet if the jurisdiction involved permits the introduction of hypnotically refreshed testimony, the *Awkard* case (chapter 3) suggests that an explanation of the use of hypnosis as a memory-enchancing device and opinions concerning its reliability are not only not necessary but are probably inadmissible in the absence of an attack on the procedure. Furthermore, the opinion of the expert concerning the reliability of hypnosis as a fact-finding device is really irrelevant. What is needed under the *Frye* doctrine is testimony regarding the consensus of opinion within the profession with regard to this issue.

If hypnosis is used to break an amnesia, testimony regarding the dynamics of the case would be helpful, but it is possible to treat an amnesia empirically without an accurate understanding of these factors. Also, hypnosis may have been used in a nonamnesic patient to enhance recollection of details. This is, of course, a more dangerous use of hypnotic memory enhancement and this should be admitted by the expert. If the courts required testimony about dynamic factors this would effectively preclude the use of lay hypnotists in forensic work. A video tape or film, though not mandated by all courts, should be an absolute requirement, since without it opposing experts have no means of evaluating the procedures used or of detecting subtle sources of error. If such a tape is available, there would appear to be no need for the expert to testify about the procedures used for they are reviewable by the court in an *in camera* inspection of the tape. Similarly, there would be no need for statements claiming the absence of improper suggestions.

Finally, the expert's opinion concerning the effectiveness of the procedure seems to be improper since, given the state of the art, no expert can say if statements made under hypnosis are veridical, and permitting one to do so encroaches on the jury's function of evaluating a witness.

Background information on the uses, techniques, and effects of hypnosis is generally admissible as foundation matter (Sarno 1979). In general, the expert should state the conditions that can affect the reliability of hypnotically influenced testimony and relate them to the situation under consideration (Herman 1964).

All of the foundation testimony of the expert is subject to cross-examination. The tapes of the session should be made available to the opposing party so that cross-examination can be based on them. The absence of a tape recording of the entire procedure necessarily implies that either the procedure was not performed by a competent expert or that the missing tape would contain material harmful to the proponent of the evidence.

From the point of view of the opposing party, the prime value of an expert witness is to review the video tapes of the procedures employed to detect defects in technique and subtle or overt suggestions concerning the testimony elicited. These can be the basis for impeaching the credibility of the hypnotically influenced witness and if gross enough can provide grounds for moving to exclude his testimony altogether because it has been contaminated by suggestions.

The opposition's expert is also in a position to help the attorney evaluate the qualifications of the other side's witnesses and to help him frame questions for use in cross-examination. He can advise the lawyer of weaknesses in the adversary's case from a technical point of view and, equally important, advise him of when the other side is on firm ground and when cross-examination could be dangerous. The opposition's expert is also in a position to explain to the court and the jury the dangers of hypnotic questioning and the possible generation of confabulations, fantasy, and other errors (Dilloff 1977). He can help the attorney draft requests for cautionary instructions concerning the evaluation of hypnotically influenced testimony for inclusion in the court's charge to the jury.

It is essential that an attorney confronted with hypnotically influenced testimony have the aid of his own experts. In several of the cases cited in chapter 3, the courts have suggested that the outcome might have been different had the defense taken a different tack on the technical issues (see, for example, *United States* v. *Adams*). To the argument that lawsuits may be converted into battles of experts that tend to confuse juries and usurp their proper function, Herman (1964) responds by asserting that it is better to decide issues on the basis of expertise than by guesswork. He asserts that if conflicting expert testimony confuses the jury, it is not the fault of expert testimony but the failure of the lawyers involved to present their cases effectively.

Orne (1979) cited a variety of cases that illustrate the role of experts in detecting defects in hypnotically influenced testimony. He reports that in *People* v. *Ritche* (1977), an analysis of the video tape showed how the witness may have been inadvertently led by the hypnotist and how inconsistencies in the witness's story suggested confabulations. Orne's testimony led to the exclusion of the hypnotic evidence as unreliable.

State v. *Douglas* (1978) involved what Orne calls the most frightening example of a witness lying, rather than being misled, by hypnosis. The complainant had claimed that she was raped by an assailant whom she was unable to identify from mug shots. Following hypnosis she identified the suspect. Because of the hypnotic identification, the previously skeptical district attorney was persuaded to prosecute. A public defender, struck by peculiarities in the handwriting of threatening notes the complainant had claimed to have received, investigated and found out that it was her own handwriting. When confronted with this, the witness admitted that the whole story was false and was intended to rekindle the interest of her husband who was in the process of divorcing her.

An interesting situation arises if the expert's opinion is adverse to the cause of the party who called him. Can the adverse party use this witness? In most jurisdictions the answer is no, for while there is clearly no doctor-patient or psychologist-patient privilege involved (since the expert was not hired for the purposes of treatment but for litigation), nevertheless, the expert is an agent of the attorney and permitting him to testify for the adversary side would be a violation of the attorney-client privilege (Warner 1979).

However, in a regrettable decision, the New York Court of Appeals in *People* v. *Edney* (1976) held that the *People* could hire a former defense psychiatrist since by asserting an insanity defense the defendant waived the doctor-patient privilege (which was never actually in existence in this case) (Warner 1979). This decision has made New York defense attorneys cautious about consulting prominent experts whom the *People* might also want to hire. Whatever the legality of hiring an opponent's former expert in a particular jurisdiction, it would seem a questionable practice on the part of the expert involved, from an ethical and a purely business point of view. What trial counsel in possession of his faculties would hire an expert witness who has changed sides in a previous case? Since an expert witness cannot be compelled to testify as to his opinion, it should be a practice of an expert once consulted by one side to be unavailable as a witness for the other side. An expert who changes sides is analogous to a defense lawyer, who after learning the facts of the case, withdraws and joins the prosecutor's staff (an act for which he would be promptly and justifiably disbarred).

6 Hypnosis and Crime

Unlike the preceding chapters, which dealt with the potential of hypnosis as a tool of law-enforcement agencies or the legal profession, this chapter will investigate its potential for criminal use. There are two major areas that require discussion in this context:

1. The psychological issues involved in the ongoing controversy concerning whether hypnosis could be misused for criminal purposes; and
2. The legal consequences that would flow from such misuse.

The alleged criminal uses of hypnosis occasionally reported or, more often, speculated about, generally involve the use of hypnosis as a vehicle to induce a subject to commit a crime; or the use of hypnosis to victimize a subject (Ladd 1902; Solomon 1952; Swain 1961; Teten 1979; Udolf 1981).

If hypnosis could be used to induce a person not otherwise so inclined to commit a crime, this would necessarily raise the issue of the status of hypnosis as a defense in a criminal action. This and other legal issues will be considered after the psychological controversies and evidence are presented.

The Potential of Hypnosis for Criminal Purposes

The question of whether hypnosis can be used to make a subject commit a crime, or to victimize subjects, has remained unresolved, although it has been debated by psychologists and legal writers since the time of Mesmer.

Those who believe that a hypnotized subject can be induced to commit a crime, either by coercion or deception, generally point to the increased suggestibility of the subject, his compliance or desire to please the hypnotist, and the fact that hypnosis is marked by distortions in perception that would make it easy to instill a belief in false premises (Allen 1934; Antitch 1967; Kline 1972; McLaughlin 1981; Rowland 1939; Watkins 1972). It is argued by proponents of this view that suggestions of posthypnotic amnesia would make the subject unaware of the real motivation for his criminal acts and hence could be used to protect the criminal hypnotist from detection. Also, it is claimed that hypnosis can render a crime victim passively submissive (Solomon 1952).

Those who do not believe that hypnotized subjects can be made to commit a crime that they would not ordinarily be willing to commit point out that a hypnotist's power over a subject is more illusory than real (Barber 1961; Conn 1972; Orne 1972). Orne (1972) notes that the reason that a hypnotist appears to have so much power over a subject is that hypnotists usually limit suggestions to those that the subject is willing to accept. A hypnotized subject is always fully conscious of what he or she is doing and is quite capable of refusing to accept a suggestion. In the therapeutic employment of hypnosis subjects commonly refuse suggestions outright or modify them in such a manner that they are willing to comply. This is why Udolf (1981) advocates that therapeutic suggestions should be worked out in advance in a conference with the subject. This can be illustrated by a classroom demonstration in which a subject was given the posthypnotic suggestion that on hearing the cue word *glasses* he would shout "Hallelujah." The subject did not respond to the cue word embedded in a sentence, but about ten minutes later he asked, "How come I didn't say 'Hallelujah' when you said *glasses?*" This subject was unwilling to act in a way that he considered would make him appear foolish, so he complied with the suggestion to say "Hallelujah" in a way that was acceptable to him. A subject always retains control over the hypnotic situation. It is the subject's imagination and cooperation that produces the effects of hypnosis, not any mysterious power that the hypnotist exerts over him or her.

Furthermore, the notion that a hypnotic subject can be deceived into accepting the reality of false premises that would justify what would otherwise be antisocial behavior is also subject to question. Hypnosis can be viewed as an ego-splitting situation in which the subject's ego divides into a participating ego, which experiences the suggestions made, and an observing ego that stands back and watches the procedure as a stranger would (Fromm 1975). Typically, good subjects have less observing ego than poor ones, but all subjects retain some observing ego. This is the reason why subjects made deaf by hypnotic suggestions recover hearing in response to verbal release signals and why subjects age-regressed to a time before they could understand a language can be brought back with verbal suggestions. It is also the reason that it is probably impossible to totally deceive a subject concerning objective reality. For example, hypnotized subjects told to negatively hallucinate a chair placed in their pathway typically do not walk into the chair but walk around it (subjects told to simulate hypnosis to deceive an experimenter are more likely to bump into it) (Orne 1962).

Finally, a posthypnotic amnesia is of such variable duration and so easily dissolved by subsequent hypnotic suggestions or by the ordinary processes of association that in reality it would give the criminal hypnotist little protection.

Ladd (1902) in an early *Yale Law Journal* article said that there was no doubt that a hypnotic subject's vulnerability to criminal abuse was greatly increased, particularly with respect to sexual assault, undue testamentary influence, and even induced suicide; but noted that the subject had some protection. This included the subject's ability to determine the character of the person he or she was willing to be hypnotized by and the fact that "fundamental moral character ordinarily asserts itself even in the hypnotic condition." Also the criminal hypnotist could not count on a complete and lasting amnesia.

The evidence used to support conflicting views on this issue has ranged from anecdotes to demonstrations, experiments, and occasionally actual criminal cases. As will be shown, there are serious problems with all of these types of evidence, which is why it is still possible for well-informed experts to differ on the issue of the potential of hypnosis as a criminal technique.

Psychological Evidence

Psychological evidence of the ability of hypnosis to cause criminal behavior or victimize a subject has generally taken the form of demonstrations of "antisocial," immoral, or self-injurious behavior. Experiments with various degrees of control have been employed in more recent work. Ladd (1902) reports that Liegeois got a young woman to "poison" her aunt with sugar and another to fire what she was told was a loaded pistol at her mother. He also reports that Sallis got a young man to fire a pistol at a servant under the suggestion that the latter was a robber about to kill him.

Orne (1972) reports a demonstration at the Salpêtrière in 1889 in which a young woman who readily accepted a series of "antisocial" suggestions, such as to stab people with a pseudodagger and to poison them with sugar, refused a suggestion to undress.

Ladd noted that the Nancy and Paris schools were opposed on the issue of whether crimes could be induced by hypnosis and he believed that the truth lay between the two extremes. He acknowledged that it does not follow that a subject who will stab with a paper knife or poison with sugar would do so with a steel knife or arsenic.

Udolf (1981) reviewed the experimental literature in this area, which will now be summarized. Hypnosis has been employed in experimental contexts to get subjects to perform all of the following kinds of so-called antisocial or dangerous behaviors, and others:

Picking up dangerous snakes or throwing acid at people (Orne and Evans 1965; Rowland 1939; Young 1952);

Minor thefts, verbal attacks on friends, and verbalizing secrets (Brenman 1942);

Revealing "military secrets" and attacking a military superior officer (Watkins 1947);

Stealing an examination (Coe, Kobayashi, and Howard 1972a, 1972b);

Calling people obscene names (Parrish 1947);

Mutilation of a flag or Bible (Levitt 1975);

Trying to buy heroin (Coe, Kobayashi, and Howard 1972a, 1972b);

Indecent exposure (Kline 1958).

Coercion and deception have both been used in these studies, and in some cases, like Rowland's work, both methods have been used to obtain compliance to the same suggestions.

The reason that such a variety of antisocial appearing behaviors has been used is that there are various requirements for the ideal experimental behavior that are not easily attained. First, the behavior should be such that most people, and especially the subjects, would normally consider it as antisocial, immoral, or unreasonably dangerous. Second, the behavior should be such that the subject can be permitted to carry it out without special protective measures taken by the experimenter. For example, in snake-grabbing experiments, the poisonous snakes must either be placed behind nonreflecting (invisible) glass shields or defanged. Also, there is no assurance that the subject can distinguish a venomous snake from a harmless one. Acid-throwing experiments also require either protection of the so-called victim or a deception of the subject concerning the nature of what is thrown.

There is little doubt that hypnotic subjects can be induced to perform all of the behaviors listed and others equally dangerous or apparently antisocial. There is considerable doubt, however, that the power of hypnosis to coerce or deceive the subject as to the nature of what he or she is doing is responsible for these results.

In most of the foregoing experiments, hypnosis was confounded with the subjects' awareness of being part of an experiment. This, in turn, implies to subjects that they are expected to follow the hypnotist's suggestions and that the hypnotist will assume responsibility for the subject's actions (Barber 1961). In addition, when subjects know that they are in experimental situations they are convinced that the experimenter, being a responsible person, will not really let them hurt themselves or others, regardless of appearances. Indeed, it is possible to get subjects to engage in an almost unlimited range of antisocial, dangerous, or just pointless behaviors by telling them it is part of an experiment (Orne and Evans 1965).

When Erikson (1939) made it clear to subjects that he would not assume responsibility for the acts of theft or violation of others' privacy that he suggested, his subjects failed to perform the same kinds of behaviors that other experimenters had elicited in their subjects. Also, as the research in this area developed, more adequately controlled studies were performed. For example, Orne and Evans (1965), unlike Rowland (1939), found that not only would hypnotized subjects pick up snakes, throw acid, or pick up a coin in a container of acid; so also would waking controls and subjects simulating hypnosis.

A major variable confounded with hypnosis in many of the earlier studies was the relationship between the hypnotist and the subject. In studies in which this relationship is separable from the effects of hypnosis, it has been found that the relationship, rather than the hypnosis, produces the compliance with suggestions (Coe, Kobayashi, and Howard 1972a, 1972b).

To summarize, the weight of the experimental evidence indicates the following conclusions.

1. In studies in which it is clear to the subjects that there is no way that the experimenter can protect them from the consequences of the suggested immoral behavior (such as mutilating a flag or Bible or getting undressed), compliance rates decline.
2. Any study in which subjects are aware that they are in experimental situations is meaningless, for this fact alone will generally produce compliant behavior without hypnosis.
3. The relationship between the experimenter and the subject, in experiments in which compliance with antisocial suggestions is obtained, is generally enough in itself to account for the subject's compliance.

In the last analysis, experimentation is unable to resolve the issue of whether hypnosis can produce criminal or self-injurious behavior, because of what Orne (1972) calls the logical unassailability of either position. On one hand, if a hypnotist fails to elicit the antisocial behavior sought, it does not establish that hypnosis cannot produce such a result. It may merely indicate a poor subject or an inept hypnotist. On the other hand, if subjects do respond as suggested, it may be that they would be willing to do the same thing when awake (Perry 1979). In some cases, hypnosis may neither deceive nor compel a subject to behave in an antisocial or immoral manner but merely serve as an excuse to act on preexisting desires.

There is no doubt that antisocial, immoral, and self-injurious behavior can be and have been produced in hypnotized subjects both in experimental contexts and in real life. There remains much doubt and controversy as to the relative effect of the hypnosis and of the interpersonal relationships involved in producing this behavior.

Cases of Hypnotically Effectuated Crimes

Just as psychological research is subject to both logical and procedural limitations in answering the question of the feasibility of hypnotically induced crime or victimization, so too are there limits to what can be learned from a study of actual criminal cases reaching the courts. A major source of error in these cases is that their operative facts are usually in issue, and it is never possible to be certain of the circumstances of the alleged hypnosis, or even whether it was employed at all (as opposed to merely being proffered as an excuse for otherwise criminal behavior). It is interesting to note, however, that in spite of all the writing and speculation on this subject few cases involving the criminal use of hypnosis have reached the courts.

Crimes Committed by or through Hypnotic Subjects

Teten (1979) claims that the use of hypnosis to induce criminal behavior deserves scant attention as the vast majority of courts have given little credence to the defense that a defendant acted under hypnotic influence. In a celebrated French murder case of the last century, Gabriele Bompard was accused of collaborating with her lover in the murder of her husband. Her defense was that she assisted in the crime only because of an irresistible impulse resulting from a hypnotic suggestion. The court's medical experts (who included Charcot) found against her and she was convicted. The court, in disallowing the defense, said that, "An honest subject resists a dishonest suggestion and if he obeys it, it is not because his will is subjugated but because he consents." (Bell 1895; Herman 1964; Ladd 1902; Solomon 1952; Swain 1961.) This psychological conclusion arrived at by the court is interesting because if true it would rule out the possibility of using hypnosis to victimize a subject.

In the case of *People* v. *Worthington* (1894), the Supreme Court of California upheld the trial court's exclusion of evidence of the effect of hypnosis, in a second-degree murder case, in which the defenses raised were hypnosis and insanity. The defendant claimed that she had killed her lover as a result of a hypnotic suggestion given to her by her husband. The court held that "Merely showing that she was told to kill the deceased and that she did it does not prove hypnotism or at least does not tend to establish a defense to a charge of murder." (Dilloff 1977; Herman 1964; Lehan 1970; Solomon 1952; Swain 1961.) The conviction was reversed and remanded for retrial on other grounds.

The 1894 Kansas cases of *State* v. *Gray* and *State* v. *McDonald* are widely reported in the literature as involving an older employer reputed to have influenced a young employee to commit a homicide by hypnotic suggestion. The employer (Gray) was convicted as an accessory before the fact and the employee (McDonald) was acquitted (Herman 1964; Ladd 1902; Solomon 1952; Swain 1961). However, Bell (1895) citing correspondence with defense counsel and the record on appeal, states that the *McDonald* case was based on the issue of self-defense, not hypnosis, and the only reference to hypnosis in the entire record was a statement by counsel to the effect that Gray had an almost hypnotic influence over McDonald. The newspapers of the time seized on this phrase and widely reported the trial as though hypnosis were an issue in it.

Reiser (1978) cites a 1934 Heidelberg case in which it was alleged that a woman was not only defrauded of money by a man posing as a doctor, but was also hypnotized by him and induced to commit prostitution and attempt to murder her husband and kill herself. A psychologist purportedly used regression to remove the woman's posthypnotic amnesia and the suspect was convicted and sentenced to ten years in prison.

Reiser also describes a 1951 case in Denmark in which the defendant robbed a bank and killed two employees. It was alleged by the accused that during World War II, when he was in prison, his cellmate repeatedly hypnotized him and made him "subservient" and that he had acted under the former cellmate's influence. Teitelbaum (1963b) cites Polgar's description of a Norwegian case in which a subject shot himself in a hypnotically anesthetized arm to collect an insurance settlement.

In 1926 in *Denis* v. *Commonwealth* the Supreme Court of Appeals of Virginia held that the opinion of a lay witness that the defendant (a priest) was acting under the hypnotic influence of another in forging and uttering a certificate of deposit, was properly excluded and sustained his conviction.

It should be noted that the claim of hypnotic influence as a defense to a crime is so uncommon that case examples have had to be excavated from the distant past or from Europe. One of the few comparatively recent American cases in which this issue was squarely presented was *People* v. *Marsh* (1959). In this case, the appellant appealed from a conviction for escaping while confined as a prisoner at the California Institution for Men at Chino. The sole defense raised at the trial was that the escape was not a voluntary act but the result of a hypnotic suggestion made by a fellow inmate, Jack A. Cox. Cox testified that he had learned hypnosis from books and had hypnotized hundreds of subjects including the appellant. The incident in question was alleged to result from a misunderstanding of a suggestion made that Marsh should "Go back where he . . . was having a good time." Cox claimed that this suggestion was intended to produce an age regression, but the subject misinterpreted it as a suggestion to leave the prison and return to the area where he formerly lived.

A psychiatrist appointed by the court at the request of the defense was qualified as an expert, in spite of her testimony that a hypnotist needs to have a rather forceful personality and a good subject should be suggestible, weak, compliant, and peaceful. She testified that Cox did not possess the personality qualities of a successful hypnotist and that Marsh lacked the qualifications of the ideal subject. She also stated that the claimed suggestion for age regression would not cause the appellant to escape. A defense request to perform a hypnotic experiment in the courtroom was refused by the trial court.

The California District Court of Appeals, in sustaining the conviction for escape, held that the rejection of the offer to demonstrate hypnosis was within the discretion of the trial judge and was not an abuse of that discretion. The appellant was estopped from contesting the expertise of the psychiatrist since he called her as an expert. The appellate court found that the appellant had had a full and fair opportunity to present his defense to the jury and they disbelieved him based on "ample evidence" (Dilloff 1977; Lehan 1970; Teten 1979).

In *United States* v. *Phillips* (1981), the defendant raised the defense of insanity or, in the alternative, that hypnosis had prevented her from forming the requisite intent. She admitted that she had shot and almost killed two United States Marshals in an attempt to help her husband escape as he was being brought into a federal courthouse. At the trial her husband testified that he had been hypnotizing the eighteen-year-old defendant since she was fifteen, sometimes ten to fifteen times a day. He said that he had made her believe that he was her mother and father and God. He claimed to have instructed her to bring a gun to court and use it to help him to escape. The insanity plea was based on the argument that since the defendant thought that her husband was God, she was unable to distinguish right from wrong for "If God tells you to do something you think it's right." The defendant was convicted on all counts except that of assault with intent to commit murder, and the case is on appeal.

Victimization of Hypnotic Subjects

The following cases involved the use of hypnosis to commit a crime, not through the agency of the subject, but against the subject. The most common type of such alleged victimization is seduction, or some type of sexual abuse, but occasionally allegations of theft or undue financial influence are made (Solomon 1952).

In 1865 in France, a vagrant named Castellan was convicted on charges of allegedly hypnotizing a twenty-six-year-old woman repeatedly and compelling her to leave home and live with him. Although authorities disagreed on whether hypnosis was actually employed, he was alleged to have completely subjugated the woman, and he received a twelve-year prison term for seduction (Herman 1964; Ladd 1902; Sloan 1924; Solomon 1952; Swain 1961).

In a similar case in Munich, Bavaria, in 1894 Czyniski was sentenced to a three-year term for seducing a thirty-eight-year-old woman of high social position by allegedly subjugating her will through hypnosis (Bell 1895; Herman 1964; Levy 1955; Sloan 1924; Solomon 1952; Swain 1961).

In an early Iowa case, *State* v. *Donovan* (1905), the supreme court of that state upheld a seduction conviction although the complainant was unable to say whether the seduction succeeded because of the defendant's hypnotic suggestions or his use of "flattery and love-making." It also sustained the admission of evidence of the defendant's use of hypnosis on other subjects as evidence of his ability to hypnotize.

Seduction is variously a crime or a tort or both in different jurisdictions, although many states have eliminated both the crime and the civil cause of action for seduction. The gist of the offense is the procurement of a sexual relationship with a female of previously chaste character. In other words, a woman can only be seduced once, since the offense requires a virginal victim. Various states have imposed other limits on the offense. For example, when a cause of action for seduction existed in New York, the seduction had to be accomplished by an unconditional promise of marriage in order to constitute the offense.

The Supreme Court of Iowa, in upholding the conviction of Donovan, noted that it was irrelevant whether hypnosis or flattery was the reason for the complainant's "debauch." It found that "A careful examination of the record has convinced us of the defendant's guilt and that he richly deserves the sentence imposed." (Dilloff 1977; Levy 1955; Solomon 1952; Swain 1961).

A New York seduction case contemporaneous with *Donovan* but grounded in tort rather than prosecuted as a crime, *Austin* v. *Barker* (1906), turned out more successfully for the defendant. The father of the alleged victim brought an action for damages against a man alleged to have used hypnosis to seduce his daughter. The claim was made that the daughter had no memory of having sexual relations with the defendant until after the birth of her child. Her memory was restored prior to the trial under hypnosis by her father's attorney. The Appellate Division of the New York Supreme Court found the testimony of the woman involved so incredible, and so unsupported by expert testimony concerning the origins of her alleged amnesia and the restoration of her memory, that it refused to permit a judgment for the plaintiff based on such evidence to stand. It declared that her testimony was simply a hearsay repetition of what had been told to her under hypnosis and was not based on actual memory (Dilloff 1977; Herman 1964; Solomon 1952; Swain 1961; Worthington 1979).

The Court of Criminal Appeals of Texas in *Tyrone* v. *State* (1915) affirmed a manslaughter conviction of a defendant whose wife had testified for the defense that the physician-victim had seduced her by means of hypnosis and she, while conscious of the doctor's acts, was powerless to resist him because of the hypnosis. A Dr. Sheppard testified for the state that it was impossible for hypnosis to permit one person to gain such control over another.

The defense moved for a new trial on grounds of newly discovered evidence, alleging that a Dr. Johnson would testify contrary to Dr. Sheppard and that it had found a book on legal medicine that said that there was no doubt that the hypnotic state could be used for sexual purposes.

The court, in denying the motion, said that it would be a reflection on the defense attorney's ability as a criminal lawyer to say that he could not have foreseen that the prosecution would attack, from every legitimate angle, the appellant's wife's "weird and unreasonable" story. Hence the evidence alleged as new should have been and would have been uncovered prior to the trial with the exercise of due diligence, and it was therefore not the kind of new evidence on which a motion for a new trial could be grounded.

Louis v. *State* (1930) involved an appeal from a conviction for common-law robbery and a sentence of ten years. The *People* alleged that the defendant, by hypnosis, had placed a spell on the complainant that compelled her to go to her home, some two miles or more from her bank, get her bankbooks, and then go to the bank, withdraw all of her money, and return to deliver some $290 to the defendant. The defendant denied these allegations, but the Court of Appeals of Alabama found that even if they were true and established by the trial evidence, the defendant's conviction of robbery could not stand. Robbery in Alabama, as in most jurisdictions, is defined as a larceny aggravated by an assault. To make a case of robbery, the *People* must prove not only an unlawful taking of valuable property but that the property was taken either by force or fear. In this case no force was used (nor could it have been used, since the victim traveled to the bank alone) and she had testified that she was not afraid. Under these operative facts the result might have been different had the defendant been convicted of larceny (by trick or device) instead of robbery (Dilloff 1977; Lehan 1970; Solomon 1952; Swain 1961; Teten 1979).

The Supreme Court of New Jersey in *State* v. *Levitt* (1961) affirmed an order of the trial court that set aside a conviction of a hypnotist for a private act of lewdness. The state's sole witness was a patient of the physician and the case turned on the issue of her credibility against that of the doctor, who denied the offense. The trial court threw out the verdict because a member of the jury after the trial disclosed to the court that some members of the jury, during their deliberations, had made remarks indicative of ethnic prejudice against the defendant.

In *Johnston* v. *State* (1967) the Court of Criminal Appeals of Texas affirmed the conviction of a thirty-six-year-old high-school guidance counselor for a homosexual sodomy committed on a sixteen-year-old student in the presence of two other teenagers. The sixteen-year-old victim claimed that the defendant had hypnotized him, while the defendant stated that neither the act in question nor the hypnosis had occurred. The two witnesses supported the victim's claims. On appeal, the defense contended that the witnesses were accomplices and that the jury should have been so instructed, for accomplice testimony requires corroboration, and one accomplice cannot corroborate another. The appellate court found that the witnesses did not participate in the offense and hence were not accomplices, and so the trial judge did not err in failing to charge that they were accomplices. This case is interesting in regard to hypnosis as a vehicle of victimization, because the trial court did charge that the victim, having participated in the sodomy, was an accomplice, and his testimony, therefore, needed corroboration. This implies that had the victim been charged with the crime of sodomy the court would probably not have been impressed with the claim that he acted under hypnotic influence.

Mirowitz v. *State* (1969) involved an aggravated sexual assault by a hypnotist on a female investigator of the Texas Board of Medical Examiners. After seeing the defendant's advertisements representing himself as a Ph.D. and a clinical psychologist dealing with marriage counseling, hypnosis, self-hypnosis, speed-reading, and emotional problems, the investigator made an appointment, pretending to have a headache. The defendant prescribed self-hypnosis and in the course of a twenty-minute session asked the complainant if she was a virgin. Thirteen days later she returned saying that the self-hypnosis had not worked and he rehypnotized her. Under hypnosis he allegedly told her that he was her boyfriend and that they were on their honeymoon. He then allegedly made sexual advances until she stopped him and got out of her reclining chair. She was then told to wait in another office until the hypnotist returned, and he would "teach her how to make love and enjoy it." At the first opportunity, she ran out of the office to where her supervisor was waiting.

The supervisor testified that the investigator had been hired to investigate whether the defendant was violating the Medical Practice Act, that she emerged from his office white and shaking, and was quite upset for some fifteen or twenty minutes. The appellant denied the investigator's story but was convicted. On appeal, he contended that the investigator was an accomplice, and, therefore, her testimony needed corroboration. The appellate court held that in this case there was no evidence to show that she had consented to being fondled, and hence she was not an accomplice. It should be noted that, according to her supervisor's testimony, she was investigating a possible violation of the Medical Practice Act, not possible immoral conduct on the part of the appellant. Had she come to his office for the latter purpose, the court may well have reached a different conclusion concerning her status as an accomplice. Also, the issue of entrapment might have arisen.

The appellant also took exception to the prosecutor's questioning of the legitimacy of his credentials and inquiries as to whether he was a "fraud," as the injection of extraneous offenses into the case. The court concluded, in the light of the appellant's negative answer, that he had not been prejudiced, and permitting the question was not, therefore, reversible error.

Perry (1979) reports an Australian case, (*Regina* v. *Palmer* 1976), in which a lay hypnotist with a long minor criminal record was convicted of sexual offenses against two female subjects. This case is interesting because the suggestions made were direct and involved neither coercion nor an attempt to deceive the subjects concerning what they were doing by the creation of false perceptions. The hypnotist, who was convicted of rape and indecent assault, freely admitted that he had used hypnosis for sexual purposes. His defense was that since it is impossible through hypnosis to coerce compliance to an act that the subject believes to be immoral, the women involved performed the sex acts with him because they were willing. The women, however, testified that they knew what they were doing, but did not want to have sex with the defendant. They said that they could not resist because of the hypnosis. A third female subject said that the defendant had also tried to seduce her but that she was able to resist. Three experts were called for the defense and two for the Queen. One of the latter two was the same bogus doctor that had trained the defendant in hypnosis, and it was the subsequent discovery of his lack of credentials and his perjury that caused the Criminal Court of Appeals to vacate the convictions.

The testimony of the complainants appears incredible on its face. They said that they could not resist the defendant's sexual advances under hypnosis, yet they were able to resist his suggestions that they sing at the party where he met them. Also, following the sexual encounter, both women paid the hypnotist's fee and made an appointment for the next visit! Furthermore, the sexualization of the hypnotic session did not seem to appear odd to them. For example, one woman came to the hypnotist for the treatment of nail-biting and she did not seem to find it peculiar that in a prehypnotic interview he asked her questions about her sex life and masturbatory practices.

It seems likely that this case is an example of hypnosis being used to give a subject an excuse to do what she was evidently willing to do. Whether the testimony of the witnesses in this case was honest rationalization to account to themselves for what happened or deliberate perjury is not so easily answered.

In an English case, reported by Hartland (1974), a twenty-year-old married woman accused an obstetrician who used hypnosis to obtain relaxation during gynecological examinations of sexually molesting her in the course of an internal examination. The doctor in question, despite twenty years of experience with hypnosis, was inadequately trained in it, having obtained most of his information from reading a book. Interestingly, the complainant denied she was hypnotized.

The fact that the subject did not believe that she was hypnotized does not mean that she was not. Many hypnotic subjects doubt that they were hypnotized on awaking because they expected to lose consciousness or experience something equally dramatic that did not happen.

Hartland testified that, based on thirty years of experience with hypnosis, he believed that it would be a matter of the "greatest possible difficulty" to get a subject to commit a crime or to submit to one. He said that the subject is not dominated by the hypnotist, is fully aware of her surroundings, and can withdraw from the hypnosis at any time. He also described the propensity of some women with hysterical personality types to produce sexual fantasies under chemical anesthetics or to project their own fantasies onto the doctor and that this sometimes occurs under hypnosis.

The defendant was acquitted, and the jury gratuitously recommended that a chaperon be present during hypnotherapy. This might be a sound idea in medical applications of hypnosis as in the instant case, but it is impractical to do so in psychotherapy, where it would interfere with the patient-therapist rapport and with the patient's need for privacy.

It seems possible that an inexperienced young woman might well confuse the procedures used in an internal examination with a sexual assault unless the doctor takes the trouble to explain them to her beforehand. Certainly this type of procedure can and should be done with a nurse present.

The Effect of Hypnosis on Criminal Liability

In 1970 Lehan noted that the defense that a defendant acted under hypnotic influence was ill-defined. This still appears to be the case. No American case has been found in which a defendant has successfully raised such a defense.

There are several reasons why the courts are hostile to such claims and counsel are reluctant to raise them. First, as previously noted, many experts, although they recognize that subjects can be influenced to perform all sorts of seemingly antisocial conduct in an experimental context, are skeptical that a subject could be coerced or deceived into committing a real crime by hypnotic means. In those few cases when actual crimes have allegedly been committed by hypnotized subjects, the relationship between the hypnotist and the subject is generally such as to account for the latter's compliance, even in the absence of hypnosis. While the author believes that hypnosis is very unlikely to cause criminal behavior by a person not inclined to it where there are not other factors at work, not all experts share this view. It is possible to find reputable and honest expert witnesses who would be willing to testify that such a thing is possible. It is also true that occasionally events of very low probability do occur. Furthermore, there are a fair number of cases in which it is quite clear that hypnotic subjects have been victimized by the hypnotist. Kline (1972) cites two cases in which subjects have been sexually abused by psychopathic hypnotists. One case involved an obstetrician who took sexual advantage of his patients and another a graduate psychology student who used hypnosis to further his homosexual pedophiliac seduction of young boys in the course of his babysitting activities. Both of these cases are probably reliable as they were reported by the hypnotists themselves during psychotherapy, not in the course of a criminal prosecution.

A second reason for the reluctance of courts to accept a defense of hypnotic influence, is the fear that such a defense would invite fraud and deception. This objection appears to be without merit, for it could be said of any defense to a criminal action. Although he advocates that hypnosis should be regarded as a defense in the same manner as force, duress, insanity, and intoxication, Lehan (1970) argues that the burden of proving that one acted under hypnosis would appear to be formidable. It is a novel notion in American criminal jurisprudence that a defendant in a criminal case should have the burden of proving anything. One who asserts a defense generally has the burden of going forward with some evidence that tends to establish it, and then the *People* have the burden of disproving the defense beyond a reasonable doubt.

When the state of New York created a new type of defense to a criminal action labeled an *affirmative defense*, the statute said that the defendant had the burden of proving such a defense by a preponderance of the evidence. This was on the theory that for some kinds of defenses the defendant was in a better position to be able to prove the facts than the *People*. It is doubtful that it would be constitutional to put the burden of negating an essential element of a crime, such as intent, on the defendant. Though instances of hypnotically induced crimes are probably few, if they occur at all, the law needs to be able to deal with uncommon as well as common events (Lehan 1970).

Canadian law distinguishes between the defense of insanity, which is based on mental disease, and the defense of automatism, which, while it also involves a negation of criminal intent, is based on some external influence such as violence, drugs, alcohol, or hypnotic suggestion (O'Regan 1978). In Canada, the defendant has the burden of proving the defense of insanity by the "balance of probabilities" while the Crown has the burden of disproving the defense of automatism "beyond a reasonable doubt." Also, a defendant acquitted as a result of the latter defense cannot be detained "during her Majesty's pleasure" as in the case of a successful insanity defense. The defense of automatism, however, has been given scant attention in American law. A recent decision of the Supreme Court of Wyoming has recognized it, and California, by statute, has recognized the defense of unconsciousness (*Fulcher* v. *State* 1981). The American Law Institute's Model Penal Code requires a voluntary act or omission as the basis for criminal liability, and it specifically states that "conduct during hypnosis or resulting from hypnotic suggestion" is not voluntary within the meaning of the proposed statute.

The basic philosophical issue in treating hypnotic influence as a defense to a crime (assuming that such an influence could be established) is the question of the role of culpability in the criminal law. In general, the function of the criminal law is to punish the defendant for unlawful actions. This is quite different from the goal of the civil law which is to remove a financial loss from the person suffering it and place it on the person whose breach of a duty caused it. The question then is, should persons who commit criminal acts they are unable to resist committing be punished, since they lack true blameworthiness?

The purposes of the criminal law also include the protection of society, deterrence, and rehabilitation (Cohn and Udolf 1979). The situation is analogous to the difference between the classical and anthropological schools of jurists. The classical school recognized free will and based punishment, at least in part, on culpability. It sought to apportion punishment to blame-worthiness. The anthropological school denied free will and inflicted punishment in the interests of society without regard to blame (Antitch 1967; Ladd 1902). The former view would excuse one who was coerced or deceived into committing a criminal act by hypnosis or otherwise, while the latter view would hold one liable without regard to fault.

Modern criminal law recognizes the distinction between *malum in se* crimes (offenses of mental culpability) and *malum prohibitum* crimes (offenses of strict liability). To commit the former type of crime the defendant must not only perform a criminal act, but also do so with a specific criminal intent or state of mind (the *mens rea*). In the latter type of crime, only a criminal act need be proven to sustain a conviction. However, even here the action must be intentional and voluntary (Cohn and Udolf 1979).

Hence, hypnotic deception would seem to negate the intent required in *malum in se* crimes whereas hypnotic coercion would negate the voluntary nature of the acts in either type of crime.

It would seem that though hypnosis is not a defense in the technical meaning of that term, hypnotic influence could function as such because if established it would effectively prevent the prosecution from proving the *corpus delicti* of a crime. It also would appear that expert testimony on the effect of hypnotic influence on a particular defendant ought to be admissible since it bears on the defendant's mental state at the time of an alleged crime. There is no stated purpose of the criminal law that would be advanced by punishing persons for crimes of which they are not culpable. Such individuals need neither punishment, deterrence, nor rehabilitation. Incarcerating them would not protect the public. The incarceration of the criminal hypnotist might.

Another theory to justify the punishment of a hypnotic subject who has been coerced or deceived into committing a crime is that hypnotic influence should be considered analogous to intoxication. The law distinguishes between voluntary and involuntary intoxication, and it is often stated that voluntary intoxication is no defense to a crime, but involuntary intoxication may be if it negates criminal intent or prevents the person from acting voluntarily. It is generally recognized that subjects cannot be hypnotized against their will, but it is possible to covertly induce hypnosis. In such a case, advocates of this position would excuse a subject for a hypnotically procured criminal act. However, if the subject voluntarily submitted to hypnosis, they would hold him liable, for the subject should have foreseen the consequences of surrendering control to the hypnotist (Allen 1934; Antitch 1967; Ladd 1902; Lehan 1970; Levy 1955; Solomon 1952; Swain 1961). This view ignores the fact that a well-informed subject would realize that the procurement of criminal behavior by hypnosis is an extremely unlikely event, and a hypnotic subject does not surrender self-control to the hypnotist. More importantly, it fails to recognize that a person submitting to hypnosis by a reputable psychologist or psychiatrist has every right to expect that the practitioner will in no way abuse the professional relationship.

In common law, it was a complete defense to a crime for a married woman if she committed the crime in the presence of her husband, because she was presumed to have been under his influence (Solomon 1952). Statutes have also provided for lesser punishment for married women who commit crimes at the direction of their husbands. However, possibly in recognition of the improbability that a hypnotist would have such influence over a subject, no commentator has advocated such a general rule concerning the hypnotist-subject relationship. Incidentally, the notion that a husband has the kind of influence postulated over his wife probably coincides with reality as rarely as the analogous notion concerning hypnotist and subject.

If there is no specific defense of hypnotic influence or automatism generally recognized in the United States, and if it is contrary to both the spirit and the purposes of the criminal law to convict defendants who are not guilty of intentional wrongdoing or criminal negligence, can hypnotic influence be raised as a defense under the prevailing rules governing the defense of insanity? This would seem important, for clearly a criminal defendant ought not be excused from criminal liability every time he or she has been the subject of hypnosis. The hypnosis may have no causal relationship to the crime at all, or it might merely have been used to suggest an act that the subject was quite willing to perform. It could even be used to enhance criminal performance by aiding a willing perpetrator to act with more assurance and confidence.

If hypnosis were treated by the courts as a form of insanity, the existing rules governing this defense would define what kinds of hypnotic influence would excuse a defendant of criminal responsibility and what kinds would not. Certainly hypnosis is neither a form of insanity nor a mental illness within the common meanings of these terms, but it may fit within the context of statutes defining them.

One of the most common tests of mental capacity to commit a crime is called the M'Naghten Rule. Under this doctrine, defendants are excused from criminal liability if they suffer from a "defect of reason" such as to preclude them from knowing the nature and quality of their acts *or* that such acts are wrong.

Some jurisdictions use the American Law Institute test that excuses individuals from criminal liability if they lack the substantial capacity to appreciate the wrongfulness of their actions *or* to conform their conduct to the requirements of the law (*United States* v. *Brawner* 1972).

The specific wording of these rules may vary from jurisdiction to jurisdiction, but they are often broad enough to encompass hypnosis, and in a proper case a court could treat hypnosis as producing a type of defect of reason or as bearing on the ability to appreciate wrongfulness or to control behavior. If this premise is correct, some predictions can be made concerning the legal effect of hypnosis on criminal liability in a variety of hypothetical situations.

In any case, and without regard to the application of either rule, hypnotists are, and should be, fully liable as principals for any crime that they have induced a subject to commit either by coercion, deception, or connivance. Hypnotists are also fully liable for any crimes committed against subjects (Levy 1955).

Even if it could be demonstrated that a subject had been coerced into committing a crime, the subject would still be criminally liable under the M'Naghten Rule because he or she knew the nature and quality of his or her actions and that they were wrong. This situation is what the law calls an "irresistible impulse," which is no defense under the M'Naghten Rule. Under the American Law Institute or Brawner Rule, it would be a defense, since the subject is assumed to be unable to conform behavior to the requirements of the law. If, however, the subject were deceived into believing his acts were proper (that he was actually acting in self-defense or retrieving his own property rather than stealing another's) then he would be excused under either rule.

If a hypnotist and a subject employed hypnosis to enhance performance on a future criminal enterprise, in addition to both being fully responsible for the crime committed, they would also both be guilty of the additional crime of conspiracy. This is an agreement between two or more people to commit a crime. No actual case where this has been alleged has been found.

If a hypnotist attempted to get a subject to commit a crime but failed, then the subject would be guilty of nothing and the hypnotist could not be guilty of conspiracy, because there was no illegal agreement consummated. However, in some states, like New York, the subject would be guilty of the crime of criminal solicitation, which consists of attempting to induce another by various means to commit a crime (Udolf 1981).

Even though the foregoing opinions concerning how the courts could deal with hypnotically induced criminal acts if the rules relating to the insanity defense were applied are based on a tenuous premise (that the defense could establish the hypnotic influence assumed), the use of hypnosis to victimize a subject rather than make the subject an accomplice seems more likely, and has been alleged in more actual cases. Since the most commonly alleged abuse of a subject has been sexual, the legal effect of such an act needs to be considered.

Rape statutes vary in wording from jurisdiction to jurisdiction. If a statute defines rape as sexual intercourse without the consent of a woman, it could be argued that the use of hypnosis by the defendant could vitiate the reality of consent (Solomon 1952; Swain 1961). Yet if the statute defines rape as intercourse against the will of the woman, some claim that this would be harder to ascribe to hypnosis (Solomon 1952; Swain 1961). Some rape statutes define the crime in alternative ways. In New York, for example, first-degree rape is sexual intercourse obtained either by force, with a female of tender years (under age eleven), or with one incapable of consenting because of physical helplessness (such as unconsciousness). If rape is defined by the age of the woman, the use or nonuse of hypnosis is irrelevant. In the case of a forceable rape, however, the effect of hypnosis is not as predictable as it might seem. It would appear that since no force is involved, a hypnotic seduction of a subject would not be rape, although it might amount to a seduction in a proper case. If the state involved did not recognize the crime of seduction, the defendant might be charged with a variety of lesser offenses, such as the crime of sexual abuse.

However, in cases involving the use of fraud rather than force to obtain sexual relations, courts have held that the fraud would be enough to sustain a rape conviction if it were clear that force would have been used had the fraud failed to achieve its purpose. Rape convictions have been obtained in various jurisdictions for sexual relations with women under anesthesia or sleeping, or by fraudulent representations that sex was a form of treatment (Solomon 1952).

The notion that a hypnotized subject will refuse to do anything suggested that is contrary to her moral standards is of no value as a defense in a rape case predicated on hypnotic influence, since it is well-established law that prostitutes can be victims of rape. Every woman, in spite of her previous sexual activity, even if with the defendant, has a right to refuse to have sex. The only exception to this rule is that in most states a husband cannot be convicted of raping his wife as a principal.

However, though not admissible as a defense, the previous sexual activity of the victim is generally relevant as evidence of the likelihood that the individual consented to the sex act in question. Some states have enacted restrictions on what the defense can ask a complainant in a rape case concerning previous sexual activities. A complainant can be asked about prior voluntary sex acts with the defendant, as this is vitally related to the issue of whether it was likely that the sex act involved in the charge was voluntary.

The probity of a defense expert's opinion that hypnosis merely gave a subject an excuse to do what the subject was willing to do in any event is a function of what this opinion is based on, and the soundness of the expert's logic and observations. This is true of all expert opinion. A statement of a conclusion without giving the jury the benefit of an explanation of how it was deduced and what evidence supports it is of little if any value. If an opinion is sound the expert ought to be able to show why it is.

In cases where it is alleged that subjects were hypnotically influenced to make gifts, to sign deeds, contracts, or promissory notes, or to execute testamentary instruments, the ordinary principles of the criminal and civil law are adequate (Antitch 1967; Ladd 1902; Solomon 1952). The criminal aspects of the theft of money or valuable property by the use of hypnosis would be covered as a form of larceny by trick and device, and if based on the creation of a false premise it would qualify as a larceny by fraud. Under civil law, any contract or will executed under the influence of hypnosis would be vulnerable to attack on the basis of undue influence (Solomon 1952).

The mere fact that a testator was hypnotized by a beneficiary would not by itself establish the existence of undue influence. The nature of the malign influence would have to be established and it would have to be demonstrated that it was such as could reasonably be expected to have overcome the testator's free agency in writing the will. It is also true that some close interpersonal relationships such as the attorney-client or doctor-patient relationship have been held to be enough in themselves to create a presumption of undue influence when the dominant party is the recipient of a legacy that would otherwise be unlikely.

Although the possibility, however remote, that a hypnotist would take advantage of his or her relationship with a subject to victimize the latter is disconcerting, perhaps even more worrisome is the possibility that a subject might wrongfully accuse an ethical practitioner of such conduct (Udolf 1981). Solomon (1952) speculates on some of the reasons that false accusations of sexual improprieties are made. In the case of an honest complainant he notes there is a susceptibility of some subjects to hallucinations and the tendency to project their own desires on to the hypnotist. In the case of dishonest complainants there is the motive of self-interest, which impels a subject, once a sex act becomes known, to attribute it to some criminal agency. Both of these notions require some discussion.

In the first place, the tendency of honest subjects to believe that they have been sexually molested, when in fact they have not, is not a result so much of the hypnotic state as of personality characteristics. Such reports are also made against innocent doctors who do not practice hypnosis. This may involve the projection of the patient's own ideas to the doctor, but it is because of a hysterical personality, not the hypnosis. Hypnotic subjects generally do not hallucinate unless it is suggested to them, and then only very good subjects are likely to do this. It is also possible that an honest subject may misinterpret a procedure, especially one that involves some physical contact between hypnotist and patient. The case of the obstetrician acquitted of sexual molestation charges cited previously may well have been such a case.

Solomon's statement concerning the dishonest subject who claims that a voluntary sexual act was hypnotically induced is somewhat misleading with regard to the culpability of the professional hypnotist. It implies that if a psychologist, psychiatrist, or physician has sex with a patient without the use of hypnosis, he or she is somehow less culpable than if hypnosis is used to accomplish this purpose. In a legal sense this is true, and Solomon was, of course, writing in a law journal. The use of hypnosis to obtain sexual relations might well be considered to be first-degree rape in some jurisdictions, while having sexual relations with a willing patient may amount only to a violation of professional ethics rather than a criminally punishable act.

However, from the point of view of a person's fitness to practice a profession, having sex with a patient is equally reprehensible whether it is accomplished with or without the aid of hypnosis. Furthermore, it is probable that in any case in which a "therapist" is able to seduce a patient by hypnotic means, the true agency of the seduction is the interpersonal relationship between the doctor and the patient, and the hypnosis is totally unnecessary. Practitioners guilty of this type of misconduct are a menace not only to their patients, but to their profession. It would seem to be of much greater value in protecting the good name of the mental-health professions if such people could be prevented from entering them in the first place, rather than being expelled following such misconduct. The personal integrity of members is a matter of vital concern to all professions, including medicine and psychology, but it is interesting to note that it is only the legal profession that attempts to screen candidates by conducting a character-committee investigation. Obviously, these procedures have not always prevented the admission to the bar of an occasional unsuitable candidate. However, the bar at least conducts a serious effort to screen out candidates who appear unlikely to adhere to its ethical standards when placed in positions of trust. The psychological and medical professions might do well to follow this example.

With respect to the equally important problem of how the ethical practitioner can be protected from unfounded charges of professional misconduct, there are no completely adequate safeguards. When hypnosis is used in a medical procedure on a patient of the opposite sex, a responsible witness can and should be present. In psychotherapy such a witness would violate the patient's right of privacy and would interfere with the therapeutic process. The same is true of the use of video or audio recording devices. The presence of a receptionist in the office can offer some protection without creating these problems (Udolf 1981). In psychotherapy there is rarely any need for physical contact between the hypnotist and the patient that may create the risk of false claims of molestation. The therapist should be especially cautious about using hypnotherapy with hysterical patients prone to erotic fantasies.

In general, the competent use of hypnosis in the proper setting by a well-trained, ethical therapist appears to be attended by very little risk of false claims of professional impropriety. Claims against hypnotists of good reputation are extremely rare, which seems to indicate that the vast majority of patients are honest and not prone to misinterpret procedures that are competently conducted.

Much of this chapter has of necessity been based on speculation and reasoning from premises concerning the establishment of facts at a trial. That this is so indicates that there has not been much case law on the subject to date compared to the volume in other areas (such as the admissibility of hypnotically induced evidence). It seems that this absence of case material is itself very convincing evidence of the fact that hypnosis does not readily lend itself to use as a method of inducing criminal behavior in subjects not otherwise inclined to such activity.

7 The Regulation of Hypnosis

In 1902, in a remarkably insightful article in the *Yale Law Journal,* Ladd considered the legal regulation of the practice of hypnosis and concluded that to suppress the phenomenon by law would be impossible, to regulate it would be difficult, and to pass laws concerning it hastily would probably be ineffective. He therefore suggested that unless and until legislators take the trouble to become familiar with the phenomenon, it would be wise to defer special legislation. He also believed that there was less need for laws dealing with hypnosis than was generally supposed, and that in most cases established legal principles were adequate. These are all conclusions that are as sound today as they were eighty years ago.

It is not realistic to expect a nonpsychologically trained legislator to become an expert in hypnotic phenomena to the degree necessary to draft sensible legislation on the subject, or to be able to evaluate the conflicting opinions of experts. This is so in spite of the fact that the majority of legislators are lawyers and, as Lincoln said, "A lawyer is a specialist in everything."

This problem exists not only with legislation concerning hypnosis but in all areas where science interfaces with the law. It accounts for why so much legislation designed to deal with specific problems often creates worse problems than it set out to solve (Cohn and Udolf 1979). The lack of technical expertise on the part of well-meaning, part-time legislators, is a major problem in a representative democracy. In addition legislators are unduly vulnerable to the demands of special-interest pressure groups. Ill-advised legislation is often passed in response to sensationalistic press reports. This is the reason that case law is often sounder than legislative enactments. Judges typically have much longer terms than legislators, and in the federal system they have lifetime tenure. They are relieved of the pressures of considering the effect of every decision on the probability of retaining their office and are free to exercise independent professional judgment. They are also more likely to be selected because they represent the highest level of professional ability than are legislators, whose most important attributes are their social and political skills. This is the major reason that the legal principles related to the use of hypnosis should be developed by the courts rather than by legislation.

There is another serious problem involved in legislation and that is the overlapping jurisdictions of the Congress and state and local legislatures. The courts may hold that if Congress has acted on a matter it has preempted the field, and so bar any legislation in this matter by the states. Often, however, if the state enactments are not in conflict with federal law, the states may be permitted to enact legislation on the same subject. The problem is even more acute at the local level because the courts have permitted local legislative bodies to enact ordinances on subjects that would better be handled uniformly throughout the state. For example, local governments have passed laws regulating smoking in public places, and even gun-control measures. Some local legislatures have enacted ordinances outlawing stage hypnosis when it was not prohibited throughout the rest of the state. This practice leads to a chaotic state of affairs in which no one can really be sure of the legality of an activity without an extensive search of both state and local statutes as well as a whole host of regulations issued by a variety of administrative agencies. Such regulations have the force of law until contested successfully in the courts (Cohn and Udolf 1979).

The practice of local legislative bodies enacting ordinances having effect only within a given municipality is necessary to deal with certain matters that should be resolved locally, such as the establishment of zoning laws. Unfortunately, both the courts and state legislatures seem extremely reluctant to limit the power of local legislatures to matters of truly local concern, particularly when the state cannot be said to have preempted the area by passing affirmative legislation on the matter.

If stage hypnosis is to be outlawed, as many professionals advocate, then this would appear to be a matter best handled by statewide legislation. All states are deemed to be sovereign political entities possessing all powers not specifically denied to them by the federal Constitution. These powers include a police power, which means the power to protect the health, morals, and public welfare of its citizens. If it is deemed that the protection of these concerns requires a municipality to declare the practice of stage hypnosis illegal, then for the same reasons the state should also outlaw it. The fact that a state legislature has not enacted such a statute when it might have ought not to be interpreted to mean that the field is open for local legislatures to act, but that the state has rejected the position that the legislation was necessary. This, of course, is based on the author's personal legal philosophy that all governments are, by their very nature, a constant threat to the personal liberties of citizens and are a necessary evil whose powers should be limited. It is a view that the author likes to think was shared by the founders of this country but is not very much in vogue today. The thinking of most politicians seems to be that every human problem can and should be solved by the passage of some law.

Typical Hypnosis Statutes

It is impossible to survey all local ordinances concerning hypnosis, but some state statutes will now be discussed to give an idea of the kinds of legislation proposed and enacted.

Three states have passed laws specifically outlawing public demonstrations of hypnosis for gain (Nebraska, Oregon, and South Dakota) (Levy 1955; Solomon 1952). These laws were primarily intended to outlaw stage hypnosis, but a Nebraska court has ruled that its statute also prohibited religious spiritualistic séances that were public and conducted for gain (Levy 1955).

Three other jurisdictions have limited their restrictions to prohibitions against the hypnotizing of children (Kansas, South Dakota, and Wyoming) (Levy 1955). The Wyoming statute prohibited any hypnosis of children while the Kansas statute was directed against using a child under eighteen in a public demonstration. Depending on how the courts interpret such statutes, the Wyoming-type statute could make hypnotic therapy with children impossible and could deny to terminally ill children the benefits of hypnosis as a supportive or a pain-control measure. A Kansas-type statute might be interpreted to outlaw demonstrations of case material involving children at professional conventions or by video recording if a court interpreted these to be public settings.

A Virginia statute was passed that limited the use of hypnosis to physicians and surgeons (Levy 1955; Solomon 1952). Such a statute, incredible on its face, is an excellent example of the problems created by ill-considered legislation. It would effectively prevent not only the use of hypnoanalysis or other forms of hypnotherapy by a well-trained psychologist but also would even deny the benefits of dental hypnosis to residents of this state.

Similarly Florida has a hypnosis law (Ch. 456.30–456.34) that restricts the use of therapeutic hypnosis to members of the "Healing Arts," which are defined to include medicine, surgery, psychiatry, dentistry, osteopathic medicine, chiropractic, neuropathy, chiropody, and optometry. Notably absent from this listing is psychology, which is the only profession other than psychiatry whose members are likely to be adequately trained in the therapeutic use of hypnosis. The enactment of such a patently maladaptive piece of legislation can only be ascribed to the ignorance of legislators of the realities of professional training and practice or their capitulation to the pressures of special-interest groups. It is interesting that while the use of the word *therapeutic* to modify the word hypnosis in the statute effectively prevents a psychologist from practicing his profession in that state (unless he consents to be supervised by a layman who may have no training at all in either psychology or hypnosis, such as a general practitioner or dentist) it does not prevent lay police officers from using hypnosis to investigate crimes and quite possibly contaminate testimony in future trials.

Tennessee has lumped hypnosis with fortune telling, clairvoyance, spiritualism, palmistry, and phrenology and protected the public in that state by requiring the practitioners of these arts to pay an occupational tax of $250 (Levy 1955). It is difficult to conceive of any court interpreting such a statute to mean what it literally says and holding that a psychiatrist or psychologist practicing hypnotherapy is within the coverage of this act. But there is the principle, respected by most courts, that it is not their function to intrude on the legislature's prerogatives and rewrite legislation. The point is that a court should not be required to have to try to interpret sensibly legislation that is intrinsically senseless. The most likely explanation of this act is that the legislators involved were simply ignorant of the fact that hypnosis is a respectable tool of therapy.

Some states have statutes that Levy (1955) believes would apply to the criminal liability of a hypnotized subject because, although not mentioning hypnosis, they exclude from criminal liability persons unconsciously committing a criminal act. It is doubtful that such a statute should exclude a hypnotic subject from criminal liability, for hypnotized persons are not unconscious in any sense of that term. They are generally aware of everything going on around them, although their attention is primarily focused on one particular thing. However, as noted in chapter 6, the courts may interpret unconscious behavior to include hypnosis, and the Model Penal Code specifically defines it as such.

In contrast, a New Hampshire statute (Ch. 626.2) lists the requirements of criminal culpability and seeks to make hypnotic subjects criminally liable in certain circumstances. The term *reckless* is defined in this statute to include a person who creates a substantial and unjustifiable risk but is unaware of this solely by reason of having voluntarily engaged in intoxication or hypnosis.

Oregon has the only statute found that attempts to specify conditions precedent for the admission of hypnotically influenced testimony (see chapter 4).

Medical Practice Acts and Psychology Statutes

The most frequent legal issue in the therapeutic practice of hypnosis is whether or not it is the practice of medicine as encompassed in the state's medical-practice act. The answer to this question is a function of the wording of the particular medical-practice act and the wording of the psychological-licensing or certification act.

All states have medical-practice acts that make the practice of medicine by an unlicensed person illegal and usually a misdemeanor. All states do not have a psychological-licensing law although some like California and Wisconsin do. Other states like New York have certification laws instead. Some states like Florida have no law on the subject, having permitted previous legislation to be repealed by their "sunset" laws.

The difference between a licensing law and a certification law is that the former defines what constitutes the practice of a profession and forbids its practice by nonlicensed persons. A certification law merely permits qualified persons to use a title, such as *psychologist*. It neither defines the practice of the profession nor excludes others from practicing it for a fee as long as they do not use the protected title. All medical and psychological licensing laws are enacted under the state's police powers and to be valid must be resonable and bear some relationship to the objectives they seek to obtain, which is the protection of the public from incompetent and unethical practitioners (Monaghan 1962). A new licensing law may be required to make exceptions for people previously considered competent to practice who do not meet the new standards imposed (*Berger* v. *Board of Psychologist Examiners* 1975).

Medical-licensing acts vary in the breadth of the terms used to define the practice of medicine. Some medical-licensing acts define the practice of medicine as the prescribing of medicines or drugs or other remedies for bodily diseases. Hypnotism in itself is probably not a violation of such an act (Monaghan 1962).

Other acts define medicine more broadly as the diagnosis or treatment of disease, physical or mental, by any method. Non-medically licensed hypnotists may well be held to violate such a statute if they use hypnosis therapeutically unless they fall within a class of persons excluded from the statute, as for example a psychologist in a state with a licensing statute that includes the use of hypnosis within the practice of psychology.

New York State has a medical-practice act broad enough to cover the administration of an aspirin by a mother to a child if the law were literally enforced. Because of the psychological-certification law, the practice of psychotherapy by psychologists is an implicit exception to the medical-practice act, although a specific definition of the practice of psychology as including psychotherapy and hypnosis [such as is contained in the psychological-licensing laws of California (Ch. 6.6 Sect. 2903, 2904, 2908) and Wisconsin (Ch. 455.01–455.11)] would be preferable. The reason that New York has never been able to pass a psychology-licensing law is that political pressure brought by other professional groups, such as social workers, who practice psychotherapy and are concerned about such legislation restricting their right to practice, has prevented legislators from acting. Of much greater concern is the opposition to such a bill mounted by lay hypnotists who are currently practicing with no training in therapy at all and who would lose a lucrative source of income if a psychology-licensing law were enacted. Lay hypnotists generally justify their practice on the fictional basis that things like antismoking or weight-control suggestions are not really therapeutic. As long as the practice of psychology is not restricted by law, anyone, however unqualified, is free to practice it for a fee. To make the situation even more complex, if an action were brought against a lay hypnotist for violating the medical-practice act of such a state, the psychological societies would probably be reluctant to support such an action, for it would render them vulnerable to the claim that the practice of psychotherapy by psychologists was a similar violation of the act, as has indeed been urged by some representatives of organized medicine.

Some states regard faith-healing or cures made by suggestion as the practice of medicine. Others such as Illinois have held it not to be. Maine passed a statute permitting cures by hypnotic techniques, and the Massachusetts Medical Practice Act (Ch. 112 Sect. 7) specifically excepted persons practicing hypnotism under certain circumstances (Monaghan 1962; Solomon 1952).

Cases

In *State* v. *Lawson* (1907) the Court of General Sessions of Delaware held that a person treating others by hypnotism and massage did not violate that state's medical-practice act by "prescribing remedies" as long as he did not give directions as to the use of drugs, medicines, or other remedies (Levy 1955; Monaghan 1962).

But in *Commonwealth* v. *Jewelle* (1908) the Supreme Judicial Court of Massachusetts sustained the conviction of a lay hypnotist for practicing medicine without requiring that it be established that he prescribed drugs. It held that the statutory exception permitting the use of hypnotism (and other nonmedical techniques) was limited to "everything that strictly belongs to each" but did not otherwise permit the unlicensed practice of medicine. The court found that the practice of medicine encompasses things other than the prescription of drugs such as the diagnosis, prevention, cure, and alleviation of disease (Monaghan 1962).

The Court of Criminal Appeals of Texas in *Masters* v. *State* (1960) held, in a case of first impression, that a person who offered to treat a physical or mental disorder by hypnosis and who was not within the class of persons exempted by that state's medical-practice act was properly convicted of the unlawful practice of medicine (Monaghan 1962).

Similarly, in *People* v. *Cantor* (1961) the appellate department of the Superior Court of California, citing the *Masters* case, sustained the conviction for practicing medicine without a license of a hypnotist who represented himself as able to treat overweight, bed-wetting, cancer, pain, tension, and migraine headache for a fee (Monaghan 1962).

The court in the *Cantor* case also cited the decision in *People* v. *Busch* that a physician who practiced as a general practitioner was not qualified as an expert in hypnosis. Thus the proper foundation was not laid for the reliability of an "analytical tool still seeking recognition in the field of psychiatry." The court did not reason, as it might have, that since a general practitioner was not an expert in hypnosis but was qualified to practice medicine, then the practice of hypnosis could not be included within the practice of medicine. Instead it went on to cite *Cornell* v. *Superior Court* in which it was held that hypnosis was recognized by medical authorities (for the nonmedical purpose of memory enhancement) and that there was no substantial legal difference between the right to use hypnosis to probe the client's unconscious and the use of a psychiatrist to determine sanity.

Having cited two cases with the conflicting conclusions that hypnosis was and was not recognized by medical authorities, for reasons clear only to itself, the Court held that "the practice of hypnotism as a curative measure by one not licensed to practice medicine amounts to the unlawful practice of medicine."

In the *Masters* case the court rejected the defense's contention that the jury should have been charged that the investigator posing as a client was an accomplice to the crime. It held that he did not instigate the commission of the offense but was merely present to collect evidence. In the *Cantor* case the court rejected a defense claim of entrapment on the part of the investigator, holding that the claim of entrapment presupposes the commission of the offense and cannot be raised by a defendant who denies commission of the crime. This seems a weak ground for a correct decision. Many jurisdictions permit the *People* to charge inconsistent offenses in the alternative and permit inconsistent defenses to be raised. The real question involved if entrapment is alleged is was the defendant merely given an opportunity to commit a crime that he was inclined to (in which case there is no entrapment) or was he induced by a law-enforcement agent to commit a crime that he was otherwise not likely to have committed. In the latter case he was entrapped. Entrapment is a defense to a crime because it is contrary to public policy to permit police officers or persons working under their direction to persuade others to commit crimes so that they can be arrested.

Posluns (1972) discussed the Ontario Hypnosis Act, which prohibits hypnosis or attempts at hypnosis, regardless of whether a fee is charged, by all but physicians, dentists, and psychologists in the practice of their respective professions or by students of these professions under supervision. Psychologists can use hypnosis only at the request of or in association with a medical practitioner under this act. One of the major reasons that the present author is opposed to legislation outlawing stage hypnosis is that statutes such as this or the Florida hypnosis law cited earlier, which purport to protect the public against the practice of hypnosis by laymen, are often used to downgrade the status of psychology as an independent profession and to treat it as though it were a branch of medical technology. In point of fact, clinical psychologists are as well or better trained in psychotherapy and hypnosis than psychiatrists, and nonpsychiatrist physicians have negligible training in either of these areas (Kiesler 1977). In effect, such a law requires a psychologist to be supervised in the practice of his profession by a layman.

There are, of course, other good reasons for opposing restrictive legislation concerning stage hypnosis. For one thing, there is little need for such laws since hypnosis in a nontherapeutic setting has been demonstrated to be a very low-risk phenomenon (J. Hilgard 1961; Orne 1965; Ryken and Coe 1977). There are also First Amendment issues involved in legislation restricting the use of a technique that involves nothing more than a verbal interchange between two people (Udolf 1981). Last, if a subject were injured by the incompetent use of hypnosis by a layman, the latter would be fully liable in tort for his or her actions without the need for any additional statutes. A professional who harmed a subject by the use of hypnosis in an incompetent manner would also be liable in malpractice with or without a statute restricting the use of hypnosis (Udolf 1981). The argument is often advanced that hypnosis is an accepted therapeutic technique and therefore to preserve its dignity it should not be permitted as an entertainment vehicle. This argument appears to overlook the fact that dignity is an attribute of people not of therapeutic techniques or natural phenomena.

Civil Misuse of Hypnosis

There has been more speculation than case law concerning the possible misuse of hypnosis in civil matters. The most common civil abuse speculated about concerns an unscrupulous hypnotist influencing a subject to make a will in the hypnotist's favor, sign a contract, deed, promissory note, or other legal instrument against the subject's own interest (Antitch 1967; Ladd 1902). The existing principles of law, including the defense of undue influence, appear more than adequate to deal with such cases if they occur (Solomon 1952). Of more concern might be the false claim that these acts were performed under hypnotic influence when, in fact, none was exerted. The risk that a false claim of undue influence could be grounded in hypnosis seems no more troublesome than the fact that defenses of any kind can be raised without merit. It is the function of juries to determine where the truth lies between the conflicting claims of the parties. If anything, a false defense based on hypnosis might be harder to maintain, for not all people are capable of being hypnotized to a significant degree, and the opposing party might seek an examination of the person asserting such claim to determine susceptibility (Antitch 1967). Solomon (1952) suggests that if a hypnotist used hypnosis to deceive or compel a subject to sign a legal instrument he or she might be convicted of forgery, on the theory that the signing was the act of the hypnotist and not the subject. Solomon also reports an experiment that shows that forgery skills of a subject were not enhanced by hypnotic suggestion but it is not clear why anyone would expect them to be.

In cases involving torts committed against the subject, such as assaults (sexual and otherwise), hypnosis without the consent of the subject, or the subject's parents if a minor, malpractice, and so on, existing legal principles also seem adequate to deal with any situations likely to arise (*Forsythe* v. *Cohen* 1969). The only exception might be the claim raised by Solomon (1952) that in states that do not recognize the crime of seduction, a sexual assault that did not meet the legal requirements of a rape might go unpunished. This appears unlikely, for in New York, which no longer recognizes seduction, the hypnotist would be guilty of the crimes of sexual misconduct or sexual abuse in some degree. These crimes range from a class-A misdemeanor to a class-D felony.

As noted in chapter 1, legal writers on the subject vary in their opinion about the need for special legislation dealing with hypnosis. Some take the view that present legislation is wholly inadequate to deal with the special problems involved, while others believe present legal principles are generally adequate without the need for new statutes. There are few who support a position midway between these extremes. Based on the foregoing considerations, the author would cast his vote with those who do not believe that special legislation is necessary or desirable. This fact seems to be generally recognized, as evidenced by the comparatively small number of states that have enacted such legislation and the further fact that some of these statutes have been repealed. The only legislation that the author would advocate, and which only indirectly affects hypnosis, would be the passage of adequate laws that define the practice of psychology and restrict it to qualified persons.

8 Summary and Conclusions

The purpose of this final chapter is to summarize the current status of forensic hypnosis, to speculate on its future, and to express the author's viewpoints on some current issues.

The use of hypnosis in a forensic context is expanding at an increasing rate. This has resulted in the burgeoning of appellate-court decisions concerning the admissibility of hypnotically influenced evidence. Some of the forensic uses of hypnosis reported in the literature are quite appropriate and likely to be productive. Others are less appropriate and are more likely to prove unproductive. Some are based on misconceptions concerning the nature of hypnosis, the fundamental principles of human behavior, or the nature and operation of our legal system, and are more accurately described as misuses of hypnosis.

Major Forensic Uses of Hypnosis

The following are the more common forensic applications of hypnosis:

1. Hypnosis is used as an investigative or discovery device to develop leads to new and independent evidence. This is the most appropriate and potentially the most productive forensic use of hypnosis. It can be used by both the prosecution and the defense in criminal matters and by either party in civil matters. It is best limited to witnesses whose testimony is not likely to be needed at the trial (because their evidence is either redundant or trivial). The common use of investigative hypnosis by the prosecution on victims or key witnesses creates serious problems. Pretrial hypnosis can contaminate future testimony and render the witness less susceptible to effective cross-examination. In some jurisdictions it also creates difficulties with the admissibility of such testimony. Even in jurisdictions permitting the introduction of hypnotically influenced testimony, the fact of pretrial hypnosis raises the issue of whether it was performed properly enough to permit the trial judge to admit the evidence. Even if the testimony is admitted, hypnosis may still impair the credibility of the witness.
2. Hypnosis is used as a device to break an amnesia of a witness or party. This use of hypnosis is appropriate from a psychological point of view.

Hypnosis is most likely to retrieve meaningful and traumatic memories that are rendered unavailable by a repressionlike process. However, from a legal viewpoint, since the subject is more likely to be needed as a witness in a future trial, all of the earlier-mentioned problems will be encountered.

3. Hypnosis is used to improve memory for significant details in a nonamnesic witness or party. Although it presents all of the foregoing legal difficulties, such use is less likely to be productive and more likely to lead to the production of inaccurate memories. However, it is a very common usage of hypnosis, particularly by police-officer hypnotists.

4. Finally, hypnosis can be used as a diagnostic procedure to evaluate a defendant's state of mind, the presence of a specific criminal intent, and sanity or capacity to stand trial. All of these are generally recognized and accepted uses of hypnosis. Hypnosis in this situation is actually a clinical technique that has been recognized as valid by the American Medical Association and the American Psychological Association. Hypnosis, though far from infallible in this regard, is as reliable a procedure for forming diagnostic impressions as any other method of which the author is aware. It may be more reliable than a poorly validated or incompetently administered psychological test, or a hastily conducted interview under adverse conditions. The fact that a subject can be hypnotized indicates that there is at least some kind of trusting relationship established between subject and hypnotist. This is not always the case in a forensic psychiatric interview.

Minor Forensic Uses of Hypnosis

The following uses of hypnosis are classified as minor only because they have been reported less frequently. In a proper case they may be quite useful and appropriate:

1. Hypnosis can be used to calm a distraught witness or defendant. Though this is psychologically appropriate, it has the legal disadvantage of raising questions about the admissibility or the credibility of future testimony. Such use should be limited to cases in which it is clearly necessary, and a video tape should be available to show that the hypnosis did not deal with any of the facts in issue in the case. If proper recording equipment is not available, such a hypnotic session might also be conducted in the presence of the court and opposing counsel, in the absence of the jury.

2. Hypnosis may be used also to distinguish malingering or hysteria from organic injuries, evaluate psychological trauma, or detect prior hypnotic tampering with a witness. These are all essentially clinical uses of

hypnosis and such sessions should be conducted by a well-trained clinician.

3. The claim of hypnotic influence as a defense to a criminal charge (or a tort claim) can be an issue. This appears to be of more theoretical than practical value, as such a defense has never been successfully interposed to the author's knowledge. This does not mean that it could not be if advocated by a skillful trial lawyer armed with a firm understanding of hypnotic phenomena and the support of a capable expert. However, hypnosis is such an unlikely vehicle for compelling or deceiving a subject into committing a crime that it seems improbable that a defense of hypnotic influence will ever become common in criminal litigation.

Forensic Misuses of Hypnosis

The following applications of hypnosis are so inappropriate from a psychological or legal standpoint, or both, that they can only be regarded as forensic abuses of hypnosis that ought never to be employed. If they are used, the resulting evidence generally is, and should be, inadmissible:

1. The deliberate creation, shaping, or distortion of testimony, if established by the opposing party, will not only cause the court to exclude the evidence obtained, it also constitutes the crime of subornation of perjury. In some cases the same results may be obtained by an honest but incompetent hypnotist using suggestive techniques. This, if demonstrated, will result in the exclusion of the hypnotically refreshed testimony, but it is not a criminal matter.

2. A confession demonstrably produced by hypnosis (whether overt or covert) is involuntary and inadmissible in evidence regardless of its truth or falsity. A conviction based on the admission of such a confession cannot stand no matter how much other evidence is available to support it. Prosecutorial agencies, particularly those who use investigative hypnosis, would be well advised to avoid even the appearance of the use of hypnosis on defendants or suspects. Otherwise, the issue of covert hypnosis may be raised by the defense in cases involving confessions or other statements made by the defendant during police interrogation. For example, police officers who do hypnotic interviewing should not be the ones selected to question suspects.

3. Hypnosis may be used to give potential witnesses confidence in the accuracy of their hypnotically refreshed memories and hence render them less vulnerable to cross-examination. The mere circumstances of a hypnotic interview conducted by an expert, the witnesses being told that everything they have ever seen is recorded somewhere in their brains, and

that the authorities believe that hypnosis will revive these critical memories, are all calculated to instill in witnesses the conviction that what they recall under hypnosis must be accurate. This, coupled with witnesses' reduced critical judgment and relaxed standards for an acceptable memory, render this artificially enhanced certainty a very real danger.

4. Hypnosis has been used to enable witnesses to bolster or corroborate their own testimony by trying to show that they told the same story under hypnosis that they did on the witness stand. Such proffered testimony is generally inadmissible. Its effectiveness depends on the jury's misconception that hypnosis assures truth and that subjects are unable to lie under hypnosis. As a matter of fact, hypnotic subjects *can* lie if they want to, and they may be able to lie more convincingly.

5. As a method of either inducing another to become an accomplice of the hypnotist in a criminal enterprise or to victimize the subject, hypnosis will in all likelihood have an extremely small probability of success. This is not to say that this situation has never occurred in the courts. It has, but the author believes that the compliant behavior of the subjects involved resulted from the interpersonal relationship between themselves and the hypnotists, and not from the hypnosis. However, if this could be accomplished, it would be a criminal act on the part of the hypnotist. The specific crimes involved would depend on what it was that the hypnotist influenced the subject to do or how the subject was victimized.

Dangers of Pretrial Hypnosis

The dangers that are summarized here are dangers to the integrity of the truth-seeking process. Psychological dangers to the subjects of forensic hypnosis, particularly when conducted by clinically untrained lay hypnotists, have not been adequately investigated. Based on studies of other episodic uses of hypnosis (such as experimental, stage, or amateur use), these dangers are likely to be substantially less than are present in the clinical use of hypnosis, but possibly greater than in other nonclinical applications because of the higher likelihood that witnesses are exposed to traumatic, anxiety-producing memories.

The legal dangers of forensic hypnosis include:

1. The creation of inaccurate testimony because of confabulations, fantasies, hallucinations, suggestive questioning, nonverbal cueing, and so on. (It should be pointed out that all of these distortion processes occur in

nonhypnotized witnesses and can be exacerbated in nonhypnotic pretrial questioning.)

2. The lowering of the criteria that witnesses set for themselves in evaluating the veridicality of a memory.

3. The rendering of subjects less susceptible to the truth-seeking test of cross-examination by instilling in them a false belief and confidence in the accuracy of their hypnotically refreshed memories. Witnesses may also confuse facts recalled after hypnosis with prehypnotic memories.

4. The drama of the hypnotic situation may unduly impress a jury, who may assume that hypnosis assures the accuracy of recalled events or at least prevents lying. (It may also have the reverse effect and cause some jurors to disbelieve accurate memories.)

5. The risk that hypnotically influenced testimony admitted into evidence for a specific purpose (for example, to show the basis of an expert's opinion) may be misused by the jury for some other purpose (such as substantive proof of the facts stated).

6. Witnesses who deliberately lie under hypnosis may have their ability to lie convincingly enhanced by the circumstances of the hypnosis and its production of feelings of relaxation and self-assurance. It is also fairly easy for dishonest witnesses to simulate hypnosis altogether or to simulate a deeper state to increase confidence in their testimony. In fact, the depth of hypnosis is probably of as little value as a predictor of the quality of hypnotically retrieved memories as it is of the success of therapeutic uses of hypnosis. In both cases, the more important variable is subject motivation.

A very real but different kind of danger of forensic hypnosis is the damage that is done to the good name of both the psychological and psychiatric professions by the bad advice given to the courts by some experts. Courts have been told such patently inaccurate things as, that the expert could tell (without extrinsic evidence) that a hypnotized subject was telling the truth, or that he or she was most likely to tell the truth, or that the expert could tell that a claim of hypnotic influence was untrue by observing the waking personality characteristics of the subject or hypnotist, and so forth.

Occasionally, cases are reported in which mental-health professionals have engaged in behavior that can only be characterized as an imposition on the courts. Perhaps the reason for these regrettable occurrences is that clinically trained people, unfamiliar with the workings of an adversarial legal system, find themselves caught in the uncomfortable role of a partisan and so lose sight of their proper function. This is to educate the trier of the facts with regard to the technical issues involved in a legal dispute without concern about what effect this has on the case of either party to the controversy. Part of this problem may be the fault of trial counsel who do not take the time to train their expert witnesses to become expert at being witnesses.

The Current Status of Hypnotically Influenced Testimony

The courts have been unanimous in refusing to permit a witness to testify while under hypnosis. They have also unanimously rejected testimony obtained while a witness was under pretrial hypnosis when such testimony was offered as substantive proof of the truth of the matters testified to. The most common reasons given for such rejection are the general unreliability of hypnosis as a fact-finding device or the status of the testimony as hearsay.

Under the majority view, testimony given under pretrial hypnosis is admissible to establish the basis of an expert's opinion, subject to the sound discretion of the trial court that its value is not outweighed by the danger that the jury will regard it as proof of the truth of the facts stated. Cautionary instructions are generally given to the jury concerning the purposes for which the evidence is received. Trial courts may selectively admit some pretrial hypnotic statements into evidence while excluding others that are either not necessary to establish the basis of expert opinion, or that relate primarily to substantive issues in the case.

The majority view treats pretrial hypnosis as merely another type of memory-jogging device such as notes, newspaper articles, or leading questions. It permits witnesses who assert that they are testifying from present memory refreshed to testify without regard to how this memory was restored. In these jurisdictions, the trial court has discretion to exclude hypnotically refreshed testimony where the circumstances show it was likely to have been contaminated by unduly suggestive hypnotic interviewing. There is a great deal of variability in these jurisdictions concerning the standards that must be met by a pretrial hypnotic interview and what must be established by a proponent of such evidence as a foundation for its admission. In general, some type of record of the hypnotic interview must be available for review by the opposing party and the fact of the hypnosis must be disclosed to the opposition to preserve its right of effective cross-examination.

A sizable minority of jurisdictions, in recent cases, have held that pretrial hypnosis under any circumstances renders a witness incompetent to testify to any matter not reported prior to the hypnosis. No court has gone so far as to hold that such a witness is totally incompetent to testify, and thus unable to testify to statements made prior to the hypnosis. Nor has any court said that purely investigative hypnosis designed to develop independent evidence is objectionable or that such independent derivative evidence is inadmissible.

Current Issues in Forensic Hypnosis

The Future Role of Hypnosis in the Courts

The expansion or contraction of the role of forensic hypnosis depends on a variety of factors. The most important of these is the quality of the advice given to the courts by experts. The current trend of the rapidly developing case law appears to reflect a tendency to limit the role of hypnotically influenced testimony, and to establish formal and more rigid standards for the circumstances under which hypnosis may be used in forensic matters. This trend seems to be largely the result of the reaction of the courts to the recent proliferation of hypnotic interrogations conducted by marginally trained lay hypnotists who are often police officers, not mental-health professionals. Often, such lay hypnotists are virtually untrained in psychology in general, and in the principles of perception and memory in particular. The effects of their inadequate preparation have been to exacerbate the intrinsic dangers of the forensic uses of hypnosis as a memory-enhancing technique and to essentially destroy potentially probative testimony. No type of formal procedural safeguard is ever likely to prevent this type of damage by non-psychologically trained hypnotists, any more than a set of formal guidelines for performing surgical operations would be likely to make surgery safe when conducted by laymen.

There are those who believe that even in expert hands hypnosis has such a potential for distorting testimony and interfering with the process of cross-examination that its use should be prohibited by the courts. Others believe that its use in the forensic field should be expanded, often on the somewhat tenuous premise that science and progress are always good and the courts should keep abreast of modern technology.

It is the author's view that forensic hypnosis is a tool and, like any tool, it has appropriate and inappropriate applications. It is one of the functions of an expert to determine whether or not a proposed application of hypnosis is appropriate, and whether hypnosis is the method of choice for the particular application contemplated. The real issue is not whether or not hypnosis should play an increasing role in litigation, but when is it appropriate and when is it not. In situations where hypnosis is likely to be the best method for aiding in the search for the truth, its increased use should be advocated. In situations where it is unlikely to contribute much to this effort or where there is a significant danger of providing inaccurate information, its use should be restricted. Since this is a matter of expert judgment, the issue of who is an expert is necessarily raised.

The Qualifications of a Forensic Hypnotist

Ideally forensic hypnotists should be trained in psychology and law as well as in hypnosis. In particular, they should be knowledgeable in the areas of perception, memory, learning, and psychodynamics. They should also be conversant with the current experimental and theoretical work in hypnosis and be aware of its limitations and problems as well as its capabilities. A well-trained forensic hypnotist needs to be able to view hypnosis in context as a branch of psychology and be able to relate hypnotic phenomena to the rest of psychological knowledge and theory.

Although it appears obvious that a layman taught to induce hypnosis, but who is ignorant of the psychological principles underlying human behavior, is unable to use the phenomenon effectively or recognize its dangers, subtle or otherwise, the need for legal training may not be so obvious. After all, psychiatrists and psychologists without such training have been testifying in court concerning the sanity and capacity of defendants to stand trial ever since such issues were recognized by the courts. The reason that some training in law is necessary for forensic hypnotists is that they are not merely observing subjects, they are performing manipulations on them that may affect their future testimony and its legal status. Hence, a procedure that is perfectly sensible and productive from a psychological point of view may have the legal effect of weakening or even destroying a party's case.

The forensic hypnotist needs both psychological and legal training, but these are not enough. Even those few psychologists and psychiatrists who also have law degrees are not necessarily competent in this subspecialty, for they also need substantial training in hypnosis. Conversely, experience in experimental or clinical hypnosis, while useful, is no assurance by itself of competency in the forensic applications of hypnosis.

Since there are comparatively few people who have all of the credentials desirable for a forensic hypnotist, it follows that as a practical matter the courts must often rely on the advice of less than optimally trained experts. In general, the courts take the position that expertise is a matter of fact, not of credentials, and an expert witness may be qualified on the basis of experience and knowledge as well as formal training. This appears to be a reasonable and pragmatic approach to the problem. In effect, it defines an expert as someone who knows much more about the technical issues of the case than the average jury member and whose opinion is likely to help the jury in its task of seeking the truth. If opposing counsel disputes the expertise of a witness permitted to testify over objections to his or her qualifications, this is a proper issue for cross-examination and raises a question of fact for the jury to determine.

With respect to the issue of police-officer hypnotists, the author is of the opinion that no amount of experience in the induction of hypnosis and the conducting of hypnotic interviewing can take the place of training in psychology. In no sense of the term can such a lay hypnotist be considered an expert. The facts that police-officer hypnotists may not be properly neutral and are unprepared to deal with atypical severe reactions to hypnosis seem less important than the fact that they may use hypnosis to affect psychological processes (such as memory retrieval) that they do not understand. The same is true for a non-psychiatrically trained physician who ought not to be permitted to testify as an expert in this area.

Although forensic hypnotists need enough legal training to be aware of the legal consequences of their work, they do not need to be lawyers. They need training in adjective or procedural law, the rules of evidence, constitutional law, and the substantive effects of mental status in a variety of legal situations. Most of the remaining content of a legal education is irrelevant to their concerns. Since experts are to testify about their opinions on psychological matters, not legal ones, legal training, though important to their functioning, is irrelevant when it comes to qualifying them as experts.

Procedural Safeguards and the Foundation Needed for Hypnotic Evidence

The purpose of procedural safeguards is twofold:

1. To minimize the foregoing risks of hypnosis. No procedural safeguards can ever eliminate these risks. They are present even without the use of hypnosis, which merely exacerbates but does not create them. The more important purpose, however, is
2. To make it possible to evaluate how likely these dangers are to have been realized in the present case. Only with this information can a court intelligently exercise its discretion to admit or reject the proffered hypnotically refreshed testimony.

The most detailed set of procedural safeguards proposed for the conduct of a pretrial hypnotic interview has been the standards recommended by Orne (chapter 2). The reactions of the courts to these suggestions have been quite variable. Different courts have adopted these standards as a requirement for the admissibility of hypnotically refreshed testimony, ignored them, adopted some of them, adopted them and then ignored them, or recommended them but stopped short of requiring them.

The author tends to favor the last view. These safeguards are designed to minimize the risks intrinsic in hypnotically refreshed testimony. No claim is made that they or any other standards can eliminate these risks. None of them, however, appears likely to increase the dangers of hypnotic memory distortion.

In any legal case the issue is not whether memory distortion is possible, but whether it is likely to have occurred in the instant case. This always requires a detailed examination of the particular procedures used and questions asked. It is possible to observe all of these safeguards and still generate distorted testimony or to ignore many of them and produce relatively little distortion. Hence, it would seem wiser not to admit hypnotically refreshed testimony routinely if the standards were met or exclude it if they were not. Each case ought to be evaluated on its own unique circumstances before the trial court decides to admit or exclude the proffered evidence. The standards, however, ought to be recommended and used as much as possible to increase the likelihood that the evidence will prove acceptable to a reviewing court.

There is one requirement that should be imposed as a foundation for the admission of hypnotically influenced testimony. This is that a video recording of all interaction between the hypnotist and the subject (before, during, and after the hypnosis) be made available to the opposing party prior to the introduction of such evidence. Without such a recording it is impossible to evaluate the probability that factual error has been introduced into the testimony as a result of faulty technique. An audio recording or a transcript of these sessions is an inadequate basis for such a review, although it may be difficult to convince a court system that still uses transcripts of trial proceedings as a basis for appellate review of this fact. Such records will fail to disclose subtle cueing by tone of voice, facial expression, body language, and so on.

Most other issues dealt with in procedural safeguards can be evaluated by an analysis of the video tape by the opposing side's experts. For example, if the hypnotist is neither an expert nor impartial, his or her lack of expertise or impartiality need not be presumed to have affected the results unless the tape demonstrates specifically how it did. Furthermore, even an impartial expert can inadvertently commit technical errors, and a review of the tapes should disclose this as well.

The proponent of the evidence should have the burden of going forward with evidence that the hypnotic session was conducted in a manner that minimized error. In support of this view the proponent should be required to submit the video tapes of the procedure. If the tapes are incomplete, defective or missing, the court should refuse to admit the hypnotically influenced evidence.

If the opposing party in a civil case contends that the procedures used were defective or unduly suggestive, this party should have the burden of going forward with expert testimony tending to establish this. The party offering the evidence should have the burden of disproving the claim by a preponderance of the evidence. In a criminal case the burden of proving the reliability of their proffered hypnotically influenced testimony beyond a reasonable doubt should always be on the *People*. They should also have the burden of proving the defense's hypnotic evidence unreliable.

The Adequacy of Existing Law to Deal with Hypnotic Issues versus the Need for New Legislation

This issue is one about which the author has ambivalent feelings. As a psychologist, cognizant of the unreliability of hypnotically refreshed testimony that is not independently corroborated, he can appreciate the position of those who would make such evidence inadmissible. Yet as a lawyer, he recognizes that a great deal of intrinsically unreliable testimony is routinely admissible in court (such as the testimony of an accomplice given in exchange for immunity from prosecution, or even ordinary eyewitness testimony). Normally, the credibility of such testimony is a matter for the jury to evaluate with the aid of cautionary instructions by the court. It is difficult to see why hypnotically influenced evidence should be treated differently. Our legal system is based on the premise that juries are competent to decide contested issues of fact and ultimate guilt or innocence based on sound instructions from the court concerning the law. If a lay jury, with the help of expert testimony, is not capable of deciding the probative value of hypnotic evidence intelligently, how can it evaluate the sanity of a defendant based on the same kind of testimony? If it can do both, there is no need for legislation concerning hypnotic evidence. If it can do neither, it makes no sense to exclude hypnotic evidence while continuing to permit juries to decide the issue of insanity. A basic restructuring of our legal system would be required.

It is often suggested that a previously hypnotized witness may not be testifying from refreshed memory as claimed, but from a hypnotic hallucination confused with a real memory. This is really similar to the problem posed by a police officer who testifies, after reading notes on an arrest, that he or she is testifying from present memory refreshed. It seems probable that, in many cases, the testimony is from the notes, not real memory. Does it make any sense to legislate one rule for hypnotically refreshed memory and retain another for note-refreshed memory when both present the same problem? It is the role of cross-examination to test the truth of the assertion that the witness is testifying from present memory. If the argument is then made that the hypnosis prevents an effective cross-examination, the answer might be that this claim could be presented to the jury by expert testimony.

Our legal system is based on the premise that juries made up of ordinary citizens are capable of reaching decisions as sound as those likely to be made by any expert or by the court itself. Jurors are also more likely to be free from political pressures. On occasion, juries have rendered verdicts more influenced by their views of the requirements of justice than the technical requirements of the law. This is another of their major advantages. It is a fundamental mistake to equate nonexpertise with lack of intelligence or to assume that a jury must be shielded from all evidence that might prove less than 100 percent reliable. Jurors are quite capable of evaluating the value of testimony intelligently if the technical issues involved are explained to them by skilled trial counsel.

There is an alternative approach to the problem of the admissibility of hypnotically refreshed testimony that the author finds appealing. Because it is somewhat foreign to our legal system, however, it is unlikely to be accepted. It is based on the belief that it is a more serious error to convict an innocent defendant than to acquit a guilty one. Hence, it might be proposed to admit hypnotically refreshed testimony of defense witnesses freely leaving the issue of their credibility to the jury while invoking stricter standards for testimony of prosecution witnesses. In effect, this situation is realized to some degree by requiring the *People* to prove their case beyond a reasonable doubt while placing no burden on a defendant to prove anything concerning the *corpus delicti* of a crime.

There are reasons, other than his general philosophic view that legislators tend to overlegislate, for the author's belief that little is needed in the way of specific legislation concerning hypnosis. Statutes are generally enacted to deal with general and often somewhat abstract problems. When applied to a variety of specific situations they often have unforeseen and unfortunate consequences. Case decisions, however, are developed to deal with specific problems. By their nature they tend to be limited to the facts involved and are less likely to have unforeseen consequences. As shown in chapter 3, when a problem arises that requires a change in legal principles, this change evolves through the case law. This is the basic method of operation of our legal system. Problems that do not arise are not dealt with on a theoretical basis by the courts as is often the case in statutory law. In the case of problems needing resolution the courts have available to them all of the careful thought and research of their colleagues and predecessors in a developing line of cases. Last, and perhaps most important, case law is very rarely influenced by either political or public pressure. It not only tends to be more carefully thought out by legal scholars but it puts the particular problem dealt with into a legal context rather than treating it in an isolated fashion.

Like any other effective tool, forensic hypnosis is capable of advancing the cause of justice when used competently in a proper case. It is also capable of doing substantial damage to this cause when misused. The optimal use of this technique will only be achieved when forensic hypnotists make the effort required to understand the special requirements of the legal system within which they practice hypnosis, and when lawyers make a similar effort to understand the nature of hypnosis and the facts and limitations of hypnotic phenomena.

Legal Glossary

Accomplice A participant in an offense charged or in another offense based on some of the same facts or conduct.

Administrative Agency A division of the fourth branch of government (in addition to the legislative, executive or judicial branches) created to administer the details of the law by the exercise of quasi-legislative, quasi-executive or quasi-judicial functions.

Administrator/Administratrix An estate representative appointed not under a will but by a court.

Admission A statement or act by a party to an action contrary to the position that he or she takes at the trial. Admissible in evidence as an exception to the hearsay rule.

Adversarial Legal System A legal system in which contested issues of fact and law are determined as a result of a contest between two opposing advocates, in contrast to an inquisitional system, in which isues are resolved by an authority who conducts the proceedings but represents neither side of the controversy.

Affidavit A factual statement sworn to under oath.

American Law Institute Test of Insanity The Brawner Rule. This states that persons are not criminally liable for their actions if, as a result of mental disease or defect, they lack substantial capacity to appreciate the wrongfulness of their conduct *or* to conform it to the requirements of the law.

Answer The civil pleading that the defendant serves on the plaintiff in response to the complaint that sets forth his position with respect to the allegations of the complaint. It may also interpose defenses to the cause of actions set forth in the complaint or assert counterclaims against the plaintiff.

Anthropological School A school of jurists committed to the view that the function of punishment is to accomplish social goals rather than to punish according to the degree of fault.

Appeal A procedure to get a superior court to review the record of a trial, to determine if there was error committed by trial judge in his rulings or charge that would require the judgement to be set aside and the case either remanded for retrial or dismissed.

Appellant The party who appeals from a lower court decision.

Arraignment A preliminary proceeding in a criminal case designed to perfect the court's jurisdiction over defendants, inform them of their rights, fix bail, and chart the course of future proceedings.

Assault   The intentional or criminally negligent injury of a person or, in some jurisdictions, putting him in fear of such injury.

Brawner Rule   See *American Law Institute Test of Insanity*

Burden of Proof   The obligation to establish the facts in issue. In a civil case if the evidence for opposing positions is equal the party with the burden of proof loses.

Business Records Rule   An exception to the hearsay rule that admits into evidence records kept in the course of a business, if timely made by a person with knowledge of the facts, for example hospital records.

Case Law   See *Common Law*

Cause of Action   The ultimate facts constituting the legal basis for the plaintiff's claim against the defendant.

Cautionary Instructions   Instructions given to the jury as part of the judge's charge advising them of special considerations related to the evidence or of limitations on the purposes for which the evidence was admitted.

***Certiorari,* Writ of** (literally, *to be informed of*)   An order issued by a superior court to an inferior court directing the latter to certify and forward the record of a pending procedure to the former for review or disposition.

Civil Case   Any lawsuit other than a criminal one includes:
1. Actions in Law - Here a judgement is limited to declaring that the defendant owes the plaintiff a sum of money.
2. Suits in Equity - Here a court may issue an injunction requiring the defendant to perform or, more commonly, abstain from performing some specified action.
3. Special Proceedings - All other civil actions e.g., applications for a writ of *habeas corpus, mandamus,* prohibition, etc.

Classical School   A school of jurists holding that the purpose of the criminal law is to punish for wrongdoing and thus the punishment should bear some relationship to the degree of culpability.

Coercion, Psychological   Any improper conduct or undue influence by a public servant or such servant's agent that undermines a defendant's ability to choose freely whether or not to make a statement, or which creates a substantial risk of false self-incrimination of the defendant or violates his or her constitutional rights.

Coercion, Physical   The use, or threatened use, of physical force on a defendant by a public servant or his agent that undermines the defendant's ability to make a free choice of whether or not to make a statement.

Collateral Issues   Issues in a trial other than the main ones defined by the pleadings, (in a civil case), or the accusatory instrument (in a criminal matter). E.g., the credibility of a witness.

Common Law   Case law based on judicial decisions and the doctrine of *stare decisis* as opposed to statutory law.

Complainant   The witness who initiates a criminal action by signing and swearing to an accusatory instrument.

Complaint
1. An accusatory instrument that initiates a criminal case.
2. In a civil action, the first pleading served by the plaintiff on the defendant which alleges the ultimate facts that constitute the plaintiff's cause of action.

Composite Sketch   A sketch made by a police artist from a description given by a witness to a crime. It may also be generated mechanically by combining pre-drawn features.

Confession   A statement made by a defendant in a criminal action admitting all of the allegations of the information or indictment.

Confession, Involuntary   A confession obtained as a result of physical or mental coercion or in violation of the constitutional rights of the accused.

Confession, Involuntary as a Matter of Law   A confession obtained, in violation of the rights of the accused, that the courts have determined will not be admitted into evidence, whether true or false, voluntary or involuntary.

Conspiracy   An agreement between two or more persons to commit a crime. This is itself a crime that is separate and distinct from the crime agreed to.

Constitutional Rights   A constitutional right is a restriction imposed by the U.S. Constitution on the power of the federal or state government to perform some action in relation to a person that it would otherwise be legally entitled to perform.

Corpus Delicti (Literally, *the body of the wrong*)   The elements of a crime that the *People* must prove beyond a reasonable doubt to obtain a conviction.

Corroboration   Additional independent evidence tending to confirm or support other evidence that it is said to corroborate. Generally, accomplice testimony and confessions require corroboration and may not be the unsupported basis of a conviction.

Crime   An act or omission prohibited by law and punished by death, imprisonment, fine, forfeiture of office or some other penalty.

Criminal Case   An action whose purpose is to punish a defendant for some criminal act, as opposed to the goal in a civil case of remedying a wrong by awarding a plaintiff money damages or injunctive relief. Unlike civil cases, criminal acts are regarded as wrongs against all society not just the victim. Hence, they are prosecuted in the name of the *People* and at public expense.

Criminal Intent   The specific state of mind that a statute defining a crime requires the criminal act to be accompanied by to constitute the offense. The *People* must prove this, as well as the criminal act, beyond a reasonable doubt.

Criminal-Justice System   A generic term that includes the functioning of all agencies involved with the processing of criminal matters from investigation to final incarceration. It includes the police agencies, the trial and appellate court systems, probation departments and correctional agencies.

Criminal Law   The body of case and statutory law dealing with the definition of the various crimes and the establishment of their punishments as well as the procedures to be followed in the prosecution of criminal cases. The defining of crimes and their elements is called substantive criminal law and the procedural rules of a criminal prosecution are called adjective criminal law.

Criminal Solicitation   The crime of attempting to induce, cajole, persuade or otherwise influence another person to commit a crime.

Cross-examination   The right of an adversary party to examine a witness after the direct examination conducted by the party calling the witness. It is for the purpose of impeaching the credibility of the witness and/or bringing out the whole truth. Leading questions are permissible under cross-examination.

Declaration against Interest   An exception to the hearsay rule which permits the introduction into evidence of statements made by a party or witness that were against his financial or proprietary interests. In some jurisdictions, statements against penal interests are also admissible.

Defamation   The twin torts of libel and slander. The tort of defamation is a violation of a person's right to have his good reputation unimpaired and not to be unjustifiably held up to scorn, ridicule or contempt.

Defendant   The party against whom either a civil or criminal action is prosecuted.

Defense
  1. The side in a criminal or civil action against whom the action was brought.
  2. A legal bar either against the plaintiff (in a civil action) or against the *People* (in a criminal action) prevailing. In a criminal case, infancy, duress, justification, entrapment, and insanity are examples of defenses.

Defense, Affirmative   In a criminal matter, an affirmative defense is one in which the defense has the burden of proof, usually by a preponderance of the evidence. This is in contrast to an ordinary defense, in which to get the benefit of the court's charge concerning the defense, the defendant need only go forward with some evidence tending to establish it. In either case, the *People* still have the burden of disproving the defense beyond a reasonable doubt.

Defense of Alibi The claim that at the time of the commission of a crime the defendant was someplace else.

Defense of Automatism The claim that, because of some temporary condition, other than mental disease or defect, a person performed an otherwise criminal act unintentionally and without conscious volition.

Defense of Duress The claim that a defendant committed an otherwise criminal act only because of the use of force or the imminent threat of force against himself or another. Such threat must be sufficient to overcome the will of a reasonably firm person.

Defense of Entrapment The claim that the defendant committed a crime, that he was not otherwise disposed to commit, because he was induced to do so by a public official or one working with a public official. Merely affording a defendant an opportunity to commit a crime he is disposed to commit is not entrapment.

Defense of Insanity The claim that a defendant is not criminally liable for his actions because at the time of their commission he suffered from some defect of reason that precluded him from being criminally responsible. In essence an insane defendant is acquitted of a crime because he lacks the mental capacity to form the required state of mind which is an essential element of the *corpus delicti* of the crime. Hence, he is in fact innocent of the crime charged. See also *M'Naghten Rule* and *Brawner Rule.*

Deposition A sworn statement of a witness, or party to an action, taken in pretrial proceedings and reduced to writing.

Dictum Remarks made by a court not necessary to its decision and not binding on it in future cases.

Direct Examination The initial questioning of a witness by the party calling him to elicit his testimony in the case. Leading questions are not generally permitted during direct examination.

Discovery Procedure A pretrial procedure in which an adversary is required to give certain information about his or her case or evidence to the opposing party.

Due Process of Law The meaning of this constitutional term has been established by the United States Supreme Court by inclusion and exclusion on a case by case basis. In substantive matters, it is generally defined by the court's notion of fairness. Procedural due process requires, as a minimum, that a defendant be given notice of an action pending against him and be given a fair opportunity to come in and defend against it. The concept of due process of law also includes other constitutional rights such as the right of the defendant to confront (cross examine) witnesses against him. These rights, originally imposed against the federal government, have been held to be assertable against the states because the Fourteenth Amendment imposed the requirements of due process of law against the states.

Dying Declarations   An exception to the hearsay rule which permits the introduction into evidence of a statement of a homicide victim, limited to identifying the slayer, provided that at the time of the statement the victim knew he was dying and had abandoned all hope of recovery. The victim must in fact have died. If he recovers, his personal testimony is still required. He also would have had to have been a competent witness if alive.

Error   An erroneous ruling on the admissibility of evidence, the conduct of a trial or a misleading or erroneous statement of the applicable law made in the trial court's charge to the jury.

Error, Reversible   An error made by a trial court that was so prejudicial to the rights of the appellant that a reviewing court must reverse the trial court's judgment and either order a new trial or a dismissal of the case.

Estoppel   An equitable doctrine that prevents a party from asserting a right, claim or defense that he would otherwise have available, because of some action on his part that would render the assertion of such right, claim or defense inequitable or inappropriate.

Evidence   Anything admissible in court that tends to prove or disprove a fact in issue. Evidence may be real or autoptic (a physical object like a gun); testimonial; or documentary.

Evidence, Clear and Convincing   A standard of proof that is more stringent than the usual civil requirement that a plaintiff must prove his or her case by a "preponderance of the evidence" but less rigorous than the criminal standard that the *People* must prove their case "beyond a reasonable doubt."

Evidence, Derivative   Evidence derived or flowing from leads supplied by other evidence. If the original evidence is not admissible the question of the admissibility of the derivative evidence relates to the reason for the inadmissibility of the original evidence. If the original evidence is inadmissible because of the unlawful conduct of a public official or the violation of the constitutional rights of an accused, the derivative evidence will also be inadmissible. If the original evidence is inadmissible because it is unreliable or because of some rule of evidence then the derivative evidence will be admissible if reliable and not violative of the rules of evidence.

Evidence, Incompetent   Evidence that is inadmissible because it violates a rule of evidence.

Evidence, Newly Discovered   To form a basis for a postconviction motion for a new trial, newly discovered evidence must be such that it could not have been discovered during the trial by the exercise of due diligence and, had it been available at the trial, it is likely that the results would have been more favorable for the defendant. The *People* cannot move for a new trial based on newly discovered evidence any more than they can appeal from a judgment of acquittal. Either situation would involve unconstitutionally subjecting the defendant to double jeopardy.

Evidence, the Probative Value of   This refers to the persuasiveness of the evidence and its ability to establish or disestablish facts in issue. It includes considerations of both the credibility of the evidence and, in the case of circumstantial evidence, its logical relationship to facts in issue.

Evidence, Rules of   The rules of evidence are the standards for determining the admissibility of proffered evidence. These rules are exclusionary, that is, any evidence tending to prove or disprove a fact in issue is admissible at a trial unless there is some specific rule against it (or, in the exercise of its discretion, the court finds that the technically admissible evidence would prove too prejudicial to admit).

Expert Opinion, The Basis of   The facts, observations and assumptions on which an expert witness' opinions are predicated. In general a jury has the right to be informed of these, to enable them to evaluate the expert's opinion.

Facts in Issue   The factual issues to be determined by the trier of the facts in a legal action. They are defined by the pleadings in civil cases and by the information or indictment in a criminal case.

Felony   The most serious classification of crime. A crime usually punishable by more than a year's imprisonment. Generally this means incarceration in a state correctional facility as opposed to a county jail and the imposition of an indeterminate sentence with a minimum and maximum term. Conviction of a felony also commonly entails the loss of certain civil rights.

First Impression   A legal case presenting an issue never resolved by a particular court system (jurisdiction) which is hence not bound by the principle of *stare decisis*.

Forensic Science Consultant   A lay investigator with some specialized training in forensic science employed by the United States Air Force in Criminal Investigations.

Forgery   The crime of falsely making or materially altering a document. A material alteration is one that changes the legal effect of an instrument.

Foundation   Preliminary evidence necessary to establish that the prime evidence to be presented meets the requirements to make it admissible.

Frye Rule   A test for the admissibility of scientific evidence as an exception to the hearsay rule. Under this rule the proponent must show that the scientific test in issue is generally recognized as reliable for the purpose used by the appropriate scientific community and that the test was conducted in accordance with recognized procedures.

Habeas Corpus, Writ of (literally, *you have the body*)   A court order to a public official or private citizen who is detaining a person, directing him or her to bring the person detained before the court to inquire into the legality of the detention. A *habeas corpus* proceeding is not an alternate form of appeal, but it may be an appropriate remedy for defendants incarcerated as the result of a criminal conviction rendered *void* by a violation of their constitutional rights.

Hearsay Evidence   The situation that results when a witness testifies to what another person said and offers this as evidence of the truth of the facts stated. This is objectionable because it deprives the opposing party of the right of cross-examination. Anytime there is no witness who can be cross-examined with regard to the truth and accuracy of the proffered testimony it amounts to hearsay.

Hypnosis Coordinator   A lay FBI agent given some training in hypnosis who coordinates FBI hypnotic investigations and who may question witnesses under hypnosis induced by a professional hypnotist.

Hypnosis, Pretrial   Refers to the hypnosis of a witness or party to a civil or criminal action prior to trial. Generally performed either as an investigative device to obtain leads to independent evidence, to break an amnesia or simply to enhance a nonamnesic witness's recollection of details.

Hypnotically Enhanced Testimony See *Hypnotically Influenced Testimony*

Hypnotically Induced Statements   Statements produced by a party, generally a defendant in a criminal action, as a result of hypnotic suggestion.

Hypnotically Influenced Testimony   This term includes at least three different situations:
1. Testimony given while under hypnosis (generally introduced by the testimony of the hypnotist or a tape recording of the hypnotic sessions).
2. Testimony given while the witness is unhypnotized but based on recollection refreshed by hypnosis.
3. Testimony following hypnosis designed not to enhance recollection but to serve some other purpose such as to compose a witness.

Hypnotically Refreshed Testimony   Waking testimony that was refreshed by prior hypnosis without regard to whether the witness had previously suffered from an amnesia or simply was unable to remember certain details of the event testified about.

Hypnotist, Certified   A meaningless term used by one court to refer to a qualified hypnotist. There are certifying boards in medical, dental, and psychological hypnosis, both experimental and clinical, but their diplomates are not certified as hypnotists. They are certified as members of their respective professions trained in the use of hypnosis. Probably the majority of well-trained professional hypnotists are not board certified.

Hypothetical Question A question put to an expert witness to elicit his opinion on one of the technical issues of the case that assumes the existence of certain facts. The assumed basis of the question should be clearly stated, for the jury must look to the evidence to see if these assumptions have been proven in order to evaluate the opinion.

Immunity from Prosecution Courts and other public officials are empowered, under certain circumstances, to grant potential defendants in criminal actions immunity from prosecution. This is a prosecutorial tool which makes it possible to compel such persons to testify against co-conspirators in criminal cases without violating their constitutional right against self-incrimination. It makes it possible for the *People* to obtain convictions against the most important figures in a crime by permitting lesser ones to escape prosecution, rather than have them all escape by means of each asserting his right against self-incrimination and refusing to testify. An agreement not to prosecute and to grant immunity in exchange for testimony against a co-defendant is enforceable against a public official. The fact that such immunity was granted is admissible to impeach the testimony of a witness testifying in exchange for it.

In Camera (literally, *In chambers*) A hearing or proceeding before a judge in his or her chambers or with all spectators excluded from the courtroom.

Indictment A written accusation of facts constituting a crime or crimes presented by a grand jury and signed by its foreman. It forms the basis of a prosecution for all felonies or misdemeanors prosecuted through a grand jury.

Information A written and verified allegation of facts that constitute a crime or offense less than a felony. The usual instrument serving as the basis for a misdemeanor prosecution.

Inquisitorial System A system of justice utilizing an impartial inquisitor who investigates the facts concerning an alleged crime in the absence of adversarial counsel for the opposing sides.

Insanity A state of mind that precludes criminal responsibility for one's actions. The concept of legal insanity has no logical relationship to the psychological concept of a psychosis.

Intoxication, Voluntary A state of intoxication produced by voluntarily drinking to excess. Generally not a defense to a criminal act.

Intoxication, Involuntary A state of intoxication involuntarily produced (such as by having one's drink spiked or the taking of prescribed medication). Involuntary intoxication is a defense to a criminal charge if it prevented the defendant from having the state of mind required by the statute at the time of the commission of an otherwise criminal act.

Irresistible Impulse   A compulsion to perform a criminal act that the defendant is unable to control because of mental illness. Not a defense under the M'Naghten Rule, but some jurisdictions admit it in addition. A defense under the Brawner Rule.

Jurisdiction
1. The power of the court to act. In general a court needs jurisdiction over the parties to the action, the subject matter of the action, and territorial jurisdiction. Any purported exercise of judicial power in the absence of jurisdiction is a nullity without force or effect.
2. A synonym for a state, territorial, or federal government.

Juvenile Delinquent
1. A law violator who is treated as a noncriminal for an otherwise criminal act because he is younger than a critical age.
2. A child who is treated as an offender for acts which would not be crimes if committed by an adult (such as being a truant or a runaway). These children are also known as status offenders.

Larceny   The taking of property with the intent to permanently deprive the owner of the goods.

Larceny by Fraud   A larceny accomplished by means of false representations of fact.

Larceny by Trick and Device   A larceny effectuated by some type of confidence operation.

Larceny, Common Law   A larceny accomplished by a physical taking of the property in question.

Leading Question   A question that suggests the desired answer.

Lie Detector   See *Polygraph.*

Lineup   An identification procedure in which a witness is asked to identify a suspect from a group of people of similar appearance. Can be done either with the suspect physically present or by means of photographs.

Malpractice   A breach of the duty of a professional person to act like a reasonable and competent member of his profession.

Malum Prohibitum **Crimes** (literally, *bad because prohibited*)   See *Offenses of Strict Liability.*

Malum in Se **Crimes** (literally, *bad in itself*)   See *Offenses of Mental Culpability.*

Mandamus, **Writ of** (literally, *we command*)   An order of a court requiring some public or corporate official to perform some purely ministerial and nondiscretionary duty that he or she is required to but has refused to perform.

Manslaughter   A homicide committed without the intent to kill.

Medical Practice Act   A statute defining the practice of medicine and limiting it to a designated class of persons.

Memory Jogging Device   Any technique that results in the refreshment of a witness's memory. Devices most commonly used are the witness's notes, newspaper articles, or leading questions if permitted.

Mens Rea (literally, *evil mind*)   See *Criminal Intent.*

Miranda **Rule**   The requirement that, immediately after being taken into custody, suspects must be informed that they have the right to remain silent, that anything they say can and will be used against them, that they have a right to consult with a lawyer prior to making any statement, to have the lawyer present during any statement they make, and that if they cannot afford a lawyer one will be appointed free of charge. Suspects must then be asked if they understand these rights and if they wish to consult a lawyer or want one appointed. Any statement resulting from a violation of these requirements, or in the absence of a lawyer after a suspect has requested one, will result in the statement being inadmissible without regard to its truth or falsity or its actual voluntary or involuntary nature.

Misdemeanor   A crime less serious than a felony. Usually a crime for which the maximum sentence that can be imposed is one year. Generally prosecuted on the basis of an information and sentence is served in local jail rather than a state prison.

M'Naghten Rule   An insanity test that holds that defendants are not criminally responsible for an act if they suffer from a defect of reason such that they either do not know the nature and quality of their actions or that these actions are wrong.

Modus Operandi (literally, *method of operation*)   The individual technique and method of operation of a criminal.

Motion   An application for a court order.

Motion for a New Trial   An application made to a trial court following conviction to set aside the verdict and grant a new trial. May be founded on any ground that would require an appellate court to grant the same relief.

Motion, Omnibus   A preliminary motion in a criminal case attacking an accusatory instrument on a wide variety of possible grounds.

Motion to Suppress Evidence or Testimony   A preliminary motion based on the grounds that the evidence was illegally obtained or is unreliable.

Murder   A homicide where the defendant intended to kill or acted with a depraved indifference to human life.

Murder, Felony   A homicide committed during the course of an ongoing felony. Generally this is murder in the first degree. In some jurisdictions any underlying felony may be the basis of a charge of felony murder while in other jurisdictions only certain enumerated felonies may be.

Negligence   The tort committed by one who fails to act as a reasonable person to protect others from injury.

Negligence, Contributory   Negligence on the part of the plaintiff in a negligence action that contributed to his injuries. Contributory negligence will bar the plaintiff's recovery in some jurisdictions. In jurisdictions having the rule of comparative negligence, it will simply diminish the amount of his recovery.

Negligence, Criminal   A failure to perceive a risk that is so substantial and unjustifiable that its disregard constitutes a gross departure from the standard of behavior of a reasonable person. A much more cavalier and extreme form of negligence than the civil variety.

Novel Impression   See *First Impression.*

Objection   A contention that proffered evidence is inadmissible. This must be made at the time the evidence is offered or the objection will be deemed waived and not the proper basis of an appeal.

Offense, Extraneous   An offense alleged to have been committed by a defendant in a criminal action other than one with which he is presently charged.

Offenses of Mental Culpability   Offenses that include as part of their *corpus delicti* the existence of a specified mental state on the part of the perpetrator.

Offenses of Strict Liability   Offenses that do not require a specific mental state at the time of their commission.

Offer of Proof   A statement of the purposes for which certain evidence that has been objected to is being offered. This may be made either to get the evidence before the jury or for purposes of establishing a record for appellate review.

Ordinance   A statute enacted by a local, as opposed to a state, legislature.

Perjury   The crime of lying under oath.

Perjury, Subornation of   The crime of inducing another to commit perjury.

Petitioner   A party that files a petition for judicial relief in a special proceeding.

Plaintiff   The party initiating a civil action.

Plea Bargain   An agreement between the prosecution and defense to permit the defendant to enter a plea of guilty to a lesser offense than the one charged. This protects the defendant from a conviction on the greater charge while assuring the People of a conviction on some charge. While the practice is often criticized in the press, it is absolutely necessary to prevent the criminal courts from being hopelessly bogged down by calendar congestion.

Plea of Guilty   This admits every allegation in the indictment or information and renders a trial unnecessary.

Plea of Not Guilty   This puts in issue every allegation in the indictment or information and requires the people to prove them all beyond a reasonable doubt. There is no narrowing of issues in a criminal case (as there is in a civil case) by admitting some allegations in an accusatory instrument and denying others.

Police Power   The power of a state to protect the health, morals and public welfare of its citizens.

Polygraph   A device that measures a variety of autonomic nervous system functions such as pulse rate, blood pressure, respiration rate and galvanic skin response. Its use to detect lies is advocated by some.

Posttrial Order   An order issued by a trial court subsequent to judgment.

Preempting the Field   When federal legislation concerning a subject is held to prevent the states from legislating concerning the same subject matter.

Premeditation   A previous consideration of an action prior to taking it. Generally applicable to murder.

Presumption, Conclusive   A substantive rule of law not subject to being set aside by any evidence. For example, a child under a certain age is conclusively presumed to be incapable of committing a crime.

Presumption, Rebuttable   A rule of evidence which satisfies the burden of proof of a party, unless evidence is introduced to overcome the presumption. For example, all persons born in wedlock are presumed legitimate, that is, the child of their mother's husband, at the time of their conception.

Principal in a Crime   All parties to a criminal conspiracy are equally guilty of the crime whether present at the scene or not. Some jurisdictions like New York have eliminated all distinctions between accessories and principals.

Privileged Communication   A communication made within the context of certain relationships that require confidential communications and that the law regards as of more importance than the production of evidence in any civil or criminal trial. These relationships include: husband–wife; attorney–client; doctor–patient; psychologist–client; certified social worker–client; clergyman–penitent; and sometimes others. The effect of a privilege is to render the professional party to such a communication incompetent as a witness to the transaction unless the privilege is waived. The privilege belongs to the client and not the professional and hence only the client can waive it.

Procedural Safeguards Procedures specified for forensic hypnotic interviews designed to minimize the risk of the development of false information.

Psychological Certification Law A statute that limits the use of the title *psychologist* to qualified people but does not define the practice of psychology nor restrict it to persons certified as psychologists.

Psychological Licensing Law A statute that defines the practice of psychology and restricts it to certain qualified persons.

Psychologist, Certified A psychologist certified under a certification statute.

Psychologist, Clinical A psychologist trained in the diagnosis and treatment of mental illness or behavior disorders.

Rape Sexual intercourse either against the will or without the consent of a woman or with a woman under the age of consent.

Reasonable Doubt The doubt that remains in the mind of a reasonable person concerning the defendant's guilt of the crime charged after considering all of the believable evidence in the case. To be proven guilty beyond a reasonable doubt requires that any reasonable view of the evidence must be incompatible with the defendant's innocence.

Redirect Examination A reexamination of a witness, by the party offering testimony following cross-examination, in an effort to rehabilitate the witness or to clarify his testimony.

Regulations Enactments of an administrative agency exercising a quasi-legislative function. Regulations of administrative agencies have the force of law unless successfully contested in the courts. Before being able to contest a regulation in the courts, the aggrieved party generally has to go through the expensive and time-consuming process of exhausting all of his remedies within the appeals system of the agency in question.

Reliability of a Scientific Test The trustworthiness or validity of the test for the purposes used. (See Psychological Glossary for the psychological meaning of this term)

Reply A plaintiff's pleading answering counterclaims made in the defendant's answer to his complaint.

Res Gestae (literally, *things done*) A spontaneous verbal exclamation made by a party to an action, before there is time to think, that is admissible in evidence as an exception to the hearsay rule.

Respondent The party who responds to a petition in a special proceeding.

Right of Confrontation (Sixth Amendment) The right of a party to cross-examine opposing witnesses.

Right to Counsel A constitutional right to be effectively represented by counsel in a criminal action.

Robbery   A larceny aggravated by an assault. The stealing of valuable property by the use of fear or force.

Seduction   Sexual intercourse with a previously chaste female by proscribed means such as an unconditional promise of marriage.

Self-Serving Statement   A prior statement of a party to an action offered to corroborate his position at the trial.

Sexual Abuse   A crime involving sexual conduct without the consent of an adult or with an underage person that does not amount to rape or sodomy.

Sexual Misconduct   A variety of sexual crimes involving nonconsensual normal or deviant sexual intercourse, bestiality, or necrophilia.

Silver Platter Doctrine   The doctrine that evidence illegally obtained by a state officer was inadmissible in a federal court if such state officer was working in conjunction with a federal officer. This doctrine was superceded by the rule that such evidence is inadmissible even in a state court.

Sodomy   A group of sexual deviations that the law treats indiscriminately. The term includes oral-genital and anal-genital sex between unmarried persons.

Stare Decisis (literally, *to stand decided*)   The principle that when a court renders a decision in a case it becomes a binding precedent to govern the resolution of similar cases, by that court and all inferior courts.

Statement   A declaration by a party or witness in a legal case prior to trial. In the case of a defendant in a criminal matter, a statement may admit or deny all or some of the allegations made in the accusatory instrument or admit some and deny others. If it admits them all it amounts to a confession.

Statements, Prior Consistent   A prior statement consistent with his present testimony, made by a witness or party to an action. This can only be used to support his present testimony if the claim is made that his story is of recent origin.

Statement, Prior Inconsistent   A prior statement of a witness or party inconsistent with his present testimony. This is admissible to impeach the testimony of that person.

Stipulation   An enforceable agreement between opposing counsel. It usually relates to the admissibility of certain evidence or the existence of certain facts. It may also be an agreement involving procedural changes or the extension of time deadlines for filing papers or pleadings. Stipulations are always subject to the court's approval.

Strict Tort Liability   Liability for certain acts without regard to the issue of negligence.

Sunset Laws   Laws automatically repealing statutes unless periodically relegislated.

Testator/Testatrix   The person executing a will.

Testimony   Evidence given by a witness under oath.

Testimony, Circumstantial   Testimony of a witness concerning a fact directly observed by him that is not in issue but which logically tends to establish or refute a fact in issue.

Testimony, Direct   Testimony given by a witness concerning facts in issue that he observed.

Testimony, Expert   Testimony by a witness who may have no personal knowledge of a fact in issue, or one logically related to such fact, but who is qualified to give his or her opinion on a technical matter at issue in the case. Ordinary witnesses are required to testify only to observations of facts. Only an expert witness is permitted to express his or her opinion.

Tort   A civil wrong. A breach of a duty not arising out of a contract.

Trial Court   A court with jurisdiction to try, and finally dispose of, a case. Also known as a court of record.

Trier of the Facts   Either a jury or the trial judge (in matters tried without a jury).

Undue Influence   A defense in an action in contract or a grounds for setting aside a gift under a will. The notion of undue influence is that there existed a relationship between the party executing an instrument and another in which the acting party was subservient to the will of the other, and that the acting party executed the instrument only because his free will was overcome by this undue and malign influence.

Voir Dire (literally, *to see, to say*)   A process by which prospective jurors are questioned and selected.

Voucher Rule   In calling a witness, a party is deemed to vouch for the witness's veracity. Hence, he is not permitted to impeach his own witness except on the basis of a prior inconsistent statement reduced to a writing and signed or one made under oath.

Waiver   The voluntary relinquishment of a known right.

Witness   One who gives testimony (generally under oath) in a judicial, administrative, or legislative proceeding.

Witness, Hostile   A witness that a party must call who is likely to be hostile to his cause. If the court grants permission to examine a witness as a hostile witness, leading questions may be asked on direct examination, but the party can still not impeach him for he has made him his own witness by calling him.

Witness, Impeachment of   Attempting to destroy the credibility of a witness by demonstrating the witness's lack of ability to observe, recall, or relate the facts or by demonstrating the witness's motive to lie.

Witness, Incompetent A witness who may not testify to certain facts because to permit him to do so would violate some rule of evidence, for example, the testimony would be violative of a privileged communication.

Psychological Glossary

Abreaction   An emotional reliving of a traumatic incident.

Acquisition   The phase of a learning situation in which the desired responses are reinforced and habit strength increases.

Age Progression   A hypnotic technique in which a subject is told that he or she is going forward in time and will have experiences in the future.

Age Regression   A hypnotic technique in which a subject is told that he or she is going back in time and will reexperience the past.

Amnesia   A forgetting of experiences over a period of time.

Amnesia, Anterograde   See *Korsakoff Syndrome*.

Amnesia, Functional   An amnesia caused by psychological as opposed to organic factors.

Amnesia, Posthypnotic   An amnesia for the events of a hypnotic trance. May be spontaneous or suggested. It may relate to the content of the hypnotic experience or to the source of information that was given under hypnosis and is retained in the subsequent waking state.

Amnesia, Retrograde   A forgetting of the experiences of a time interval in the past.

Anxiety   A free-floating fear (fear without an object). Synonymous with neurotic anxiety. In Freudian terms it is the emotion associated with a repressed thought, which is beginning to break through into consciousness, because of the failure of repression, while the thought itself remains unconscious.

Association   A link in the psychically determined chain of connections between ideas.

Automatic Talking   A hypnotic technique, analogous to automatic writing, in which a subject is told that, on a signal, a part of his or her psyche that knows things that he or she is unaware of (the hidden observer) will answer questions.

Automatic Writing   A hypnotic technique for tapping unconscious ideation, in which a subject's hand is instructed to write out material without any conscious awareness on the part of the subject of what it is writing or even what it is doing.

Autonomic Nervous System   The division of the nervous system concerned with the automatic regulation of life processes, such as respiration, heart rate, blood pressure, and so on. A series of servomechanisms that maintain homeostasis.

Borderline Personality   In Freudian terms a primitively fixated personality with marked defects in ego development, a poor sense of self and little capacity to integrate the positive and negative qualities of others.

Catalepsy   A muscular rigidity suggested under hypnosis. Similar to the fixed, symbolic posturing sometimes displayed by catatonic schizophrenics.

Chaperone Technique   A technique to induce hypnosis in reluctant or fearful subjects by having them witness what is described as the hypnosis of another.

Chunking   The organization of bits of information into larger functional units: organizing letters into words or words into phrases.

Closure   The perceptual completing of an incomplete unit.

Cocktail Party Effect   The ability to tune into one particular conversation while ignoring several simultaneous ones.

Coding   The organization of material prior to entry into long-term memory. Most often verbal material is encoded into semantic categories for this purpose. For example, apples, bananas and pears are encoded as fruit.

Cognitive System   Refers to the higher mental processes such as thinking, reasoning, and logic as opposed to sensation.

Compliance   A desire on the part of a hypnotic subject to please the hypnotist by doing or saying what it seems the latter desires.

Confabulation   A filling in of forgotten details between remembered events, in accordance with what witnesses deduce should have occurred as opposed to what they actually remember. This is generally done unintentionally by witnesses and they may fail to distinguish between confabulations and actual memory.

Confounding Variables   Having more than one independent variable in an experiment, combined so that the effects of one cannot be separated from the effects of the other.

Constancies, Perceptual   The learned tendency of a subject to perceive objects as permanent unchanging entities that do not vary in regard to such attributes as size, shape, and color under changing conditions of observation.

Constructive Theory of Memory   The notion that memories are constantly undergoing reconstruction and change, as opposed to the notion they are simply recordings that can be played back like a video tape.

Contraindications for Hypnosis   Reasons that make hypnosis inadvisable for a particular subject or application; factors that would create undue risks of an adverse reaction on the part of the subject or produce unreliable results in a forensic context.

Control Group   A group of subjects in an experiment treated identically to the experimental group except for the application of the independent variable.

Countertransference   A transference reaction on the part of an analyst directed toward the patient.

Cybernetics   The electronic simulation of the functioning of the nervous system.

Deafness, Hypnotic   A suggested (and selective) loss of hearing in a hypnotic subject.

Delusion   A false belief tenaciously held despite all evidence to the contrary. May be created by hypnotic suggestion in normal subjects but is generally a symptom of a psychosis.

Dissociation   The separation in consciousness of two concurrent activities so that each is conducted in isolation from the other, such as automatic writing.

Dream, Hypnotically Induced   A dream produced by hypnotic suggestion. May occur during hypnosis or posthypnotically. Specific content and other specifications may be imposed on such a dream.

Dream, Nocturnal   The spontaneous dreams that generally occur during Stage 1, REM sleep.

Dream Work   The unconscious mechanism that distorts the latent content of a dream into the relatively innocuous manifest content.

Dynamics, Intrapersonal   The intrapsychic personality factors that affect a person's behavior.

Echo   An auditory afterimage.

Ego Functions   The psychic functions assigned to the ego system by Freud or ego psychologists, such as sensing, cognition, identification, integration, defense, and planning.

Ego, Observing   That portion of the ego that observes a dream or hypnotic experience as if it were a stranger to the event.

Ego, Participating   That part of the ego that subjectively experiences the events of a dream or hypnotic suggestions.

Ego Splitting   The division of the ego into functionally diverse units such as into observing and participating egos.

Eidetic Imagery   A photographic memory. A memory with perceptionlike clarity.

Exact Copy Theory of Memory   The notion that memories are recorded in the brain accurately and permanently as on a video tape.

Experimental Group   The group in an experiment that differs from the control group only in that it is exposed to the action of the independent variable.

Fantasy   In the generic sense of the term it is a synonym for primary process thinking (fantasy, dreams, and hallucinations). In its specific sense, as used in this book, it is synonymous with daydream or imagination.

Figure   The enduring object into which perception organizes a group of sensory elements.

Flower Method of Hypnotic Induction   A method of induction in which subjects are instructed to open and close their eyes as they count, and told that they will eventually be unable to open them, at which time they will be deeply hypnotized. In this procedure all of the instructions given to subjects are massed at the beginning of the induction.

Forgetting   The weakening of memory traces with the passage of time. Not the same as *extinction* which refers to an active unlearning process produced by the elicitation of a learned response which is not re-inforced.

Ground   The background formed by all of the sensory elements not organized into a figure.

Hallucination   A perception in the absence of a real external stimulus. Can be suggested under hypnosis with a good subject and may occur in normal people under certain conditions. Otherwise it is a symptom of a psychosis.

Hallucination, Negative   The failure to perceive a real external stimulus.

Hand Attraction (or Repulsion)   The attraction (or repulsion) of the hands as a result of a hypnotic or prehypnotic suggestion that this effect will be experienced.

Hidden Observer Technique   See *Automatic Talking*.

Hypermnesia   Increased recall ability.

Hypersuggestibility   A state of enhanced suggestibility or likelihood of accepting suggestions.

Hypnoanalysis   Psychoanalysis conducted while the patient is in a hypnotic state.

Hypnoidal State   A prehypnotic or a very shallow hypnotic state.

Hypnosis, Clinical   Hypnosis employed in a clinical context, that is, in the treatment of physical or mental conditions.

Hypnosis, Episodic   Hypnosis in a context in which it is viewed by both the subject and hypnotist as an isolated event and not part of a clinical procedure designed to alter the personality of the subject.

Hypnosis, Forensic   Hypnosis employed in a legal context.

Hypnosis, Investigative   Hypnosis used solely as a device to generate leads to independent evidence and employed on a subject not likely to be a witness at a future trial.

Hypnosis, Involuntary   Hypnosis produced without the explicit consent of the subject, as opposed to hypnosis against the will of the subject. The latter means hypnosis produced despite the subject's active opposition, which is extremely unlikely if not impossible.

Hypnotechnician   A lay hypnotist who purports to limit his or her work in hypnosis to nontherapeutic suggestions or to suggestions by prescription of a physician or psychologist.

Hypnotherapy   The use of hypnosis as an ancillary technique in any type of psychotherapy.

Icon   A visual afterimage.

Ideomotor Questioning   Questioning a subject under hypnosis who has been trained to make an ideomotor response for *yes* or *no*. It purports to be a dissociative method for communicating with the unconscious.

Ideomotor Response   An ideomotor response is an involuntary-type response, produced by the subject's imagining that it is happening, as opposed to performing it intentionally. Arm levitation is an example.

Illusion   A common misperception of external reality. Illusions occur in all sensory modalities and are universal.

Importations   Material introduced into memory that was not present in the original event.

Induced Emotions   Emotions suggested to a subject under hypnosis or, induced in a patient or therapist by the behavior of the other (as opposed to transference or countertransference reactions which are produced by internal dynamics and not another person).

Induction Procedure (Ritual)   The particular suggestions made and procedures followed to formally induce a trance state.

Interference Theory of Forgetting   The theory that the retrieval of older memories is interfered with by subsequently acquired information, rather than by the mere passage of time.

Korsakoff Syndrome   An impairment of the ability to record new memories, while the ability to recall previously recorded material remains intact. Usually attributed to organic brain disease.

Lay Hypnotist   A hypnotist untrained in Psychology or Psychiatry. See also *Hypnotechnician.*

Learning   A relatively permanent change in behavior potential due to reinforced practice (Hilgard and Marquis 1961). The modification of behavior as a result of experience.

Levitation   An ideomotor response, such as the raising of an arm, in response to suggestions to imagine that the arm is floating up all by itself.

Meaningfulness   As used in the learning and memory studies cited in this book, the meaningfulness of a word or nonsense syllable generally refers to the number of associations that subjects can produce when the word or nonsense syllable is used as a stimulus.

Memory Bank   The hypothetical repository of past experiences that can be retrieved into consciousness when required.

Memory Block   An emotional factor that prevents the retrieval of a given memory.

Memory Centers in Brain   The inaccurate position that certain regions in the temporal lobes of the cerebrum are specialized for recording memories.

Memory Consolidation   Refers to the observation that long term memories require a certain period of time to set or become permanent.

Memory, Long-term   Memories of events that were experienced more than one minute ago. All memories other than short-term memories.

Memory, Pseudo-   Confabulations, fantasies, and other distortions that a subject confuses with true memory.

Memory, Screen   False memories unconsciously produced to protect the subject from actual but traumatic recollections.

Memory, Short-term   Transitory memories lasting for a period of approximately one minute. The contents of short-term memory are either encoded into long-term memory or forgotten permanently.

Memory Span   The time duration of short-term memory or the number of items within the capacity of short-term memory.

Memory, Traumatic   The memory of an event associated with an aversive affect, such as fear or anger.

Mental-Health Professional   An indefinite term that refers to a person trained in one of the professions dealing with mentally ill people. The term is used differently by various writers. Some would limit it to psychologists or psychiatrists while others would include physicians, certified social workers, and psychiatric nurses.

Mental Illness   An ambiguous term referring to a behavior disorder without regard to whether it is functional (that is, psychologically caused) or organic (caused by a physiological disorder).

Monoideism   The narrowing of the field of consciousness to a single idea or stimulus.

Motivation   Technically, motivation refers to a secondary or learned need but the term is often used to apply to primary drives such as sex. It refers to the factors that energize or drive goal-directed behavior.

Movie-screen Technique   See *Video-recorder Technique.*

Narcoanalysis   Psychoanalysis conducted while the patient is under the influence of a drug designed to facilitate free verbalization.

Neo-Dissociation Theory   The theory, that contrary to the classic view of hypnotic dissociation, when two activities are performed simultaneously, one on a conscious and the other on an unconscious level, they are each performed less efficiently than if they were both performed consciously. This is because, in addition to the normal amount of interference between the two tasks, the psychic energy necessary to keep one task unconscious also detracts from performance.

Nonsense Syllable A syllable having no meaning that is used in verbal learning studies to eliminate or control for preexperimental associations to the material to be learned.

Paralysis, Hysterical A paralysis having a psychological as opposed to an organic etiology.

Passive Decay of Memory Traces, Theory of The theory that forgetting is caused by the impermanence of the chemical recording processes in the brain.

Perception The reception and organization of incoming sensory information into meaningful entities (figures).

Persistence of Vision See *Icon*

Positive Afterimage See *Icon*

Preconscious The hypothetical region of the psyche in which material is recorded that is freely accessible to consciousness when required.

Primacy Effect Refers to the fact that, in learning a serial list of words or nonsense syllables, items at the beginning of the list are learned before items in the middle.

Professional Hypnotist In this book the term refers to a psychologist or psychiatrist with specialized training in hypnosis. Some writers use the term to refer to lay hypnotists who practice hypnosis for a fee.

Psychiatrist A physician specializing in mental disorders (functional or organic). The term implies residency training in psychiatry but may legally be used by any physician who limits his or her practice to psychiatry, even in the absence of such training or board certification.

Psychological Test A sample of behavior taken under standard conditions and used as a basis for making inferences about future behavior.

Psychologist A person having a Ph.D. in some branch of psychology who has passed a licensing or certification examination by a state board of psychology examiners.

Psychosis A severe form of mental illness characterized by symptom formation (in the sense of symbolic behavior) that is so disabling that the patient is often unable to function in everyday life.

Rationalization A Freudian defense mechanism by which the patient conceals the real motivation for his behavior from himself by fabricating good reasons for it.

Reality, Objective A person's life situation as perceived by disinterested observers.

Reality, Subjective　A person's life situation as he or she perceives it.

Recall　A method of testing memory that requires the subject to retrieve material unaided.

Recency Effect　Refers to the fact that, in learning a serial list of words or nonsense syllables, items at the end of the list are learned before items in the middle.

Recognition　A method of testing memory in which the subject is required to recognize the item to be remembered in a field of different items.

Relearning Method　A method of testing memory in which the subject is given the opportunity to relearn the material in question. The reduction in the number of learning trials needed to achieve the original criterion of learning, expressed as a percentage of the original number of learning trials, is taken as an index of memory.

Reliability　In psychology, this term refers to the repeatability of a measurement. In legal writings on hypnosis, the term refers to the validity or objective accuracy of statements elicited under hypnosis.

Replication (of research results)　Refers to the ability of other researchers to repeat a study and get the same results. The fact that a study is replicable increases confidence that the results of the original study were real and not merely the result of chance.

Repression　The hypothetical Freudian mechanism by which anxiety-laden ideas are consigned to the unconscious and kept there.

Retention Phase　The phase in a memory study between learning or acquisition and the testing of memory.

Retrieval Categorization　The semantic categories under which long-term memory is searched to retrieve an item filed there.

Retrieval Phase　The final phase of a memory study during which memory for previous learning is tested.

Retroactive Facilitation　The effect of learning which when interspersed between acquisition and retrieval facilitates recall of the previously learned material.

Retroactive Inhibition　The effect of learning which when interspersed between acquisition and retrieval inhibits the recall of previously learned material.

Revivification　A perceptionlike reliving of a past experience accompanied by the temporary forgetting of all subsequent experience.

Role Playing　Producing behavior appropriate to a role adopted by or assigned to a subject.

Savings Method　See *Relearning Method*

Secondary Elaboration　The filling in of details in a dream or memory to make a smooth, coherent story.

Sensory Modality   A distinct type of sensory information: visual, auditory, tactile, sharp pain, hot, cold, and so on.

Sensory Registers   A hypothetical structure that holds sensory information in raw or unprocessed form for a brief period of time while it is being processed.

Serial Position Effect   The observation that the beginnings and ends of serial lists, of words or nonsense syllables, are learned more rapidly than the middle. A result of primacy and recency effects.

Simulators   Subjects used in hypnotic research who are not hypnotized but are instructed to behave as though they were and to try to deceive the experimenter.

Sodium Amytal   See *Truth Serum.*

Sodium Brevital   See *Truth Serum.*

Somnambulistic State   A deep hypnotic trance.

Subconscious   A colloquialism for the term *unconscious.*

Suggestions, Hypnotic   A statement made to a hypnotized subject designed to elicit a nonvolitional response, usually involving an ideomotor reaction, a perception, or an affective reaction. For example, "Your hand is becoming so light that it is floating up in the air all by itself," is a suggestion. "Raise your hand up in the air," is a command. In the case of a suggestion the subject does not intentionally raise his hand. In the case of a command he does.

Suggestion, Posthypnotic   A suggestion made under hypnosis that is intended to be acted on in the subsequent waking state, either on the occurrence of some signal or at a certain time. It may also involve the continuation into the waking state of a response made while under hypnosis.

Suppression   The conscious counterpart of repression. The conscious decision to avoid thinking about an anxiety-producing idea.

Susceptibility, Hypnotic   The ability of a subject to achieve a given level of hypnosis under standardized conditions

Task-Motivating Instructions   Instructions given to subjects to the effect that what they are requested to do will be easy and that if they do not do it, the entire experiment will be a waste of time.

Trance   The condition of being hypnotized or a series of responses to trance-inducing suggestions.

Trance Capacity   See *Susceptibility, Hypnotic*

Trance Depth   This is generally specified by the kinds of suggestions that the subject is capable of accepting. The more difficult the suggestion accepted (that is, the lower its probability of acceptance) the deeper the trance is considered to be.

Trance, Hyperempiric   An active as opposed to a relaxed type of trance.

Trance, Mini   Refers to Erickson's notion that there is a reinstatement of a trance state whenever a subject acts on a posthypnotic suggestion.

Trance, Spontaneous   A trance state induced unintentionally and without the assistance of a hypnotist.

Transference   The directing of intense emotions, which are not appropriate to the objective situation, toward the therapist by the patient.

Transpositions   The interchanging of the time sequence of items in a memory or story.

Truth Serum   A drug purported to prevent lying by facilitating talking while removing inhibitions. The subject can supposedly be responsive to questions while cognitive ability to control responses is diminished. No drug has been demonstrated to be able to do this, but drugs that produce an appreciably altered state of consciousness might be expected to weaken memory associations.

Unconscious   A hypothetical Freudian structure. The part of the psyche that contains repressed material unavailable to consciousness without the employment of special techniques.

Video-Recorder Technique   A method of retrieving memories under hypnosis by having the subject see events formerly witnessed displayed on an imagined giant television screen.

Video-Recorder Theory of Memory   See *Exact Copy Theory of Memory*.

Table of Cases and
Case Index

Desist v. United States, 394 U.S. 244, 89 S. Ct. 1048, 22 L.Ed. 248 (1969).
    Pg. 109.
Durham v. United States, 214 F.2d 862 (D.C. Cir. 1954).
Eaton v. State, 394 A.2d 217 (Del. Sup. Ct. 1978). Pg. 68.
Emmett v. Ricketts, 397 F. Supp. 1025 (N.D. Ga. 1975). Pp. 46, 91, 92, 93.
Emmett v. State, 232 Ga. 110, 205 S.E.2d 231 (1974).
Fleischer v. C.I.R., 403 F.2d 403 (2d Cir. 1968).
Forsythe v. Cohen, 305 F. Supp. 1194 (D.R.I. 1969). Pg. 155
Frye v. United States, 203 F. 1013 (D.C. Cir. 1923). Pp. 62, 65, 71, 73, 77,
    80, 82, 88, 89, 116, 122, 177.
Fulcher v. State, 633 P.2d 142 (Wyo. Sup. Ct. 1981). Pg. 139.
Goldberg v. United States, 425 U.S. 94, 96 S. Ct. 1338, 47 L.Ed.2d 603
    (1976). Pg. 91.
Greenfield v. Commonwealth, 214 Va. 710, 204 S.E.2d 414 (1974). Pp. 67,
    71.
Greenfield v. Robinson, 413 F. Supp. 1113 (W.D. Va. 1976).
Harding v. State, 5 Md. App. 230, 246 A.2d 302 (Ct. Spec. App. 1968),
    Cert. denied 395 U.S. 949 (1968). Pp. 72, 73, 74, 75, 78, 88, 118.
Hewitt v. Maryland State Board of Censors, 243 Md. 574, 221 A.2d 894
    (1966). Pg. 73.
Hird v. General Motors Corp., 61 App. Div. 2d 832 (N.Y. 1978).
Jackson v. Denno, 378 U.S. 368, 84 S. Ct. 1774, 12 L.Ed. 908 (1964). Pg.
    101, 109.
Johnston v. State, 418 S.W.2d 522 (Tex. Crim. App. 1967). Pg. 135.
Jones v. State, 542 P.2d 1316 (Okla. Crim. App. 1975). Pg. 64.
In Re Ketchel, 68 Cal. 2d 397, 438 P.2d 625, 66 Cal. Rptr. 881 (1968). Pg.
    57.
Kline v. Ford Motor Co., Inc., 523 F.2d 1067 (9th Cir. 1975). Pp. 75, 78,
    94, 95.
Lawson v. State, 280 N.W.2d 400 (Iowa Sup. Ct. 1979). Pg. 93.
Lemieux v. Superior Court, 132 Ariz. 214, 644 P.2d 1300 (1982).
Leyra v. Denno, 347 U.S. 556 (1954), cert. denied 345 U.S. 918 (1952),
    hab. corp. denied 113 F. Supp. 556 (D.N.Y. 1953), aff'd 208 F.2d 605
    (2d Cir. 1953). Pg. 108.
Louis v. State, 24 Ala. App. 120, 130 So. 904 (Ct. App. 1930). Pg. 134.
Mapp v. Ohio, 367 U.S. 643 (1961). Pg. 111.
Masters v. State, 341 S.W.2d 938, 85 A.L.R. 2d 1123 (Tex. Crim. App.
    1960). Pp. 152, 153.
McGraph v. Rohde, 53 Ill. 2d 56, 289 N.E.2d 619 (1972). Pg. 14.
McMillen v. Arthritis Foundation, 432 F. Supp. 430 (S.D.N.Y. 1977).
Merrifield v. State, 74 Ind. Dec. 213, 400 N.E.2d 146 (Sup. Ct. 1980). Pg.
    81.
Miranda v. Arizona, 384 U.S. 436 (1966). Pp. 100, 101, 181.

People v. Modesto, 59 Cal. 2d 722, 382 P.2d 33, 31 Cal. Rptr. 225 (1963). Pp. 66, 69.

People v. Morse, 60 Cal. 2d 631, 36 Cal. Rptr. 201 (1964). Pg. 66.

People v. Norcutt, 44 Ill. 2d 256, 255 N.E.2d 442 (1970). Pg. 109.

People v. Pennington, 66 Cal. 2d 508, 426 P.2d 942, 58 Cal. Rptr. 374 (1967). Pg. 118.

People v. Peters, 4 Crim. 5996 (1974). Pg. 75.

People v. Ritche, No. C-36932 (Cal. Super. Ct. April 7, 1977). Pg. 123.

People v. Shelly, Ind. No. 1340/73 (N.Y. Sup. Ct. 1973). Pg. 109.

People v. Shirley, 31 Cal. 3d 18, 641 P.2d 775, 181 Cal. Rptr. 243 (1982). Pp. 85, 89.

People v. Sirhan, 7 Cal. 3d 710, 497 P.2d 1121, 102 Cal. Rptr. 385 (1972). Pg. 70.

People v. Smrekar, 68 Ill. App. 3d 379, 385 N.E.2d 848, 24 Ill. Dec. 707 (App. Ct. 1979). Pp. 79, 219.

People v. Tait, 99 Mich. App. 19, 297 N.W.2d 853 (Ct. App. 1980). Pg. 96.

People v. Therapeutic Hypnosis, 57 App. Div. 2d 979 (1977), 52 App. Div. 2d 1017 (1976), 38 N.Y.2d 740 (1975), 83 Misc. 2d 1068 (1975).

People v. Thomas, Crim. No. 3274 (Cal. Ct. App. Jan. 9, 1969). Pg. 70.

People v. Ubbes, 374 Mich. 571 (1965). Pg. 101.

People v. Wallach, 312 N.W.2d 387, 110 Mich. App. 37 (Mich. App., 1981).

People v. White, No. J-3665 (Wisc. Milwaukee Cir. Ct. Mar. 27, 1979). Pp. 54, 55.

People v. Williams, 132 Cal. App. 3d 920 (1982).

People v. Wofford, 59 App. Div. 2d 562 (N.Y. 1977). Pg. 72.

People v. Worthington, 105 Cal. 166, 38 P. 689 (1894). Pg. 130.

Polk v. State, 48 Md. App. 382, 427 A.2d 1041 (Ct. Special App. 1981). Pg. 88.

Quaglino v. People, *Cert. denied*, 99 S. Ct. 212, *rehear. denied*, 99 S. Ct. 599 (1978). Pg. 54.

Reed v. Maryland, 283 Md. 374, 391 A.2d 364 (1978). Pg. 62.

Regina v. K, 10 C.R. 3d 235, 47 C.C.C. 2d 436 (Canad. Prov. Ct. Fam. Div. 1979). Pg. 84.

Regina v. Palmer, (Austl. New So. Wales Sup. Ct. 1976). Pg. 136.

Regina v. Pitt, 68 D.L.R. 2d 513 (Canad. B.C. Sup. Ct. 1967). Pp. 67, 68.

Rex v. Booher, 4 D.L.R. 795 (Canad. Alta. Sup. Ct. 1928). Pp. 105, 106.

Rochin v. California, 342 U.S. 165 (1952). Pg. 111.

Rodriguez v. State, 327 So.2d 903 (Fla. Dist. Ct. App. 1976). Pg. 71.

Rucker v. Wabash Railroad Company, 418 F.2d 146 (7th Cir. 1969). Pg. 64.

Shaw v. Garrison, 467 F.2d 113 (5th Cir. 1972).

Sheppard v. Koblentz, 174 Ohio St. 120, 187 N.E.2d 40 (Sup. Ct. 1962). Pg. 57.

State v. Valdez, 91 Ariz. 274, 371 P.2d 894 (1962). Pg. 60.
State v. Walker, 416, S.W.2d 134 (Mo. Sup. Ct. 1967). Pg. 109.
Stevenson v. Boles, 221 F. Supp. 411 (N.D.W.V. 1963). Pg. 103.
Strong v. State, 435 N.E.2d 969 (Ind. 1982).
Tyrone v. State, 77 Tex. Crim. 493, 180 S.W. 125 (Ct. Crim. App. 1915).
    Pg. 134.
United States v. Adams, 581 F. 2d 193 (9th Cir. 1978), *cert. denied*, 439
    U.S. 1006 (1978). Pp. 94, 123.
United States v. Andrews, GCM No. 75–14, N.E. Jud. Cir. Navy-Marine
    Corp. Judiciary Phila. Pa. (1975). Pp. 76, 77.
United States v. Awkard, 597 F. 2d 667 (9th Cir. 1979), *cert. denied,* 444
    U.S. 885 (1979). Pp. 94, 122.
United States v. Barnard, 490 F.2d 907 (9th Cir. 1973), *cert. denied*, 416
    U.S. 959, 94 S. Ct. 1976, 40 L.Ed.2d 310 (1974). Pg. 95.
United States v. Brawner, 471 F.2d 969 (D.C. Cir. 1972). Pp. 141, 142,
    171, 172, 175, 180.
United States v. DeBetham, 348 F. Supp. 1377 (S.D. Cal. 1972). Pg. 62.
United States v. Kimberlin, 527 F. Supp. 1010 (S.D. Ind. 1981). Pg. 98.
United States v. Miller, 411 F.2d 825 (2d Cir. 1969), 296 F. Supp. 422
    (D.C. Conn. 1968). Pp. 90, 93, 96.
United States v. Narciso, 446 F. Supp. 252 (E.D. Mich. 1977). Pp. 77, 78,
    83.
United States v. Phillips, 515 F. Supp. 758 (E.D. Ky. 1981). Pg. 132.
Weeks v. United States, 232 U.S. 383 (1914). Pg. 111.
Wolf v. Colorado, 338 U.S. 25 (1949). Pg. 111.
Wyller et al. v. Fairchild Hiller Corporation, 503 F.2d 506 (9th Cir. 1974).
    Pp. 75, 76, 78, 94, 95.

References and Bibliography

Abrams, S. 1973. Validity of the polygraph, a bibliography. *Polygraph* 1, No. 2: 97–101.

Adams, J.A. 1976. *Learning and memory, an introduction.* Homewood, Ill.: Dorsey Press.

Alderman, E.M., and Barrette, J.A. 1982. Hypnosis on trial; a practical perspective on the application of forensic hypnosis in criminal cases. *Criminal Law Bulletin* 18: 5–37.

Allen, G.S. 1934. Hypnotism and its legal import. *Canadian Bar Review* 12, No. 1: 14–22.

Anonymous. 1982a. Witnesses questioned under hypnosis may not testify in Arizona trials. *Criminal Law Reporter* 30, No. 18: 2348–50.

Anonymous. 1982b. Witness whose memory was refreshed by hypnosis could testify. *Criminal Law Reporter,* 30, No. 17: 2335–36.

Anonymous. 1982c. Nebraska court thumbs its nose at hypnosis. *Law Enforcement News* 7, No. 1: 1–10.

Anonymous. 1982d. Perspective. *Law Officer's Bulletin* 6, No. 13: 78.

Anonymous. 1981a. Hypnotically refreshed testimony may not be admitted in Pennsylvania. *Criminal Law Reporter* 30, No. 7: 2133–35.

Anonymous. 1981b. Fair trial—hypnosis—defense request. *Criminal Law Reporter* 29, No. 22: 2486.

Anonymous. 1981c. New Jersey approves admission of hypnotically refreshed testimony. *Criminal Law Reporter* 29, No. 19: 2398–99.

Anonymous. 1981d. Evidence—hypnosis. *Criminal Law Reporter* 29, No. 12: 2251.

Anonymous. 1981e. Reliability of hypnotically refreshed memory must be established. *Criminal Law Reporter* 29, No. 5: 2103–04.

Anonymous. 1981f. Witness questioned under hypnosis may not later testify at trial. *Criminal Law Reporter* 28, No. 23: 2518–19.

Anonymous. 1981g. Evidence—hypnotically refreshed testimony. *Criminal Law Reporter* 28, No. 21: 2484.

Anonymous. 1981h. Evidence—hypnotically refreshed testimony. *Criminal Law Reporter* 28, No. 16: 2372.

Anonymous. 1981i. Investigative and forensic hypnosis. *Enforcement J.* 20, No. 1: 76–77.

Anonymous. 1981j. Witness: admissibility of testimony of witnesses who have been questioned while under hypnosis. *IACP Law Enforcement Legal Review* 111: 12.

Anonymous. 1981k. Witness: admissibility of testimony of witnesses who have been questioned while under hypnosis; safeguards. *IACP Law Enforcement Legal Review* 111: 13–14.

Anonymous. 1981l. Voluntariness; effect of prior hypnosis. *IACP Law Enforcement Legal Review* 104: 13.

Anonymous. 1981m. Training key #306 looks at investigative hypnosis. *Police Chief* 48, No. 10: 13.

Anonymous. 1980a. Judge should have let defense question witness about his hypnosis. *Criminal Law Reporter* 28, No. 12: 2275–76.

Anonymous. 1980b. Evidence obtained by hypnosis suffers from reliability problems. *Criminal Law Reporter* 27, No. 11: 2242–43.

Anonymous. 1980c. Hypnosis may be used to refresh victim's memory of assailant. *Criminal Law Reporter* 27, No. 10: 2209–10.

Anonymous. 1980d. Hypnosis evidence: admissibility; safeguards. *IACP Law Enforcement Legal Review* 101: 9.

Anonymous. 1980e. Investigative hypnosis; its operation. *IACP Training Key*, 13, No. 307: 1–6.

Anonymous. 1980f. Investigative hypnosis: its function. *IACP Training Key* 13, No. 306: 1–6.

Anonymous. 1979a. Evidence—hypnosis. *Criminal Law Reporter* 26, No. 8: 2168.

Anonymous. 1979b. Hypnosis: can it aid in security investigations? *Security Letter* 9, No. 18: 3.

Anonymous. 1978a. Criminal justice—hypnotized witnesses may remember too much. *American Bar Association J.* 64: 187.

Anonymous. 1978b. Witnesses—hypnosis. *Criminal Law Reporter* 23, No. 19: 2435.

Anonymous. 1978c. Witnesses—hypnosis. *Criminal Law Reporter* 23, No. 16: 2368–69.

Anonymous. 1978d. LAPD uses hypnosis as crime fighting technique. *Security Management* 22, No. 9: 97.

Anonymous. 1978e. Hypnosis as a police tool. *Security World* 15, No. 1: 11.

Anonymous. 1977a. LAPD hypnosis program earns award. *Systems, Technology and Science for Law Enforcement and Security* 9, No. 7: 2.

Anonymous. 1977b. LAPD to provide hypnosis training to other departments. *Training Aids Digest* 2, No. 11: 4.

Anonymous. 1977c. Los Angeles police cited for hypnosis work. *Trial* 13, No. 2: 15.

Anonymous. 1975. Hypnosis: new tool for fighting crime. *Law Enforcement J.* 5, No. 4: 2.

Anonymous. 1969. Hypnosis as a defense tactic. *Toledo Law Review* (1969) 691–708.

Antitch, J.L.S. 1967. Legal regulations concerning the practice of hypnosis. *J. of American Society of Psychosomatic Dentistry and Medicine* 14: 3–12.

Arons, H. 1977. *Hypnosis in criminal investigation.* So. Orange, N.J.: Power Pub.

As, A. 1962. The recovery of forgotten language knowledge through hypnotic age regression: a case report. *American J. of Clinical Hypnosis* 5: 21–29.

Asch, G.B. 1981. Evidence—hypnotically induced testimony: the pendulum swings towards admissibility. *Suffolk U.L. Rev.* 15: 1372–84.

Ashman, A. 1980. Criminal law—testimony by hypnosis. *American Bar Association J.* 66: 1291.

Associated Press. 1979. Cautious use of investigative hypnosis is growing. *New York Times,* August 19, 1979: 49.

Ault, R.L., Jr. 1980. Hypnosis, the FBI's team approach. *FBI Law Enforcement Bulletin* 49, No. 1: 5–8.

⸻. 1979. FBI guidelines for use of hypnosis. *International J. of Clinical and Experimental Hypnosis* 27, No. 4: 449–451.

Baddeley, A.D. 1966. Short term memory for word sequences as a function of acoustic, semantic and formal similarity. *Quarterly J. of Experimental Psychology* 18: 362–65.

Bailey, D.B., and Shapiro, S.L. 1982. Hypnosis: should hypnotically induced testimony be excluded? *Washburn Law J.* 21: 607–25.

Barber, T.X. 1965. The effects of "hypnosis" on learning and recall: a methodological critique. *J. of Clinical Psychology* 21: 19–25.

⸻. 1962a. Toward a theory of "hypnotic" behavior: the "hypnotically induced dream." *J. of Nervous and Mental Disease* 135: 206–21.

⸻. 1962b. Hypnotic age regression: a critical review. *Psychosomatic Medicine* 24, No. 3: 286–99.

⸻. 1961a. Antisocial and criminal acts induced by "hypnosis": a review of experimental and clinical findings. *Archives of General Psychiatry* 5: 301–12.

⸻. 1961b. Experimental evidence for a theory of hypnotic behavior. Vol. II. Experimental controls in hypnotic age regression. *International J. of Clinical and Experimental Hypnosis* 9, No. 4: 181–93.

Barber, T.X., and Calverley, D.S. 1966. Effects on recall of hypnotic induction, motivational suggestions, and suggested regressions: a methodological and experimental analysis. *J. of Abnormal Psychology* 71: 169–80.

Barr, D., and Spurgeon, L. 1982. Testimony by previously hypnotized witnesses: should it be admissible? *Idaho Law Rev.* 18: 111–32.

Bartlett, F.C. 1932. *Remembering: a study in experimental and social psychology.* Cambridge, England: Cambridge University Press.

Bazelon, D.L. 1974. Psychiatrists and the adversary process. *Scientific America* 230, No. 6: 18–23.

Bell, C. 1895. Hypnotism and the law. *Medico–Legal J.* 13: 47–56.

Berger, N. 1982. Evidence—hypnotically induced testimony admissible if reasonably likely to result in recall comparable to normal memory. *Seton Hall Law Rev.* 12: 404–06.

Best, H.L., and Michaels, R.M. 1954. Living out "future" experiences under hypnosis. *Science* 120: 1077.

Block, E.B. 1976. *Hypnosis—a new tool in crime detection.* New York: David McKay Co.

Bloom, R.F. 1972. Review of H. Arons, *Hypnosis in criminal investigation. International J. of Clinical and Experimental Hypnosis.* 20, No. 2: 132–34.

Bodine, L. 1981. Hypnosis, fingerprints and the Lindberg baby. *National Law J.* 3: 39.

Bodine, L., and Lavine, D. 1980. Hypnosis runs into court wall: 2 key state rulings bar testimony induced by "unreliable" technique. *National Law J.* 2: 1.

Bousfield, W.A. 1953. The occurrence of clustering in the recall of randomly arranged associates. *J. of General Psychology* 49: 229–40.

Bower, G.H. 1970. Organizational factors in memory. *Cognitive Psychology* 1: 18–46.

Boyd, J.A. 1973. Evidence—admissibility of the neutron activation analysis test. *St. Louis Law J.* 18, No. 2: 235–55.

Brenman, M. 1942. Experiments in the hypnotic production of anti-social and self-injurious behavior. *Psychiatry* 5: 49–61.

Brody, J.E. 1980. Hypnotism vs. crime: a powerful weapon—or an abused tool? *New York Times*, October 14, 1980: c1, c2.

Brooks, C.L. 1981. Hypnosis: the state of the art in Arizona. *Arizona Law Rev.* 23: 1475–86.

Brunn, J.T. 1968. Retrograde amnesia in a murder suspect. *American J. of Clinical Hypnosis* 10, No. 3: 209–13.

Bryan, W.J., Jr. 1962. *Legal aspects of hypnosis.* Springfield, Ill.: Charles C. Thomas.

Burrows, G.D. 1981. Forensic aspects of hypnosis. *Austl. J. of Forensic Science* 13: 120–25.

Ciollo, R. 1978. Teich hypnosis tape is an issue in trial. *Newsday*, March 13, 1978.

Coe, W.C. 1977. The problem of relevance versus ethics in researching hypnosis and antisocial conduct. *Annals of New York Academy of Sciences* 296: 90–104.

Coe, W.C., Kobayashi, K., and Howard, M.L. 1972a. An approach toward isolating factors that influence antisocial conduct in hypnosis. *International J. of Clinical and Experimental Hypnosis* 20, No. 2: 118–31.

————. 1972b. More on experimental design in evaluating the influence of hypnosis in antisocial conduct. *Proceedings, 80th Annual Convention of the American Psychological Association* 861–62.

Coe, W.C., and Ryken, K. 1979. Hypnosis and risks to human subjects. *American Psychologist* 34, No. 8: 673–81.

Cohn, A., and Udolf, R. 1979. *The criminal justice system and its psychology.* New York: Van Nostrand Reinhold Co.

Conn, J.H. 1972. Is hypnosis really dangerous? *International J. of Clinical and Experimental Hypnosis* 20, No. 2: 61–79.

Conour, W.F. 1980. Criminal justice notes—hypnosis. *Res Gestae* 24: 370–72.

Conrad, R. 1972. Speech and reading. In J.F. Kavanagh, and I.G. Mattingly, eds. *Language by ear and by eye: the relationship between speech and reading.* Cambridge, Mass.: MIT Press.

Cooper, L.M., and London, P. 1973. Reactivation of memory by hypnosis and suggestion. *International J. of Clinical and Experimental Hypnosis* 21, No. 4: 312–23.

Crasilneck, H.B., and Michael, C.M. 1957. Performance on the Bender under hypnotic age regression. *J. of Abnormal and Social Psychology* 54: 319.

Creager, R.T. 1981. The admissibility of testimony influenced by hypnosis. *Virginia Law Rev.* 67: 1203–33.

Danto, B.L. 1979. The use of brevital sodium in police investigation. *Police Chief* 46, No. 5: 53–55.

Darwin, C.J., Turvey, M.T., and Crowder, R.G. 1972. An auditory analogue of the Sperling partial report procedure: evidence for brief auditory storage. *Cognitive Psychology* 3: 255–67.

Das, J.P. 1961. Learning and recall under hypnosis and in the waking state: a comparison. *Archives of General Psychiatry* 4: 517–21.

Davidson, P.A. 1976. Refreshing the memory of a witness through hypnosis. *UCLA–Alaska Law Rev.* 5: 266–83.

Davis, R.E. 1982. The admissibility of hypnotically induced recollection. *Ky. Law J.* 70: 187–202.

Davis, R.P. 1960. Counsel's right in consulting with accused as client to be accompanied by psychiatrist, psychologist, hypnotist or similar practitioner. *ALR 2d* 72: 1120–21.

Day, J.E. 1980. Use of investigative hypnosis. *Detective* 8, No. 2: 6–10.

Dhanens, T.P., and Lundy, R.M. 1975. Hypnotic and waking suggestions and recall. *International J. of Clinical and Experimental Hypnosis* 23, No. 1: 68–79.

Diamond, B.L. 1980. Inherent problems in the use of pretrial hynosis on a prospective witness. *California Law Rev.* 68, No. 2: 313–49.

Dilloff, N.J. 1977. The admissibility of hypnotically influenced testimony. *Ohio Northern University Law Rev.* 4, No. 1: 1–23.

Di Vesta, F.J., Ingersoll, G., and Sunshine, P. 1971. A factor analysis of imagery tests. *J. of Verbal Learning and Verbal Behavior* 10: 471–79.

Dorcus, R.M. 1960. Recall under hypnosis of amnestic events. *International J. of Clinical and Experimental Hypnosis* 8: 57–60.

Douce, R.G. 1979. Hypnosis: a scientific aid in crime detection. *Police Chief* 46, No. 5: 60, 61, 80.

Edmonston, W.E., Jr. 1960. An experimental investigation of hypnotic age regression. *American J. of Clinical Hypnosis* 3: 127.

Erickson, M.H. 1939. An experimental investigation of the possible antisocial use of hypnosis. *Psychiatry* 2: 391–414.

Estabrooks, G.H. 1951. The possible antisocial use of hypnotism. *Personality: Symposia on Topical Issues*, 1: 294–99.

Falick, P. 1968. The lie detector and the right to privacy. *N.Y. State Bar J.* 40, No. 2: 102–10.

Feldman, S.L. 1981. Hypnosis: look me in the eyes and tell me that's admissible. *Barrister* 4, No. 6: 4–6, 52–54.

Fowler, W.L. 1961. Hypnosis and learning. *International J. of Clinical and Experimental Hypnosis* 9: 223–32.

Fromm, E. 1975. Self-hypnosis: a new area of research. *Psychotherapy: Theory, Research and Practice* 12, No. 3: 295–301.

Galton, F. 1883. *Inquiries into human faculty and its development.* London: Macmillan.

Gibbons, D.E. 1976. Hypnotic vs. hyperempiric induction procedures: an experimental comparison. *Perceptual and Motor Skills* 42, No. 3: 834.

Gibson, H.B. 1982. The use of hypnosis in police investigations. *Bulletin of the British Psychological Society* 35: 138–42.

Gilbert, J.E., and Barber, T.X. 1972. Effects of hypnotic induction, motivational suggestions, and level of suggestibility on cognitive performance. *International J. of Clinical and Experimental Hypnosis* 20, No. 3: 156–68.

Gillette, P. 1981. Hypnosis on trial: while the state supreme court deliberates, the debate continues over its validity as a courtroom tool. *Cal. Law* 1, No. 5: 22–23, 65–66, 77.

Gleitman, H. 1981. *Psychology.* New York: W.W. Norton, 271–311.

———. 1971. Forgetting of long-term memories in animals. In W.K. Honig and P.H.R. James, eds. *Animal Memory.* New York: Academic Press, 2–46.

Gold, A.D. 1980. Hypnosis-induced testimony—voice-prints. *Criminal Law Quarterly* 22: 178–81.

Graham, E.L. 1980. Hypnosis as a security tool. *Security Management* 24, No. 9: 18–22.

Gravitz, M.A. 1983 (in press). An early case of investigative hypnosis. *American J. of Clinical Hypnosis.*

———. 1980. Discussion at symposium on forensic hypnosis at 22nd annual meeting of American Society of Clinical Hypnosis in November 1979 in San Francisco. *American J. of Clinical Hypnosis* 23, No. 2: 103–11.

Griffin, G.R. 1980. Hypnosis: Towards a logical approach in using hypnosis in law enforcement agencies. *J. of Police Science and Administration* 8, No. 4: 385–89.

Griffiths, G.L. 1979. Investigative and forensic hypnosis. *Detective* 7, No. 3: 14–20.

Gros, R.E. 1980. Clinical hypnosis. *Fire and Arson Investigator* 31, No. 1: 55–58.

Gurley, K. 1980. Hypnosis a dream of a crime solver. *Law Enforcement J.* 9, No. 10: 7.

Gurston, S.A. 1934. Hypnotism and its legal import. *Canadian Bar Rev.* 12, No. 1: 14–22.

Hammer, E.F. 1954. Posthypnotic suggestion and test performance. *J. of Clinical and Experimental Hypnosis* 2: 178–85.

Hammerschlag, H.E. 1957. *Hypnotism and crime.* Hollywood, Calif.: Wilshire Book Co.

Hartland, J. 1974. An alleged case of criminal assault upon a married woman under hypnosis. *American J. of Clinical Hypnosis* 16, No. 3: 188–98.

Haward, L., and Ashworth, A. 1980. Some problems of evidence obtained by hypnosis. *Criminal Law Rev.* 469–85.

Herman, L. 1964. The use of hypno-induced statements in criminal cases. *Ohio State Law J.* 25, No. 1: 1–59.

Hibbard, W.S., and Worring, R.W. 1981. *Forensic hypnosis: The practical application of hypnosis in criminal investigations.* Springfield, Ill.: Charles C. Thomas.

Hibler, N.S. 1979. The use of hypnosis in United States Air Force investigations. Paper presented at the American Psychological Association 87th annual convention, New York City, September 1979.

Hilgard, E.R. 1973a. A neo-dissociation interpretation of pain reduction in hypnosis. *Psychological Rev.* 80: 396–411.

———. 1973b. *Dissociation revisited.* In M. Henle, J. James, and J. Sullivan, eds., *Historical conceptions of psychology.* New York: Springer Pub. Co., 205–19.

. 1968. *The experience of hypnosis.* New York: Harcourt, Brace and World.

Hilgard, E.R., and Loftus, E.F. 1979. Effective interrogation of the eyewitness. *International J. of Clinical and Experimental Hypnosis* 27, No. 4: 342–57.

Hilgard, E.R., and Marquis, D.G. 1961. (Revised by Kimble, G.A.) *Conditioning and Learning* 2d Ed. New York: Appleton-Century-Crofts.

Hilgard, J.R. 1974. Sequelae to hypnosis. *International J. of Clinical and Experimental Hypnosis* 22, No. 4: 281–98.

Hilgard, J.R., Hilgard, E.R., and Newman, M.F. 1961. Sequelae to hypnotic induction with special reference to earlier chemical anesthesia. *J. Nervous and Mental Disease* 133: 461–78.

Hirschberg, H.G. 1962. Validity of legislation regulating licensing or prescribing for certification of psychologists. *ALR 2d* 81: 791–93.

Holden, C. 1980. Forensic use of hypnosis on the increase. *Science* 208, No. 4451: 1443–44.

Houston, J.P. 1981. *Fundamentals of learning and memory.* New York: Academic Press.

Hunt, S.M. 1979. Hypnosis as obedience behavior. *British J. of Social and Clinical Psychology* 18, No. 1: 21–27.

Huse, B. 1930. Does the hypnotic trance favor the recall of faint memories? *J. of Experimental Psychology* 13: 519–29.

Ikemi, Y., and Nakagawa, S. 1962. A psychosomatic study of contagious dermatitis. *Kyushu J. of Medical Science* 13: 335–50.

Illovsky, J. 1963. An experience with group hypnosis in reading disability in primary behavior disorders. *J. Genetic Psychology* 102: 61–67.

International Society of Hypnosis. 1979. Resolution adopted August 1979. *International J. of Clinical and Experimental Hypnosis* 27, No. 4: 453.

Jaffe, J.R. 1980. Hypnosis—its use and limitations in police and criminal investigations. *Police J.* 53, No. 3: 233–39.

Jenkins, J.A. 1980. Hypnosis: a new technique in crime detection. *Student lawyer* 26, No. 4: 24, 25, 33, 34.

Jenkins, J.G., and Dallenbach, K.M. 1924. Obliviscence during sleep and waking. *American J. of Psychology* 35: 605–12.

Johnson, J.A., Jr. 1981. Hypnosis as a criminal technique in the Department of Defense. *A.F.L. Rev.* 22: 20–58.

Jordan, J.D. 1982. Evaluating the admissibility of the testimony of previously hypnotized witnesses. *Okla. B. J.* 53, No. 16: 1023–28.

Kadish, M.J., Brofman, R.A., Peskin, S., and Baccus, L.T. 1981. The polygraph, hypnosis, truth drugs and the psychological stress evaluator: admissibility in a criminal trial. *American J. Trial Advocacy* 4: 593–614.

Kassinger, E.T. 1979. A review of workshops at the IACUSD conference at Hot Springs, Arkansas June 24–28, 1979. *Campus Law Enforcement* 9, No. 4: 10–14.

Kaufman, M.R. 1958. Medical uses of hypnosis. *J. of American Medical Association* 168: 186–89.

Kennedy, A. 1957. The medical use of hypnotism. *British Medical J.* 1: 1317–19.

Kiesler, C.A. 1977. The training of psychiatrists and psychologists. *American Psychologist* 32, No. 2: 107–108.

Killmier, T.R. 1981. Evidence obtained by hypnosis. *Criminal Law Rev.* 518–19.

Kleinhauz, M., Horowitz, I., and Tobin, Y. 1977. The use of hypnosis in police investigation: a preliminary communication. *J. of Forensic Science Society* 17, Nos. 2 and 3: 77–80.

Kline, M.V. 1979. Defending the mentally ill: the insanity defense and the role of forensic hypnosis. *International J. of Clinical and Experimental Hypnosis* 27, No. 4: 375–401.

———. 1976. Dangerous aspects of the practice of hypnosis and the need for legislative regulation. *Clinical Psychologist* 29, No. 2: 3–6.

———. 1972. The production of antisocial behavior through hypnosis: new clinical data. *International J. of Clinical and Experimental Hypnosis* 20, No. 2: 80–94.

———. 1958. The dynamics of hypnotically induced antisocial behavior. *J. Psychology* 45: 239–45.

Kroger, W.S., and Douce, R.G. 1980. Forensic uses of hypnosis. *American J. of Clinical Hypnosis* 23, No. 2: 86–93.

———. 1979. Hypnosis in criminal investigation. *International J. of Clinical and Experimental Hypnosis* 27, No. 4: 358–74.

Krosney, M.S. 1981. Israeli police keep pace with newest detection devices. *Police Chief* 48, No. 5: 34–35.

Ladd, G.T. 1902. Legal aspects of hypnotism. *Yale Law J.* 11, No. 4: 173–94.

Leask, J., Haber, R.N., and Haber, R.B. 1969. Eidetic imagery in children II: Longitudinal and experimental results. *Psychonomic Monograph Supplements* 3 (Whole No. 35): 25–48.

Lehan, J.M. 1970. Hypnotism as a criminal defense. *California Western Law Rev.* 6: 303–15.

Levinthal, C.F. 1979. *The physiological approach in psychology*. Englewood Cliffs, N.J.: Prentice-Hall, p. 398.

Levitt, E.E. 1981. The use of hypnosis to "freshen" the memory of witnesses or victims. *Trial* 17, No. 4: 56–59, 63.

Levitt, E.E., Aronoff, G., Morgan, C.D., Overley, T.M., and Parrish, M.J. 1975. Testing the coercive powers of hypnosis: objectionable acts.

International J. of Clinical and Experimental Hypnosis 23, No. 1: 59–67.

Levitt, E.E., Overley, T.M., and Rubinstein, D. 1975. The objectionable act as a mechanism for testing the coercive power of the hypnotic state. *American J. of Clinical Hypnosis* 17, No. 4: 263–66.

Levy, S.S. 1955. Hypnosis and legal immutability. *J. Crim. L. C. and P. S.* 46: 333–46.

Lieber, E. 1981. Trial testimony of hypnotized witness rejected by D.C.A. *L.A. Daily J.* 94: 1.

Loftus, E.F. 1975. Leading questions and the eyewitness report. *Cognitive Psychology* 7: 560–72.

Loftus, E.F., and Zanni, G. 1975. Eyewitness testimony. The influence of the wording of a question. *Bulletin of the psychonomic Society* 5: 86–88.

London, P., Convant, M., and Davison, G.C. 1966. More hypnosis in the unhypnotizable: effects of hypnosis and exhortation on rote learning. *J. Personality* 34: 71–79.

Mandler, G. 1967. *Organization and memory*. In K.W. Spence and J.T. Spence, eds., *The psychology of learning and motivation,* Vol. 1. New York: Academic Press, 327–72.

Mandler, G., and Pearlstone, Z. 1966. Free and constrained concept learning and subsequent recall. *J. of Verbal Learning and Verbal Behavior* 5: 126–31.

Manolis, C.G. 1982. The admissibility of polygraph and hypnotic evidence to test the credibility of a witness. *Det. C. L. Rev.* 97–125.

Marcuse, F.L. 1953. Antisocial behavior and hypnosis. *J. Clinical and Experimental Hypnosis* 1: 18–20.

Margolin, E. 1981. Hypnosis-enhanced testimony: valid evidence or prosecutor's tool? *Trial* 17, No. 10: 42–46.

Marshall, J. 1969. The evidence—do we see and hear what is? Or do our senses lie? *Psychology Today* 2, No. 9: 48–52.

Matlosz, H.S., Jr. 1977. Hypnosis as an investigative aid. *Detective* 6, No. 2: 9–15.

McCord, H. 1962. A note on attitudes for and against being hypnotized. *British J. of Medical Hypnotism* 13, No. 2: 20–22.

McCranie, E.J., and Crasilneck, H.B. 1955. The conditioned reflex in hypnotic age regression. *J. of Clinical and Experimental Psychopathology* 16: 120.

McLaughlin, J.A. 1981. Hypnosis—its role and current admissibility in the criminal law. *Willamette Law Rev.* 17: 665–92.

McPherson, D. 1982. The use of hypnosis in police investigation. *Bulletin of the British Psychological Society* 35: 253.

Miller, G.A. 1956. The magical number seven plus or minus two: some limits on our capacity for processing information. *Psychological Review* 63: 81–97.

Millwee, S.C. 1979. The hypnosis unit in today's law enforcement. *Police Chief* 46, No. 5: 65–70.

Minami, H., and Dallenback, K.M. 1946. The effect of activity upon learning and retention in the cockroach. *American J. of Psychology* 59: 1–58.

Miron, M.S. 1980. Issues of psychological evidence: discussion. *Annals of N.Y. Academy of Science* 347: 100–07.

Mishkin, B.D. 1979. Hypnosis—from sideshows to crime fighting. *Law Enforcement J.* 8, No. 10: 4, 9.

Mitchell, M.B. 1932. Retroactive inhibition and hypnosis. *J. General Psychology* 7: 343–59.

Monaghan, F.J. 1981. Warning: doctors may be dangerous to the health of your investigation. *Police Chief* 47, No. 8: 73–76.

Monaghan, F.J. 1980. *Hypnosis in criminal investigation.* Dubuque, Iowa: Kendall/Hunt.

Monaghan, J.R. 1962. Hypnotism as the illegal practice of medicine. *ALR 2d* 85: 1128–30.

Monrose, R. 1978. Justice with glazed eyes—the growing use of hypnotism in law enforcement. *Juris Doctor* 54–57.

Morton, J. 1981. The use of hypnosis in criminal cases. *New L. J.* 131:1109.

Mutter, C. B. 1980. Critique of videotape presentation on forensic hypnotic regression: "the case of Dora." *American J. of Clinical Hypnosis* 23, No. 2: 99–101.

———. 1979. Regressive hypnosis and the polygraph: a case study. *American J. of Clinical Hypnosis* 22, No. 1: 47–50.

O'Brien, R.M., Kramer, C.E., Chiglinsky, A.B., Stevens, G.E., Nunan, L.J., and Fritzo, J.A. 1977. Moral development examined through hypnotic and task motivated age regression. *American J. of Clinical Hypnosis* 19, No. 4: 209–13.

O'Connell, D.N., Shor, R.E., and Orne, M.T. 1970. Hypnotic age regression: an empirical and methodological analysis. *J. Abnormal Psychology Monograph Supp.* 76: 3.

O'Regan, R.S. 1978. Automatism and insanity under the Australian state criminal codes. *Australian Law J.* 52, No. 4: 208–14.

Orne, M.T. 1982. Seminar on the use of hypnosis in treatment at the Institute of Pennsylvania Hospital. Philadelphia, January 29, 30, and 31, 1982.

———. 1979. The use and misuse of hypnosis in court. *International J. of Clinical and Experimental Hypnosis* 27, No. 4: 311–41.

_____. 1972. Can a hypnotized subject be compelled to carry out otherwise unacceptable behavior? *International J. of Clinical and Experimental Hypnosis* 20, No. 2: 101–17.

_____. 1965. Undesirable effects of hypnosis: the determinants and management. *International J. of Clinical and Experimental Hypnosis* 23, No. 4: 226–37.

_____. 1962a. *Antisocial behavior and hypnosis: problems of control and validation in empirical studies.* In G.H. Estabrooks, ed., *Hypnosis: current problems.* New York: Harper and Row, 137–92.

_____. 1962b. *Hypnotically induced hallucinations.* In L.J. West, ed., *Hallucinations.* New York: Grune and Stratton, 211–19.

_____. 1959. The nature of hypnosis: artifact and essence. *J. of Abnormal and Social Psychology* 58, No. 3: 277–99.

_____. 1951. The mechanisms of hypnotic age regression: an experimental study. *J. of Abnormal and Social Psychology* 46, No. 2: 213–25.

Orne, M.T., and Evans, F.J. 1965. Social control in the psychological experiment: antisocial behavior and hypnosis. *J. of Personality and Social Psychology* 1, No. 3: 189–200.

Packer, E. 1979. A study of the expert opinion of a panel of hypnotherapists on the use of hypnosis in the courts. *Dissertation Abstracts International* 40, No. 4B: 1907.

Packer, I.K. 1981. The use of hypnotic techniques in the evaluation of criminal defendants. *J. Psychiatry and Law* 9: 313–27.

Palmer, T.L., and Sims, J. 1970. Hypno-induced statements; safeguards for admissibility. *Law and Social Order* 99: 97–120.

Parker, P.D., and Barber, T.X. 1964. Hypnosis, task-motivating instructions and learning performance. *J. of Abnormal and Social Psychology* 69:499–504.

Parrish, M.J. 1974. Moral predisposition and hypnotic influence of "immoral" behavior: an exploratory study. *American J. of Clinical Hypnosis* 17, No. 2: 115–24.

Paterson, A.S. 1974. Hypnosis as an adjunct to the treatment of alcoholics and drug addicts. *International J. of Offender Therapy and Comparative Criminology* 18, No. 1: 40–45.

Pelanda, K.L. 1981. The probative value of testimony from the hypnotically refreshed recollection. *Akron Law Rev.* 14: 609–31.

Penfield, W. 1958. *The excitable cortex in conscious man.* Liverpool, England: Liverpool: Liverpool University Press.

Perry, C. 1979. Hypnotic coercion and compliance to it: a review of evidence presented in a legal case. *International J. of Clinical and Experimental Hypnosis* 27, No. 3: 187–218.

Perry, C., and Chisholm, W. 1973. Hypnotic age regression and the Ponzo and Poggendorff illusions. *International J. of Clinical and Experimental Hypnosis* 21, No. 3: 192–204.

Peterson, L.B., and Peterson, M.J. 1959. Short term retention of individual items. *J. of Experimental Psychology* 58: 193–98.

Platonow, K.I. 1933. On the objective proof of the experimental personality age regression. *J. General Psychology* 9: 190.

Posluns, D. 1972. Legal aspects of psychology. *Ontario Psychologist* 4, No. 2: 78–91.

Postman, L. 1969. *Mechanisms of interference in forgetting.* In G.A. Talland and N.C. Waugh, eds., *The pathology of memory.* New York: Academic Press, 195–210.

Putnam, W.H. 1979a. Some precautions regarding the use of hypnosis in criminal investigations. *Police Chief* 46, No. 5: 62–64.

———. 1979b. Hypnosis and distortions in eyewitness memory. *International J. of Clinical and Experimental Hypnosis* 27, No. 4: 437–48.

Raginsky, B.B. 1969. Hypnotic recall of an aircrash cause. *International J. of Clinical and Experimental Hypnosis* 27, No. 1: 1–19.

Reiff, R., and Scheerer, M. 1959. *Memory and hypnotic age regression: developmental aspects of cognitive function explored through hypnosis.* New York: International Universities Press.

Reiser, M. 1980. *Handbook of investigative hypnosis.* Los Angeles, Calif.: LEHI Pub. Co.

———. 1978. Hypnosis and its uses in law enforcement. *Police J.* 5, No. 1: 24–33.

———. 1976. Hypnosis as a tool in criminal investigation. *Police Chief* 43, No. 11: 36, 39, 40.

———. 1974. Hypnosis as an aid in a homicide investigation. *American J. of Clinical Hypnosis* 17, No. 2: 84–87.

Reiser, M., and Nielson, M. 1980. Investigative hypnosis: a developing specialty. *American J. of Clinical Hypnosis* 23, No. 2: 75–77.

Reiter, P.J. 1958. *Antisocial or criminal acts and hypnosis: a case study.* Springfield, Ill.: Charles C. Thomas.

Reitman, J.S. 1974. Without surreptitious rehearsal, information in short term memory decays. *J. of Verbal Learning and Verbal Behavior* 13: 365–77.

Restak, R.M. 1982. Will hypnotism entrance the police? *Newsday,* Nov. 23, p. 19.

Rieber, R.W., and Vetter, H.J. 1978. *The psychological foundations of criminal justice.* Vol. I. New York: John Jay Press.

Robinson, L.W. 1979. Hypnosis: an investigative tool. *Campus Law Enforcement* 9, No. 4: 15–20.

Robitscher, J.B. 1974. Psychosurgery and other somatic means of altering behavior. *Bulletin of American Academy of Psychiatry and the Law* 2, No. 1: 7–33.

Rosenhan, D., and London, P. 1963. Hypnosis in the unhypnotizable: a study in rote learning. *J. of Experimental Psychology* 65: 30–34.

Rosenthal, B.G. 1944. Hypnotic recall of material learned under anxiety and non-anxiety producing conditions. *J. Experimental Psychology* 34: 369–89.

Rothblatt, H.B. 1981. The mental probe continued—hypnosis and witness preparation. *American J. Trial Advocacy* 4: 615–20.

Rowland, L.W. 1939. Will hypnotized persons try to harm themselves or others? *J. of Abnormal and Social Psychology* 34: 114–17.

Russell, W.R. 1959. *Brain, memory and learning: a neurologist's view.* Oxford, England: Oxford University Press.

Ryken, K., and Coe, W.C. 1977. Sequelae to hypnosis in perspective. Paper presented to the annual convention of the American Psychological Association, San Francisco, August 1977.

Salzberg, H.C. 1977. The hypnotic interview in crime detection. *American J. of Clinical Hypnosis* 19, No. 4: 255–58.

_____. 1960. The effects of hypnotic, posthypnotic and waking suggestions on performance using tasks varied in complexity. *International J. of Clinical and Experimental Hypnosis* 8: 251–58.

Sanders, G.S., and Simmons, W.L. 1983 (forthcoming). The use of hypnosis to enhance eyewitness accuracy: does it work? *J. of Applied Psych.*

Sannito, T., and Mueller, P. 1980. The use of hypnosis in a double manslaughter defense. *Trial Diplomacy J.* 3: 30–35.

Sarbin, T.R. 1950. Mental changes in experimental regression. *J. Personality* 19: 221.

Sarbin, T.R., and Farberow, N.L. 1952. Contributions to role taking theory: a clinical study of self and role. *J. Abnormal and Social Psychology* 47: 117.

Sarno, G.G. 1979. Admissibility of hypnotic evidence at criminal trial. *ALR 3d* 92: 442–68.

Schachtel, E. 1949. On memory and childhood amnesia. In P. Mullahy, ed., *A study of interpersonal relations.* New York: Hermitage, 3–49.

Schafer, D.W., and Rubio, R. 1978. Hypnosis to aid the recall of witnesses. *International J. of Clinical and Experimental Hypnosis* 26, No. 2: 81–91.

Schneck, J.M. 1977. Hypnotic elucidation of isolation and displacement following a sexual assault. *J. of Clinical Psychiatry* 38, No. 11: 934–35.

_____. 1967. Hypnoanalytic study of a false confession. *International J. of Clinical and Experimental Hypnosis* 15, No. 1: 11–18.

Schulman, R.E., and London, P. 1963. Hypnosis and verbal learning. *J. Abnormal and Social Psychology* 67: 363–70.

Schwed, L. 1981. Down the primrose path. *Soc. Act. and Law* 7: 27–29.

Schwitzgebel, R.L., and Schwitzgebel, R.K. 1980. *Law and psychological practice*. New York: John Wiley and Sons.

Scott, E.M. 1981. Hypnosis in criminal psychiatry. *International J. of Offender Therapy and Comparative Criminology* 25: 11–22.

————. 1979. Paranoid prisoners. *International J. of Offender Therapy and Comparative Criminology* 23, No. 1: 25–34.

————. 1977. Hypnosis in the courtroom. *American J. of Clinical Hypnosis* 19, No. 3: 163–65.

Sears, A.B. 1954. A comparison of hypnotic and waking recall. *J. of Clinical and Experimental Hypnosis* 2: 296–304.

Shaul, R.D. 1978. Eyewitness testimony and hypnotic hypermnesia. *Dissertation Abstracts International* 39, No. 5B: 2521.

Sloan, G.E. 1924. Hypnotism as a defense to crime. *Medico-legal J.* 41: 37–49.

Society for Clinical and Experimental Hypnosis. 1979. Resolution adopted October 1978. *International J. of Clinical and Experimental Hypnosis* 27, No. 4: 452.

Solomon, J. 1952. Hypnotism, suggestibility and the law. *Nebraska Law Rev.* 575–96.

Spector, R.G., and Foster, T.E. 1979. The utility of hypno-induced statements in the trial process: reflections on *People* v. *Smrekar*. *Loy. Chi. Law J.* 10: 691–707.

————. 1977. Admissibility of hypnotic statements: is the law of evidence susceptible? *Ohio State Law J.* 38, No. 3: 567–613.

Sperling, G. 1960. The information available in brief visual presentations. *Psychological Monographs* 74 (whole No. 11).

Spiegel, H. 1980. Hypnosis and evidence: help or hindrance? *Annals of N.Y. Academy of Science* 347: 73–85.

Spiegel, H., Shor, J., and Fishman, S. 1945. An hypnotic ablation technique for the study of personality development. *Psychosomatic Medicine* 7: 273.

Stalnaker, J.M., and Riddle, E.E. 1932. The effect of hypnosis on long delayed recall. *J. of General Psychology* 6: 429–40.

Steele, H.M. 1895. Hypnotism and justice. *North American Rev.* 116: 503–05.

Sternberg, S. 1969. Memory-scanning: mental processes revealed by reaction time experiments. *American Scientist* 57: 421–57.

Stevenson, J.H. 1976. Effect of posthypnotic dissociation on the performance of interfering tasks. *J. of Abnormal Psychology* 85, No. 4: 398–407.

Stratton, J.G. 1980. Psychological services for police. *J. of Police Science and Administration* 8, No. 1: 31–39.

————. 1977. The use of hypnosis in law enforcement criminal investigations: a pilot program. *J. of Police Science and Administration* 5, No. 4: 399–406.

Sudduth, W.X. 1895. Hypnotism and crime. *Medico-Legal J.* 13: 239–44, 250–51.

Swain, W.P. 1961. Hypnotism and the law. *Vanderbilt Law Rev.* 14: 1509–24.

Swiercinsky, D., and Coe, W.C. 1971. The effect of "alert" hypnosis and hypnotic responsiveness on reading comprehension. *International J. of Clinical and Experimental Hypnosis* 19, No. 3: 146–53.

————. 1970. Hypnosis, hypnotic responsiveness, and learning meaningful material. *International J. of Clinical and Experimental Hypnosis* 18, No. 3: 217–22.

Teitelbaum, M. 1965. *Hypnosis induction techniques.* 4th ed. Springfield, Ill.: Charles C. Thomas.

————. 1963a. Admissibility of hypnotically adduced evidence and the Arthur Nebb Case. *St. Louis Law J.* 8: 205–14.

————. 1963b. Personal injury law and hypnotism. *Medical Trial Technique Quarterly* 95–101.

Teten, H.D. 1979. A discussion of the precepts surrounding the use of hypnosis as an investigative aid by the Federal Bureau of Investigation. Paper presented at the American Psychological Association, 87th Annual Convention, New York City, September 1979.

Thigpen, J.G. 1981. Safeguards against suggestiveness: a means for admissibility of hypno-induced testimony. *Washington and Lee Law Rev.* 38: 197–212.

Timm, H.W. 1981. The effect of forensic hypnosis techniques on eyewitness recall and recognition. *J. Police Sci. & Ad.* 9, No. 2: 188–94.

True, R.M. 1949. Experimental control in hypnotic age regression states. *Science* 110: 583–84.

Tulving, E. 1972. Episodic and semantic memory. In E. Tulving and W. Donaldson, eds., *Organization and memory.* New York: Academic Press.

Tulving, E., and Pearlstone, Z. 1966. Availability versus accessibility of information in memory for words. *J. of Verbal Learning and Verbal Behavior* 5: 381–91.

Twerski, A.J., and Naar, R. 1976. Guilt clarification via age regression. *American J. of Clinical Hypnosis* 18, No. 3: 204–06.

Udolf, R. 1981. *Handbook of hypnosis for professionals.* New York: Van Nostrand Reinhold Co.

Vandiver, J.V. 1977. You the investigator. *Law Enforcement J.* 7, No. 9: 6.

W., S. 1969. Recent cases. *McGill Law J.,* 15:189–91.

Wagstaff, G.F. 1982. Recall of witnesses under hypnosis. *J. of Forensic Science Society* 22, No. 1: 33–39.

_____. 1981a. Recall of witnesses under hypnosis. *J. of Forensic Science Society* 21, No. 3: 249.

_____. 1981b. The use of hypnosis in police investigation. *J. of Forensic Science Society* 21, No. 1: 3–7.

Walker, N.S., Garrett, J.B., and Wallace, B. 1976. Restoration of eidetic imagery via hypnotic age regression: a preliminary report. *J. of Abnormal Psychology* 85, No. 3: 335–37.

Wall, P.D., and Lieberman, L. R. 1976. Effects of task motivation and hypnotic induction on hypermnesia. *American J. of Clinical Hypnosis* 18, No. 4: 250–53.

Warner, K.E. 1979. The use of hypnosis in the defense of criminal cases. *International J. of Clinical and Experimental Hypnosis* 27, No. 4: 417–36.

Warren, M.A., and Roberts, A.C. 1980. Challenging the use of hypnotically induced evidence. *Colorado Lawyer* 9: 1142–52.

Wasowicz, L. 1981. High Court asked to review hypnosis testimony use. *L.A. Daily J.* 94: 3.

Watkins, J.G. 1972. Antisocial behavior under hypnosis: possible or impossible? *International J. of Clinical and Experimental Hypnosis* 20, No. 2: 95–100.

_____. 1947. Antisocial compulsions induced under hypnotic trance. *J. of Abnormal and Social Psychology* 42: 256–59.

Weinstein, E., Abrams, S., and Gibbons, D. 1970. The validity of the polygraph with hypnotically induced repression and guilt. *American J. of Psychiatry* 126, No. 8: 1159–62.

Weitzenhoffer, A.M. 1949. The production of antisocial acts under hypnosis. *J. of Abnormal and Social Psychology* 44: 420–22.

Wells, W.R. 1941. Experiments in the hypnotic production of crime. *J. Psychology* 11: 63–102.

West, L.J., and Deckert, G.H. 1965. Dangers of hypnosis. *J. American Medical Association* 192: 9–12.

White, J.R., Hogan, J.L., and Roberts, H.G. 1979. Training officers in investigative hypnosis. *Police Chief* 46, No. 10: 96–98.

White, R.W., Fox, G.F., and Harris, W.W. 1940. Hypnotic hypermnesia for recently learned material. *J. Abnormal and Social Psychology* 35: 88–103.

Wickelgren, W.A. 1977. *Learning and Memory.* Englewood Cliffs, N.J.: Prentice-Hall.

Wilson, R. 1979. Hypnosis: investigating the subconscious. *Police Magazine* 2, No. 1: 14–20.

Worthington, T.S. 1979. The use in court of hypnotically enhanced testimony. *International J. of Clinical and Experimental Hypnosis* 27, No. 4: 402–16.

Young, P.C. 1952. *Antisocial uses of hypnosis.* In L.M. LeCron, ed., *Experimental Hypnosis.* New York: Macmillan.

_____. 1940. Hypnotic regression—fact or artifact? *J. Abnormal and Social Psychology* 35: 273.

_____. 1925. An experimental study of mental and physical functions in the normal and hypnotic states. *American J. of Psychology* 36: 214–32.

Zeichner, I.B. 1981. Hypnosis-prompted recollection. *Law and Order* 29, No. 3: 18, 20–21.

_____. 1980. Admissibility of hypnotically induced recollection. *Law and Order* 28, No. 8: 35.

Zelig, M., and Beidleman, W.B. 1981. The investigative use of hypnosis: a word of caution. *International J. of Clinical and Experimental Hypnosis* 29, No. 4: 401–12.

Zonana, H.V. 1982. Court witnesses treated with hypnosis. *Hospital and Community Psychiatry* 33, No. 7: 531.

_____. 1979. Hypnosis, sodium amytal and confessions. *Bulletin American Academy of Psychiatry and Law* 7, No. 1: 18–28.

Name Index

Subject Index

About the Author

Roy Udolf is a graduate of New York University, College of Engineering (B.E.E. 1950); Brooklyn Law School (J.D. 1954); Hofstra University (M.A. 1963), and Adelphi University (Ph.D. 1971). He has completed postdoctoral training at the Advanced Institute for Analytic Psychotherapy and is listed in the National Register of Health Service Providers in Psychology. He is a diplomate of the American Board of Forensic Psychology.

He has written four other books including *Handbook of Hypnosis for Professionals* and *The Criminal Justice System and its Psychology*, with Alfred Cohn, in addition to a variety of professional-journal articles.

Dr. Udolf has had professional experience in engineering, criminal law, and psychology. He has been at Hofstra University since 1967 where he is currently a teaching fellow and professor of psychology at its New College.